Praise for

THE LIFE OF

YOGANANDA

"Philip Goldberg sheds new light on the incredible story
and illuminates the forces that made Yogananda a
spiritual teacher and role model for the ages."

— **Deepak Chopra, M.D.**, author of *The Healing Self*

"*The Life of Yogananda* is a profound and exquisitely written
account of the life of one of the most renowned spiritual masters
of our time, and is essential reading for anyone on a spiritual
path. . . . In a mysterious but unmistakable way, this book
pulsates with the very presence, blessing, and transmission of
Yogananda's limitless wisdom and grace. With insight, clarity,
and his own depth of consciousness, Philip Goldberg takes you
on a virtual pilgrimage that will uplift you, inspire you, and
illuminate your own journey of awakening."

— **Dr. Barbara De Angelis**, #1 *New York Times* best-selling author
of *Soul Shifts* and *The Choice for Love*

"A brilliant account of what history will recognize as one of the most
significant lives of the 20th century. . . . Sympathetic yet critical, the
book brings to light an enormous number of facets of Yogananda's
life, times, spiritual realization, culture clashes, and personal
dimensions. . . . I highly recommend you read this book, and get
a profound reminder of what the spiritual search is all about."

— **Ken Wilber**, author of *The Religion of Tomorrow*

"In this intensely researched book, Phil Goldberg describes the
deep commitment and tireless effort of Paramahansa Yogananda
to bring the spiritual teachings of India to the West. He reveals
the many obstacles that Yogananda had to overcome in
order to bring a light into the darkness."

— **Krishna Das**, Chantmaster and author of *Chants of a Lifetime*

"A precious dive into the life and times of America's most
famous yogi. Anyone who has read the classic *Autobiography
of a Yogi* . . . will thrill to the untold story of Yogananda's life
in this graceful, insightful biography. It is a worthy companion
to Yogananda's masterwork, informed both by Goldberg's
scholarship and by his deep spiritual practice."

— **Joan Borysenko, Ph.D.**, author of *Minding the Body,
Mending the Mind* and *Seven Paths to God*

"With spiritual elegance and integrity, Goldberg provides an intimate portrait of the life of Yogananda. . . . Through engaging stories and unique perspectives, Paramahansaji shines through this biography as an enlightened master and creator of a great spiritual legacy."

— **Michael Bernard Beckwith**, founder of Agape International Spiritual Center and author of *Spiritual Liberation*

"Paramahansa Yogananda is probably the dominant figure behind the Western Yoga movement and its spiritual roots, the veritable father of Yoga in the Western world, living and teaching in America for more than three decades. Philip Goldberg presents a detailed and informative biography of the great master."

— **Dr. David Frawley, D. Litt.**, director of American Institute of Vedic Studies and author of *Yoga and Ayurveda*

"This exceptionally written, wise, profound biography of one of the 20th century's greatest spiritual pioneers is essential reading for all those who want to understand deeply the growing marriage between Eastern and Western spirituality. I am so moved by and grateful for Phil Goldberg's humble mastery of tone and truth in this marvelous book."

— **Andrew Harvey**, author of *The Hope* and co-author of *Savage Grace*

"Philip Goldberg has masterfully assembled a colorful tapestry of stories detailing the intricacies and complexities that comprise the life of Paramahansa Yogananda. Goldberg's work enables us to understand Yogananda as both mundanely human and extraordinary, while providing a detailed inside understanding of this remarkable human being and spiritual leader."

— **Richard Miller, Ph.D.**, author of *Yoga Nidra* and the CD *iRest Meditation: Restorative Practices for Health, Resiliency, and Well-Being*

"*The Life of Yogananda* is a tremendous gift: a chance to meet from the 'outside' the spiritual genius we met on the 'inside' in *Autobiography of a Yogi*. That book shared what was important to Yogananda; this biography shares why Yogananda is important to you. If you've read the Autobiography, you must read the biography. If you haven't read either, you must read both."

— **Rabbi Rami Shapiro**, author of *Holy Rascals*

"Yogananda was more than just a popular guru who brought Indian spirituality to the United States. He was also a spiritual genius in the art of living, and his impact and legacy transcend the traditional divides of race, ethnicity, nationality, politics, and religion. In *The Life of Yogananda*, Philip Goldberg meticulously peels back the mystical layers in order to reveal the man behind the myth [and] continues his extraordinary work as our foremost chronicler of Hinduism in the United States."

— **Varun Soni, Ph.D.**, Dean of Religious Life and Vice Provost for Campus Wellness and Crisis Intervention, University of Southern California

"When I was 15, Ram Dass gave me a copy of *Autobiography of a Yogi* and the gates of the universe opened. Yogananda's account of his spiritual journey emboldened me to commence mine. Now, all these years later, Phil Goldberg has compiled the stories behind the stories! What a treasure."

— **Mirabai Starr**, author of *God of Love* and *Caravan of No Despair*

"This book is a gift for anyone interested in the yogic journey. Deeply informed by Phil Goldberg's years of practice and study, it explores the life of one of the great spiritual masters of the 20th century. . . . A delightfully written, juicy, and inspiring portrait that takes us right into the heart of the yogic experience."

— **Sally Kempton**, author of *Meditation for the Love of It* and *Awakening Shakti*

"Learning who Yogananda was historically can help us to understand who he *is* spiritually. As with all great spiritual masters, understanding who Yogananda is spiritually helps us to understand who we deep down really are and are called to be."

— **James Finley, Ph.D.**, core teacher at the Center for Action and Contemplation, author of *Merton's Palace of Nowhere* and *Christian Meditation*

"The story of meditative, 'Eastern' spirituality in the West doesn't exist without Yogananda; yet the story of Yogananda, in anything like a full telling, hasn't existed till now. Philip Goldberg, with the clear eyes of the diligent scholar and the open heart of the passionate, lifelong spiritual voyager, is the right person to tell it."

— **Dean Sluyter**, author of *Fear Less* and *Natural Meditation*

"When I was informed about the author's intention to write this book, I knew that gathering information from reliable sources almost seven decades after the subject's passing would be a major endeavor. The result is satisfying. It is enjoyable to read, presented in a clear, forthright manner, and is fair and honest."

— **Roy Eugene Davis**, direct disciple of Paramahansa Yogananda and founder of Center for Spiritual Awareness

"The book admirers of Yogananda and scholars of Yoga alike have been waiting for. . . . Religious culture, across nations and traditions, continues to be informed and influenced by [Yogananda's] unique vision—whether acknowledged or not. This book tells the story of how he accomplished the extraordinary and, thereby, transformed millions of mundane lives into ones worth living."

— **Rita D. Sherma, Ph.D.**, director and associate professor, Shingal Center for Dharma Studies at Graduate Theological Union, Berkeley

"Every yoga teacher and yoga student owes an enormous debt to Yogananda. Goldberg has done a great service with this engaging book, adding vital details to what the iconic *Autobiography of a Yogi* revealed about Yogananda's fascinating life."

— **Larry Payne, Ph.D.**, co-author of *Yoga for Dummies* and founder of Yoga Therapy Rx and Prime of Life Yoga

"Through this work, one gains a sense of what guided Yogananda toward greatness: the cities that shaped his youth, including Gorakhnath, the birthplace of Hatha Yoga, Varanasi, India's spiritual center, and Serampore, the home of missionaries who taught him about Jesus. His success in building schools and meditation centers as well his adept adaptation of new learning technologies all receive fuller treatment here than in any earlier resources."

— **Christopher Key Chapple**, Doshi Professor and Director, Master of Arts in Yoga Studies, Loyola Marymount University

"In making *Awake*, we discovered what a monumental task it is to represent a spiritual giant like Yogananda. . . . Philip Goldberg has done a terrific job of capturing the complexities of such a world teacher."

— **Paola di Florio, Lisa Leeman, and Peter Rader**, filmmakers of *Awake: The Life of Yogananda*

"Among its many virtues, this book fleshes out many parts of Yogananda's life that have not been previously revealed. . . . Goldberg manages to convey with clear eyes Yogananda's human quirks and foibles while simultaneously maintaining respect for the mysteries and depth of his spiritual powers."

— **Danny Goldberg**, author of *In Search of the Lost Chord: 1967 and the Hippie Idea*

THE LIFE OF
YOGANANDA

ALSO BY PHILIP GOLDBERG

American Veda: From Emerson and the Beatles to Yoga and Meditation, How Indian Spirituality Changed the West

Roadsigns: On the Spiritual Path—Living at the Heart of Paradox

The Intuitive Edge: Understanding Intuition and Applying It in Everyday Life

Get Out of Your Own Way: Overcoming Self-Defeating Behavior (with Mark Goulston, M.D.)

THE LIFE OF
YOGANANDA

The Story of the Yogi Who Became
the First Modern Guru

PHILIP GOLDBERG

HAY HOUSE, INC.
Carlsbad, California • New York City
London • Sydney • Johannesburg
Vancouver • New Delhi

Published and distributed in the United States by: Hay House, Inc.: www
.hayhouse.com® • *Published and distributed in Australia by:* Hay House
Australia Pty. Ltd.: www.hayhouse.com.au • *Published and distributed in the
United Kingdom by:* Hay House UK, Ltd.: www.hayhouse.co.uk • *Distributed in
Canada by:* Raincoast Books: www.raincoast.com • *Published in India by:* Hay
House Publishers India: www.hayhouse.co.in

Indexer: Jay Kreider
Cover design: Scott Breidenthal • *Interior design:* Nick C. Welch

Library of Congress Cataloging-in-Publication Data

Names: Goldberg, Philip, 1944- author.
Title: The real life of Yogananda : the story of the yogi who became the
   first modern guru / Philip Goldberg.
Description: Carlsbad, California : Hay House, Inc., 2018.
Identifiers: LCCN 2017060608 | ISBN 9781401952181 (hardback)
Subjects: LCSH: Yogananda, Paramahansa, 1893-1952. | Yogis--India--Biogra-
phy.
   | Self-Realization Fellowship. | BISAC: BIOGRAPHY & AUTOBIOGRAPHY /
   Religious. | RELIGION / Spirituality. | RELIGION / Hinduism / General.
Classification: LCC BP605.S43 Y634 2018 | DDC 294.5092 [B] --dc23 LC record
available at https://lccn.loc.gov/2017060608

Hardcover ISBN: 978-1-4019-5218-1

10 9 8 7 6 5 4 3 2 1
1st edition, April 2018

Printed in the United States of America

To all the yogis who,
like Yogananda, have blessed the world
with their practical wisdom.

We are here today, tomorrow we are gone; mere shadows in a cosmic dream. But behind the unreality of these fleeting pictures is the immortal reality of Spirit.

– PARAMAHANSA YOGANANDA

CONTENTS

INTRODUCTION

The question I was asked most frequently while working on this book was "Why do we need a biography of Yogananda when we have *Autobiography of a Yogi*?" The broad answer is this: in the life of any important historical figure there is room for many books. The specific answers are: 1) Yogananda's iconic memoir is as much about other people as it is about himself, 2) There are major gaps in his narrative, including spans of several years that are summarized in one or two sentences, and 3) While Yogananda spent almost all his adult years in America, less than 10 percent of the autobiography is about that immensely productive and historically significant period. The prospect of filling in those spaces seemed both enticing and important.

Several books have been written about Yogananda by direct disciples. These are valuable firsthand accounts of who he was and what he was like. They are, however, more like tributes than biographies. My goal was to draw a more complete portrait of Yogananda the human being—an extraordinary human being to be sure, but human nonetheless, with all the complexity that term implies. The book's central narrative is the saga of a profoundly spiritual being navigating the material realm, attempting to unite fully with the Divine while skillfully playing his role in the human drama—just as he taught so many to do themselves. No book can capture the true essence of a soul like Yogananda, but it can describe the footprints he left on the sands of time and space. My goal was to render an accurate, fact-based description of those exceptional footprints.

To many, Yogananda was a saint. To some, he was an avatar, an incarnation of God. I am not qualified to make such evaluations. For me it was enough that his contribution to the spiritual history of East and West is unparalleled, and that his life unfolded in a compelling narrative spanning two hemispheres, two vastly different cultures, two world wars, massive economic upheavals, and unprecedented social changes. I set out to tell that remarkable story as truthfully and thoroughly as I could, knowing full well that I could not do justice to it in 3,000 pages, let alone 300.

In choosing to emphasize Yogananda the man, I found validation in the words of one of his most important disciples. Mrinalini Mata was close to him in the last seven years of his life and she served as president of Self-Realization Fellowship (the organization he founded) from 2011 until her passing in 2017. "Some who come onto the path seem to want to 'dehumanize' Master, to think of him only in terms of God incarnate," she once said, adding, "Too often, there is a tendency to take away from Gurudeva [Yogananda] that beautiful human personality which is such an integral part of his spiritual nature."[1] Precisely.

When asked if he has to admire the people he writes about, David McCullough, the celebrated biographer of Harry S. Truman, John Adams, and others, said he needs to admire what they did, but he does not expect them to be perfect. In fact, he adds, "Perfection is boring." I have no idea how the term perfection could be applied to any human being. But I do know that Yogananda had a fascinating personality, with quirks and idiosyncrasies and peculiarities that were shaped by the mysteries of karma and a specific upbringing in a specific family in a specific culture at a specific time. He made decisions; he expressed feelings; he learned and grew; he experienced ups and downs, victories and defeats, pleasures and sorrows. It may add up to perfection in the eyes of some of his disciples, but to this writer it is enough that it forms a one-of-a-kind, eminently distinguished life.

To be clear, I am not a disciple of Yogananda. I was never a formal student of his. I never enrolled in a course he designed or that is taught by an organization teaching in his name. I am, to say the least, a great admirer. I have held him in high esteem ever since I read his *Autobiography of a Yogi* in 1970. The book that launched thousands of spiritual paths augmented and accelerated mine. I was already meditating every day; I had already plunged into the Upanishads, the *Bhagavad Gita*, and other major texts; and I was preparing to train as a meditation teacher with Maharishi Mahesh Yogi. Yogananda's unique, intimate portrait of a bona fide yogi, his depictions of India, and his snapshots of saints, sages, and miracle workers—it was all intriguing, illuminating, and inspiring. I still have the hardcover I read back then. The cover says it cost $5. Since I was unlikely to have had five bucks to spare, I probably borrowed it and never returned it. I remain grateful to whoever loaned it to me. I am repaying that karmic debt with this book.

In the course of hundreds of conversations over the decades, I came to realize how many lives Yogananda has impacted. While researching my book *American Veda* I came to see him as a teacher for the ages, whose contribution to the transmission of India's ancient wisdom to the West was incomparable. I also came to see how moving and compelling his life story was, and the frustration of having to summarize it in one chapter became the seed for this biography. My fascination only increased with every book, document, article, and e-mail I read, and every interview I conducted and every relevant site I visited in the U.S. and India.

Writers have to make choices. One of mine was to devote less space to what Yogananda taught and more to what he did—less to his ideas and more to the events of his life and the decisions he made. As a spiritual teacher of the highest order, he is the best source of his own teachings. Thousands of pages of his writings are available. I saw no reason to explicate his works beyond what was necessary to capture their essence and advance his story.

I also chose to emphasize what is not in *Autobiography of a Yogi*, on the assumption that many readers of this book will already have read Yogananda's memoir, and those who haven't should. Hence, nearly two-thirds of the book is devoted to the second half of his life, spent mostly in America. His formative years in India are covered thoroughly, however, and the narrative contains details not found in previous accounts (readers are advised not to let unfamiliar Indian names and places slow them down). I would be pleased if people finished this book and immediately purchased the autobiography.

Another choice had to do with controversial episodes in Yogananda's life. I thought hard about what to include and not include. My primary goal was to be fair and objective, neither sugarcoating nor sensationalizing the known facts. Some disciples will say I should not have gone to those places at all because the mere mention of what they regard as mean-spirited rumor demeans Yogananda. Other people will say I wasn't tough enough. I expect e-mails from all sides telling me I left out vital information. In the end, I chose brevity because it would have been impossible to do justice to every point of view, or to describe every related document and hypothesis without consuming an inordinate number of pages. And that would have shrouded far more important facets of a highly consequential life. I kept it concise and stuck to the evidence.

Along those same lines, I fully expect some devotees to say I wasn't reverent enough in my treatment of a saintly life, while skeptics will accuse me of being a Yogananda apologist and too much of a fan. While researching this book, I spoke to dozens of people with strong but disparate views about Yogananda, from ardent disciples to casual students to cynics to outright antagonists. I heard it all. He was perfect; he was deeply flawed. He did the will of God and was unattached to the fruits of his actions; he was ambitious, egotistical, and obsessed with money. He was a man of pristine integrity and moral recti- tude; he was ethically and morally compromised. He was a true renunciate, beyond earthly desires; he ran a harem and fathered children. He faithfully represented his tradition; he sold out to the Christian West. And on and on and on. I began this project with no preconceived opinions, and I ruled out none of the conflicting assertions I encountered during my research. Care- ful consideration was given to all reasonable sources. To those who feel I left out or misconstrued important information, I encourage you to write your own book. Yogananda deserves multiple biographies.

Elements of exceptional lives are, by definition, beyond the scope of the ordinary person's experience, including the biographer's. That's what makes them compelling. We read about creative geniuses and world leaders because there are precious few of them, and they are different from the rest of us. We want to partake of their uniqueness and also their humanness. The job of biographers, as I see it, is to try to capture what is extraordinary about their subjects and also depict their human struggles and inconsistencies so readers can, to whatever degree, relate to them.

In the case of Yogananda, an additional challenge presents itself to both writer and reader. As a monk, an Indian immigrant in early-20th-century America, a world-class yogi, and a spiritual teacher with a global reach, his life was in many ways even further removed from the average person's experience than that of a genius or a head of state. Not only were his life circumstances vastly different from most; he had challenges and responsibilities that few individuals have, even other gurus. He also had something more subtle and more profound: a qualitatively different state of consciousness. Self-realized yogic masters (and there is no reason to doubt that he was one) operate from a different awareness, with different modes of perception, attunement, intuition, and connection to unseen dimensions of existence.

All of which presented daily challenges in researching and writing this book. I did my best to remain objective, honest, and discerning without disguising my respect for my subject. I sincerely hope that every reader will find something of value in the book, and that even Yogananda's most earnest students will learn something they did not know before. More important, as a highly practical guru, Yogananda would, I believe, want any book about him to not only inform but transform. It is my hope that readers will be enriched, expanded, and deepened by this humble account of his life.

CHAPTER 1

THE BOY MUKUNDA

The child who became Paramahansa Yogananda was born on Thursday, January 5, 1893, in Gorakhpur, a small city by Indian standards, not far from the Nepal border and the birthplace of Buddha. The time, according to most sources, was 8:38 P.M. In one of several naming customs, the first sound of the newborn's name was astrologically determined; in this case it was *Mu*. The parents, Bhagabati Charan Ghosh and Gyana Prabha Ghosh, chose Mukunda and added a common middle name, Lal.

The birth of Mukunda Lal Ghosh was not the only 1893 event that would help shape the historic transmission of India's spiritual wisdom to the West. Later that year, Mohandas K. Gandhi, then a struggling lawyer in Bombay, would accept a position in South Africa, where his socio-spiritual activism would be ignited; Aurobindo Ghose would return to India from his schooling in England to become, first, a radical thorn in the British side and then, as Sri Aurobindo, one of India's leading philosopher-sages[1]; and, in September, Swami Vivekananda would steal the show at the World's Parliament of Religions in Chicago.

The family astrologer predicted that Mukunda would have three marriages, with the first two spouses dying young. As a boy, Mukunda would beg to differ, setting his horoscope aflame one day in a flagrant act of defiance. From an early age, he saw himself becoming a monk, and several modern astrologers have said that the planets at the time of his birth were indeed aligned for asceticism and detachment, only lived

1

out in public rather than in seclusion and accompanied by exceptional achievement. Vedic scholar and astrologer David Frawley[2] says Yogananda's birth chart points not only to renunciation and a spiritual temperament, but to "high intelligence and probing insight," a "devotional nature," and "good yogic powers," but also loss and weakened health. All of which, as we will see, turned out to be so.

"I was conscious in my mother's womb," Yogananda once claimed, "feeling the movements in her body, aware of my own helpless state. . . . Occasionally the darkness of the womb would be dispelled, and light would visit me. On one side, I wanted to express myself as a human being, yet on the other side I didn't, because I felt I was Spirit."[3] Skeptics might attribute that statement to imagination, not memory, but the tension it describes between the spiritual and the material could not have been more real. If there was one overarching conflict or a single ongoing trial in Yogananda's nearly six decades of embodiment, it was between renunciation and engagement. To be in the world but not of it has been a struggle for spiritual seekers throughout the ages, but few have lived it as publicly, or expressed it as memorably, as Yogananda.

The womb he claimed to remember had borne three children before him: brother Ananta (in 1883) and sisters Roma (1887) and Uma (1890). Two more sisters and two more brothers would join the clan by the time Mukunda was 10 and a half. As the second oldest brother in a Bengali family, he would be called Mejda. His father was from a humble village family of the *kayasthas* caste, a subset of the *kshatriyas*, which traditionally consisted of rulers and warriors. When his own father died young, it fell upon Bhagabati, the eldest son, to support his mother and siblings. He scraped his way through college, became an accountant, and eventually worked his way up to a high-ranking position in the vast, British-run railway system. But he never forgot the hardship and penury of his early years, remaining frugal and austere despite the affluence he achieved.

In *Autobiography of a Yogi*,[4] Yogananda describes his parents as saintly: "A perfect parental harmony was the calm center for the revolving tumult of eight young lives." His father was "kind, grave, at times stern" and "guided principally by his intellect." His mother was "a queen of hearts, and taught us only through love."[5] Other sources suggest that Mrs. Ghosh may actually have been worthy of the halo that typically encircles the memory of mothers who die young. She was said to be humble, devoted, compassionate, and kind. It was also said that young Mukunda bore a strong facial resemblance to his mother—a fortunate trait according to Bengali lore—and indeed, the dark eyes in photographs of her remind one of the mesmerizing, sagacious eyes that peer from the cover of her son's seminal memoir. Clearly, his mother was a major psychological influence on Mukunda, and she continued to be one long after she was gone. As an adult, Yogananda would exhibit his mother's good-hearted warmth and spiritual depth as well as his father's grit, discipline, and sense of responsibility.

Hindu tradition holds that highly evolved souls are likely to be reincarnated into a family of yogis. That seems to have been the case with Mukunda Lal Ghosh. In the opening passages of the *AY*, as Yogananda's autobiography is known, he claims to have recalled in infancy a past life as a Himalayan ascetic, and his parents in the life we're exploring in this book were committed to the path of householder yogis. While Mrs. Ghosh was raised in a wealthy home and Mr. Ghosh's salary afforded his family far more creature comforts than the average Indians of the period, they disdained luxury, preferring a lifestyle that Yogananda called spartan. They were diligent in their daily *sadhana* (spiritual practice), observant of traditional rituals and holy days, reverent toward gurus, swamis, and learned *pandits*, and rigorous about upholding Hindu ideals of right behavior. Mrs. Ghosh drew on episodes from the great epics the *Mahabharata* and the *Ramayana* to teach her children moral and spiritual lessons, and she evidently modeled empathy for the less fortunate, often persuading her husband, a generous man by any standard, to open his wallet wider than he otherwise would have.

As readers of Yogananda's autobiography know, his parents' spiritual dedication included the intimacies of marital life. He said that his parents slept together once a year for the purpose of having children. This was not based on what we think of as religious dogma or fear of divine retribution. Rather, it was rooted in yogic guidelines for directing primal sexual energy to higher purposes. That distinction, between religious compliance and pragmatic adherence to methods known to advance spiritual development, would be a cornerstone of Yogananda's teaching, as it has been with virtually every guru who has come to the West.

Young Mukunda learned to perform *pujas* (devotional rituals) at his mother's side and, at an exceptionally early age, began performing them by himself. He made daily offerings to a homemade image of the goddess Kali, and would sometimes withdraw behind a curtain to meditate privately. Kali's was not the only sacred image in the Ghosh home. Like most Hindu families with a *bhakti* (devotional) bent, they displayed other favored deities and holy figures. Chief among them was a photograph of Lahiri Mahasaya[6], Bhagabati and Gyana Prabha's beloved guru.

Born Shyama Charan Lahiri in Bengal and raised in the holy city of Benares (now Varanasi), where he spent most of his life, Lahiri was a family man. That placed him in a distinct minority among sainted Indian masters, most of whom have been renunciates. His transformation from ordinary accountant in the British government's Military Engineering Department to revered holy man began dramatically at age 33 when he was on assignment in the Himalayan foothills. There, the story goes, he encountered an ascetic cave dweller said to be the legendary and ageless Mahavatar Babaji. The meeting did not occur by chance, he was told, but by an esoteric arrangement orchestrated by the saint himself. Babaji, who is alleged to be hundreds of years old and reportedly still appears from time to time to a chosen few, initiated Shyama Charan into the spiritual methods of his Kriya Yoga tradition and charged him with the task of reviving the dormant science after centuries of nonuse, or at least severely limited use.[7]

The Sanskrit word *kriya* derives from the same root as the now-familiar term *karma*. Usually translated as action, deed, or effort, in the context of spiritual discipline it refers to an action taken to achieve a specific result. Many yogic lineages use the term to describe their favored techniques. Here, Kriya Yoga refers to the specific method that Babaji is said to have taught Lahiri Mahasaya and that Yogananda would one day make widely available. In a footnote early in his autobiography, he defines Kriya Yoga this way: "A yogic technique, taught by Lahiri Mahasaya, whereby the sensory tumult is stilled, permitting man to achieve an ever-increasing identity with cosmic consciousness."[8]

He adds that Babaji originally decreed that only Lahiri Mahasaya could teach the practice, but Lahiri asked that he be allowed to authorize others to do so as well. This laid the foundation for a lineage that would instruct a wider range of seekers than ever before, including those who engaged in worldly affairs, like Lahiri himself. He began teaching at his Benares home. In time, his following grew from a handful of students to legions of disciples whose spiritual lives he guided while upholding his duties as a husband and a father. Among those he trained was a guru known to us as Sri Yukteswar, who tasked his disciple Yogananda with the democratization and proliferation of Kriya Yoga.

Bhagabati Ghosh was not looking for a guru when Lahiri Mahasaya entered his life. One day, an employee of his in the Gorakhpur offices of the Bengal Nagpur Railway, a man named Abinash, asked for a week's leave so he could visit his guru in Benares. Mr. Ghosh ridiculed the request. What followed is the first of innumerable tales of miracles, wonders, and yogic powers in Yogananda's celebrated autobiography. Mr. Ghosh was walking home with Abinash when Lahiri Mahasaya appeared out of nowhere and told him he was treating his employee too harshly. He then promptly vanished. The astonished boss not only gave his employee leave, but he and his wife accompanied him to Benares to meet the apparent miracle maker.

They became initiates and ardent disciples. When Mrs. Ghosh was pregnant with Mukunda, the guru prophesized that their child would one day transmit Kriya Yoga to the masses. He reinforced the prediction later when the infant was brought to Benares for his blessing. Holding the boy on his lap, the guru placed his hand on the child's forehead and said, most likely in Bengali, "Little mother, thy son will be a yogi. As a spiritual engine, he will carry many souls to God's kingdom."[9]

In between those twin prophecies, the spirit of Lahiri is said to have played a key role in Mukunda's birth. As is often the case with spiritual luminaries, Yogananda's nativity narrative contains an element of the miraculous. According to his brother, Sananda, in *Mejda*, his book about his illustrious sibling, Mrs. Ghosh suffered from severe labor pains and beseeched Lahiri Mahasaya for help. "Suddenly a celestial light filled the room," Sananda reported, "and from the concentrated rays in the center emerged the form of Lahiri Mahasaya. Mother's pain vanished instantly. The divine light continued to illumine the room till Mejda was born."[10] Whether the tale is embellished family lore or an accurate depiction of a metaphysical event is, of course, unknowable. At the very least, its persistence reinforces the special place Mukunda occupied in his family from the start.

Lahiri Mahasaya's impact on Yogananda's life would prove to be monumental, not just because he was his parents' spiritual guide, but because he was Yogananda's own *paramguru*—the guru of the guru to whom he would one day bow as a disciple. He would meet that master teacher, Sri Yukteswar, after graduating from high school. But Lahiri Mahasaya was a powerful and living presence in his life from the time he was born and beyond the guru's passing in 1895, when Mukunda was not yet three. A handsomely framed picture of Lahiri—the origin of which is depicted as miraculous in the *AY*—had a profound influence on him. He would meditate and make offerings before the guru's photo, and sometimes, he claimed, the image would step out of its two-dimensional space and, in fleshly and "luminous" form,[11] sit down in front of him. He does not explicitly say whether the visions occurred within his mind or to his external sense of sight. He does say that when he tried to touch Lahiri's feet in the traditional gesture of reverence, the figure would return to pictorial form.

When he was eight, he says, he experienced a miraculous healing by Lahiri Mahasaya's grace. Stricken by Asiatic cholera, an infectious disease that claimed many lives in that era, he lay enfeebled on what his family feared was his deathbed. His mother implored him to "inwardly kneel" in supplication to the guru. He did so, gazing at the photograph, and soon saw what he called "a blinding light" permeate the room.[12] His symptoms immediately disappeared, he says.

Copies of that sanctified photo now adorn the altar of every center and temple in Yogananda's lineage, as well as the altars, bureaus, and tabletops of millions of devotees. It even played a role in literary history. As a young man, J. D. Salinger, the celebrated author of *The Catcher in the Rye* and other classics, was determined to achieve enlightenment. Convinced that the lofty goal required renouncing worldly desires, he struggled to overcome a strong urge to mate. When he read in *Autobiography of a Yogi* that Lahiri Mahasaya had been a family man, he realized he'd been wrong. Wife and children followed, along with initiation into Yogananda's teachings. He reportedly gave his kids that photo of Lahiri to carry with them.

The spiritual inclinations Mukunda displayed at an early age were nourished not only at home but by the town in which he spent his first eight years. Gorakhpur was named for one of the many religious reformers in Indian history.[13] Gorakhnath (aka Gorakshanath) was a sainted yogi who is thought to have lived in the 11th century C.E. He is credited with founding the Nath order of ascetics, although some say the tradition actually predates him and his role was to solidify and expand it. Every Sunday, Mukunda's parents would take him with them to worship at the 12th-century Gorakhnath temple about a mile from their home. One Sunday, they skipped the temple because they were hosting a ceremonial event. Late that night, when the festivities had ended, Mukunda was not to be found. Anxious family and friends scoured the neighborhood to no avail. Then his mother thought of checking the temple. Her son was there, meditating.

Despite the lateness of the hour and the trouble he had caused, his parents let him finish his sadhana.

The traits on display in that story, extraordinary devotion and an independent spirit, would characterize Yogananda's life as a celebrated guru. So would another quality: indomitable will. By way of illustration, he once recalled the time he was drawn to orange candies in a drugstore. He wanted some of that candy. His nurse refused and wheeled him home in his carriage. After dinner, he reiterated his desire to his mother. She too said no. He repeated the demand more loudly. She again refused. Mukunda was unrelenting; he grew more adamant with each shout, until his mother finally gave in. By then it was so late that she had to wake up the store owner to get her son the treat. The victory was sweeter than the candy itself. He was branded as naughty, but he had learned a vital lesson about the power of will. He would grow up using his will to accomplish extraordinary things, including teaching others how to harness the power of their own will.

Other childhood traits would also serve Yogananda well later in life. One was a facility for language. The Ghoshes spoke their native Bengali but also needed enough Hindi and English to get by outside of Bengal. At St. Andrew's, an all-boys school in Gorakhpur where Mukunda's education began, the British and Christian influence was strong, and English was part of the curriculum. By all indications, he was an articulate child who knew how to use his verbal skills to get what he wanted. He also displayed a knack for prose and poetry, foreshadowing Yogananda's prolific literary output. As is recalled in *Mejda*, his first known poem was composed when he was eight. Heartbroken over the death of his treasured goldfish, he wrote, in English:

my
red fish is die[14]

Mukunda was also relentlessly persistent—so much so that less tolerant parents might have labeled him obstinate or stubborn and disciplined him accordingly. The Ghoshes, however, seemed to have recognized something special in their little Moko; they responded to his willful and often inconvenient behavior with patience and perhaps a certain amount of pride. That may have been because so many of the child's demands were motivated by spiritual objectives that are rare among adults, much less eight- or nine-year-olds. But, as we saw with the orange candy, even when an ordinary childhood desire was thwarted, his determination to get what he wanted could be intrepid.

In one telling instance, he resorted to the kind of ascetic rigor we associate with nonviolent resisters like Mahatma Gandhi. It occurred shortly before his ninth birthday, after the family had moved to Lahore (now a major city in Pakistan). When Mukunda was not permitted to attend a traveling exhibition featuring a pair of famous wrestlers, he locked himself in his father's room. He stayed there for 24 hours, refusing food and causing his father to miss time at work because he could not access his clothing. The protest succeeded. "Mejda unbolted the door and came out of the room as though he had conquered the world," says Sananda Ghosh.[15] He got to see the wrestlers.

While he loved amusements, candy, and play as much as any other kid, Mukunda's principal passion was as rare as a cold front in an Indian August. He was a spiritual prodigy, attracted to tales of saints and yogis the way other boys were to athletes and warriors, and he was drawn to solitary silence at an age normally associated with clamor and attention seeking. His brother Sananda reported in *Mejda* that Mukunda would frequently sit in secluded places and meditate with his eyes closed, or half-closed, sometimes murmuring inaudibly in the manner of someone praying or voicing an invocation.

If the stories that came down to us are true, Mukunda's devotion was rewarded by spectacular spiritual experiences. At one point, jealous that his elders received letters in the mail and he did not, he wrote to God (as reproduced in English in *Mejda*):[16]

To Your beautiful lotus feet, my Bhagavan.[17]
How are you? Are you ill? I talk to You every day and ask You to send me a letter. Probably You have forgotten my request? I am very hurt. You know that many letters come to my father and mother and eldest brother; but no one sends a letter to me. Certainly You will send me a letter. Please write quickly. Don't forget about it. What else shall I write? Father and Mother are well.
Thus bowed,
Mukunda

He mailed it in a sealed envelope addressed "To Splendid God, Heaven." Every day he watched eagerly for the postman. He cried, he prayed, and he scolded the Lord. Then, it is said, he was awakened one night in the presence of brilliant celestial light. He was certain that the visitation was the long-awaited reply from God.

Another experience would have a lasting impact on Yogananda's life. Alone in his room one morning, he slipped into a reverie. A philosophical query arose: "What is behind the darkness of closed eyes?" Instead of being dispelled by thoughts of football or homework, as it might have with most children, the query triggered an inner vision of bright celestial light, and then, as he later described it, "Divine shapes of saints, sitting in meditation posture in mountain caves, formed like miniature cinema pictures on the large screen of radiance within my forehead." He asked them who they were.

"We are the Himalayan yogis," they said.

He expressed a desire to emulate them. The beings promptly disappeared, "but the silvery beams expanded in ever-widening circles to infinity," and a voice said, "I am Iswara.[18] I am Light."[19]

The presence faded, but in the aftermath of the ecstatic experience Yogananda came away impassioned with the determination to find God. The inspiration would last a lifetime, and the beneficiaries of that inspiration number in the millions.

CHAPTER 2

LOVE, LOSS, AND LORE

Between November 1902, when Mukunda was two months shy of his 10th birthday, and July 1906, when he was 13 and a half, the Ghosh family lived in three different cities, as Mr. Ghosh was transferred to offices within the railway complex. The first move was 1,300 kilometers west and north to Lahore. The capital of Punjab state, with a population of approximately 200,000 at the time, Lahore was larger and more cosmopolitan than Gorakhpur.[1] Its proximity to Afghanistan and Persia (now Iran) and its location on a vital trade route made it a highly valued possession to the British, as it had been to previous rulers over centuries of conquest and counterconquest. As a result, Lahore was more ethnically and religiously diverse than most Indian cities.

How much the cosmopolitan atmosphere influenced young Mukunda can only be inferred. Conceivably, he learned lessons that would serve him well as a foreign spiritual teacher in a nation known as a melting pot. Then again, he may have been relatively sheltered from Lahore's hustle and bustle. The Ghoshes had a spacious home in a quiet area, and Mukunda spent a good deal of time in the makeshift temple he'd created in a corner of a second-floor balcony, with a newly acquired picture of goddess Kali on the altar.

In the spring of 1904, the family once again uprooted, this time to Bareilly, in Uttar Pradesh, about 260 kilometers east of Delhi. Mr. Ghosh had been promoted to a position with a typically tortured bureaucratic title: Deputy Examiner in the Office of the Government Superintendent of Accounts, Establishment Department, Rohilkund and Kumaon Railway. Situated on the Ramganga River, Bareilly was about half the size of Lahore and less heterogeneous. The family lived there for two eventful years before they moved to Chittagong, a seaport on the Bay of Bengal in what is now Bangladesh. Only two months later they were off to Calcutta.

Most of the stories that found their way into print about those three and a half years reflect Yogananda's lifelong fascination—some might say preoccupation—with the miraculous. If the tales are true, he was, as Mukunda, psychically gifted to say the least. There is the story, well known among devotees, about the time he responded to teasing from his older sister Uma by using his willpower to make a large boil appear on his arm overnight and make Uma's boil double in size. On another occasion, Uma challenged his belief that Divine Mother would give him anything he asked for by requesting the two kites that were floating above their home in Lahore. Mukunda closed his eyes and silently prayed. Before long, the story goes, a kite string broke, the wind suddenly ceased, a string got caught in a cactus plant, and, one after the other, the kites drifted close enough to grasp.[2] Then there was the time when he, at ten, suddenly made unreasonable demands on his mother, forcing her to stand up and move, with her newborn son in her arms, just as a skylight broke and a shower of glass fell on the chair on which they'd been seated. He was even given credit, at 13, for silencing a frightful storm.[3]

Did these events occur exactly as they've come down to us? Are the tales embellished versions of ordinary occurrences? Mythology often accrues around celebrated spiritual masters, but so do events that defy explanation. This, at least, can be said: The stories boast a certain consistency, both among themselves and with the miraculous events Yogananda described in his memoir. They attest to his lifelong faith in the powers available to a mind in tune with Divine intelligence.

One psychic occurrence played a role in the biggest trauma of Yogananda's life. It occurred in Bareilly when the Ghosh family was settling into their newly rented home. Eldest son Ananta, then 21, was soon to be married. Mrs. Ghosh took some of her children to Calcutta, about 1,200 kilometers to the southeast, to take charge of wedding preparations. Mukunda and his father remained in Bareilly. The two eldest Ghosh daughters, Uma and Roma, had already wed in gala fashion, but the marriage of an eldest son was traditionally of a higher order of splendor. To accommodate the maximum number of guests, the family rented a large house at 50 Amherst Street[4] for lodging and a base of operations. When they first set foot in the house, Mrs. Ghosh said she could feel the presence of a bad omen—"as if the building would devour us," according to *Mejda*.[5] Sure enough, it would soon play host to a dark tragedy and, in an ironic twist, several years later it would be an important source of light in Yogananda's life.

Traditional Hindu weddings are colorful, elaborate affairs that last for days, with a cast of hundreds, music, dance, religious rituals, and enough food to sustain the Indian army. Mrs. Ghosh attacked the preparatory tasks with grace and skill, aided by a bevy of relatives. Then the family karma took a dreadful turn. Ananta's same-age cousin and companion, Jnanada, was stricken by the fearsome Asiatic cholera and died. Mrs. Ghosh, who had attempted to nurse her nephew back to health, also came down with the contagious disease.

None of this was known to Mukunda and his father back in Bareilly. They were attending to their day-to-day duties and preparing to join the family for the wedding festivities. One night, around midnight, as he and his father slept on the patio to escape the heat, Mukunda was awakened by the fluttering of the net with which Indians encircle their beds as protection against mosquitos. The unmistakable form of his mother appeared before him, he says, and commanded him to wake up his father and tell him they must catch the 4 A.M. train to Calcutta if they wished to see their wife and mother again. The terrified Mukunda did as he was told. "Mother is dying!" he cried.

As most parents would, Mr. Ghosh brushed off his son's alarm as a nightmare or hallucination. He told Mukunda to go back to sleep, adding that if anything had actually gone wrong they would deal with it the next day. His son declared that he would never forgive him, and predicted that his father would never forgive himself.

In the morning, a telegram sent by Ananta arrived: "Mother dangerously ill. Marriage postponed. Come at once."[6] They left on the next train, but Mrs. Ghosh passed away before they arrived. The date was April 26, 1904. Yogananda says he collapsed when he entered the Amherst Street house, overwhelmed by the reality of death. In Sananda's account, Mukunda called out to his mother frantically, then ran toward the door, shouting that he would find her and bring her back. Ananta restrained him. Mukunda struggled to no avail and soon collapsed and lost consciousness.

"I loved Mother as my dearest friend on earth," he wrote in the *AY*. "Her solacing black eyes had been my refuge in the trifling tragedies of childhood."[7] He would compose a poem about those eyes. Titled "The Lost Two Black Eyes" (sometimes shortened to "Two Black Eyes"), it occupies more than three pages in collections of Yogananda's poems. In this stanza, Divine Mother tells the author why his mother was taken from him:

I stole away those imprisoning two black eyes
That thou might'st be free
To find those eyes
In My eyes,
And in the eyes of all black-eyed mothers[8]

Yogananda called the tear in the fabric of his family irreparable. Mr. Ghosh, bitterly reminded of the transitory nature of worldly life, converted his grief into a single-minded focus on spiritual deepening. He dutifully fulfilled his added parental responsibilities. Yogananda said he became a more tender and attentive father. But each day, when his duties to his company and children were completed, he retired to his austere room to practice late into the night the Kriya Yoga methods he'd learned from Lahiri Mahasaya. He was so intent on yogic purity that his room was lit only by oil lamps and candles; he eschewed movies and theaters; his diet was as simple as a monk's; he disdained luxuries so much that he refused even to wear the gold-rimmed glasses his wife had given him; he rarely accepted a social invitation; and he would not have a mirror in his room because he did not want to become too attached to his body. He lived another 38 years[9] and never remarried, rejecting out of hand any suggestion of a match.

Yogananda's own grief was profound and enduring. By all accounts, the impact lasted for years, but at the same time the loss of the mother who bore him in the flesh strengthened his devotion to the Divine Mother. Eventually, he says, his persistent grief-stricken cries drew that sacred feminine presence to him, and She delivered to him these healing words: "It is I who have watched over thee, life after life, in the tenderness of many mothers! See in My gaze the two black eyes, the lost beautiful eyes, thou seekest!"[10]

After the cremation rites were performed, the bereft family returned to Bareilly and a home with a cavernous emotional hole. Ananta's marriage was postponed for the customary one-year mourning period. Mukunda created a mourning ritual of his own. Each dawn he sat by a *sheoli* tree in a field next to the house, aching with longing for the Divine presence and feeling pulled toward the Himalayas. Traditional tales of *sadhus* (wandering ascetics) and hermetic yogis who awakened to higher consciousness in high-altitude caves and forests charmed him the way stories of warriors and kings excited other boys. He wanted to emulate those spiritual heroes, and his father and older brother knew it. They were determined to discourage his Himalayan wanderlust and, if need be, thwart it. Mukunda, after all, was only 11.

One afternoon he took off on the pilgrimage he'd dreamed about. He either walked the three kilometers to the train station or rode there in a *tonga* (a horse-drawn carriage), avoiding detection by his family and neighbors. His goal would have been Kathgodam, the nearest station to Nainital, a well-trod point of embarkation for Himalayan trekkers and yogis, 130 kilometers from Bareilly and 1,800 meters higher. The train would have taken about three hours, and the tonga ride to Nainital about the same amount of time. But he never reached the mountain abode of gods and saints. Ananta discovered his brother missing, deduced his destination, and tracked him down, probably by boarding the same or a subsequent train. An 11-year-old traveling alone would not have been inconspicuous. Back in Bareilly, the saddened Mukunda resumed his morning ritual by the sheoli tree. "My heart wept for the two lost Mothers: one human, one divine," he wrote.

Indian history boasts a long list of precocious spiritual prodigies who set off from home to wander in search of the highest attainment. Some never return to the ordinary world, while others do so when their spiritual goal has been achieved, to serve humanity as gurus and sages. Mukunda's karma clearly dictated a different narrative.

The accounts of Mukunda's life between ages 10 and 13 reveal several qualities Yogananda exhibited in adult form. One was a commitment to the ethical principle of *ahimsa*, or nonviolence, and its dietary complement, vegetarianism. Contrary to popular belief, not all Hindus are vegetarians; in fact, vegetarians are a minority in some regions of India, including Bengal. Mukunda was an exception, even in his family. According to brother Sananda, when others were indulging the flesh of a bird, Mukunda ate rice and vegetables in silence and would later scold his brother for being complicit in the sin of killing helpless creatures.

His commitment to ahimsa was not entirely Gandhian, however. His righteous willingness to stand up for principle was sometimes muscular. A bully at the school he briefly attended in Chittagong intimidated, humiliated, and occasionally beat up on

smaller lads. Mukunda was outraged, and one day challenged the
bully to a fight. As is reported in *Mejda*, his antagonist pounced;
the combatants scuffled; the bully lifted Mukunda off the ground
and threw him down with a thud. He was poised to deliver a
decisive blow when Mukunda wrapped his neck in an armlock.
He held on tightly as the bully maneuvered into position and
repeatedly slammed Mukunda's head on the ground. Despite his
bloody skull, Mukunda held the neck grip until, finally, the bully
was red-faced and gasping for air. Mukunda would not let him go
until he promised never to pick on others again.

Mukunda later regretted that fight; he'd learned that anger
is an obstacle to a yogi's spiritual advancement, not to mention
a social menace. The next time he confronted bullies, he stood
erectly before them, and when they shoved him, he roared like
a lion. The aggressors backed off and extended their friendship.
As a guru, Yogananda would explain that practicing ahimsa
does not prevent you from hissing like a snake.

Mukunda was also possessed of an outsized wanderlust, and
not just in relation to spiritual pilgrimage. He had a tourist's
passion for exploring the earth's natural wonders and observing human life in all its variety. Aided by his father's ability
to obtain railroad passes, he toured much of the vast Indian
subcontinent throughout his youth, and later would relish the
landscapes and cityscapes of North America and Europe. "Time
has never dimmed my delight in new scenes and strange faces,"
he wrote in his celebrated memoir.[11] He remained an inveterate
sightseer and a collector of exotic artifacts until the final years
of his life, when an intense desire to complete essential writing
projects pinned him down in Southern California.

But his prime motive for travel was always spiritual, first
as a seeker and later as a teacher. While the family was still
in Bareilly, Mukunda persuaded his father to let him venture,
alone, to Benares, the holiest of holy cities. Perhaps to satisfy his
son's hunger for pilgrimage while keeping him under watchful
eyes, Mr. Ghosh gave him a round-trip pass, enough rupees to
sustain a brief adventure, and letters of introduction. In Yogananda's telling, there is no description of the city that charmed

Mark Twain, who said, "Benares is older than history, older than tradition, older even than legend and looks twice as old as all of them put together."[12] Nor is there anything about the sights and sounds and smells that enchant visitors even today, when the sacred Ganga is a virtual sewer and the city of Shiva is choked by motor vehicles; nothing about the cremation rites, the sunrise rituals, and the sunset chanting along the great river. The title of the six-page chapter about his trip reveals what mattered most to Yogananda: "The Saint with Two Bodies."

That saint was Swami Pranabananda, a former business colleague of Bhagabati Ghosh who had renounced the world. The tale, with the swami's mysterious appearance in two places at the same time, is one of the more eye-opening episodes in the *AY*. Yogananda attempts to explain bilocation in footnotes referencing both material science and the yogic science of consciousness. Skeptics would argue that young Mukunda had an overly active imagination, or that Pranabananda was one of India's many trickster ascetics, who create magician-like illusions to open the minds of seekers or, in some cases, swindle them. Then again, perhaps the swami was, as Yogananda posited, a *siddha* (a yogic adept) whose mind was so firmly anchored in the Infinite that he could manipulate the subatomic vibrations of matter and blithely materialize a duplicate body. Yogananda contended that one who awakens to the realization that all of creation is light becomes capable of miracles: "A master is able to employ his divine knowledge of light phenomena to project instantly into perceptible manifestation the ubiquitous light atoms."[13]

The central mind-boggling incident aside, the Benares episode offered an important takeaway for young Mukunda. It came in the form of confirmation of the destiny he'd begun to intuit. "Your life belongs to the path of renunciation and yoga," Swami Pranabananda told him.[14]

Two other miraculous stories from this period of Mukunda's life stand out because, if true, they point to his special role in the cosmic drama. The first is not in the *AY*, a curious absence in a book filled from start to finish with occult events, some of which entail visitations from departed souls, as does this one. It took place during the Ghoshes' brief stay in Chittagong, when Mukunda was a mischievous 13-year-old with a rebellious streak. On one of the occasions when he would do something forbidden and drag Sananda along for the ride, the boys stopped on the way home to pick lichis from a grove of trees. In the gathering dusk, they heard a voice call out Mukunda's name. A smiling man in white garments beckoned to them. They walked toward him, and as they drew closer his form seemed lustrous. Mukunda bent low and touched the man's feet in the Indian gesture of deepest respect. In turn, the man embraced the youngster, kissed him on the head, and said, "You have come on earth as God's representative to fulfill His wishes. Your body is His temple, sanctified by prayer and meditation. Do not run after material pleasures or satisfaction. You will show the way that leads to true happiness; and by your spiritual knowledge you will deliver those who are suffering in ignorance." He advised Mukunda to always think of God and always remember his inseparable oneness with the Divine. And he promised he would always be protected: "One day your ideals of Yoga will inspire all mankind. Mukunda, march onward!"[15]

The figure promptly vanished. When the awestruck boys arrived at home, after their curfew but undetected, Mukunda showed his brother a photograph hanging on a wall. It was a portrait of the man they had just met, their parents' guru, Lahiri Mahasaya.

The second tale adds a note of mystery and wonder to the tragedy of Gyana Prabha Ghosh's death. As Yogananda tells it, one day in Lahore a wandering sadhu came to the family's home with a portentous message for his mother: her next illness would be her last. The sadhu went on to say that the next day a silver amulet would materialize in her hand. Her son Ananta was to give it to Mukunda one year after her death. Mukunda would know the meaning of the sacred object at the proper time, the sadhu added, and once it had served its purpose the amulet would vanish.

Fourteen months later, in June 1905, when the family was in Bareilly, Ananta fulfilled his mother's deathbed assignment, albeit two months late. He handed Mukunda a small box and verbally delivered a message from their mother. (In *Mejda* it is reported that Ananta had written down the message and inserted it in the box to be given to Mukunda.) In her message, Mrs. Ghosh describes the visit from the mysterious sadhu and says she had known of Mukunda's special destiny from the time Lahiri Mahasaya blessed him in her womb. The day after the sadhu's appearance at her home, as she sat in meditation, a silver amulet appeared in her hands. Now, as planned, the precious object was passed to Mukunda. His mother's final words were "Do not grieve for me, as I shall have been ushered by my great guru into the arms of the Infinite. Farewell, my child; the Cosmic Mother will protect you."[16]

When Ananta gave him the amulet, Yogananda said, he was enveloped by a form of illumination, and he knew that the amulet had come to him from past-life teachers who were serving as his guides in the present. That conclusion, he said, was not just an intuitive flash but was communicated—whether explicitly or implicitly is not clear—by a Sanskrit inscription on the amulet itself. The inscription was a mantra, he added, a term known to very few Westerners at the time he wrote his memoir. And the amulet itself, despite its solid appearance, was not an ordinary material object, but rather "astrally produced" and "structurally evanescent." Mukunda would keep the holy object close to him for the next five years, as a reminder and an inspiration. Then, he tells us, shortly before he met his guru, the amulet disappeared as prophesied.[17]

Once again, we are left to wonder about the wonders in Yogananda's life. And once again we would be advised to curb, at least momentarily, the tendency to dismiss them as fiction. "When the Yogi becomes perfect, there will be nothing in nature not under his control," Swami Vivekananda, Yogananda's great predecessor, once said. "If he orders the gods or the souls of the departed to come, they will come at his bidding. All the forces of nature will obey him as slaves. When the ignorant see these powers of the Yogi, they call them the miracles."[18]

When Mukunda was 13, his family's movement from place to place came to an end. Why Mr. Ghosh was transferred again after only two months in Chittagong and why they had to leave on one week's notice are unclear. It may have been a simple bureaucratic decision, or it may have been due to the social unrest that had erupted in the region. Six months earlier, Bengal had been divided into two separate provinces; Chittagong was now part of East Bengal. A great many Indians had risen up in protest, viewing the change as another example of Britain's divide-and-rule tactics.[19] Whatever the reason for their sudden departure, in July 1906, the Ghosh family boarded a steamboat for Calcutta in West Bengal. There they would find permanence in a sophisticated metropolis whose religious and cultural climate did much to shape the teenage Mukunda into the grown-up Yogananda. In *Mejda*, Sananda Ghosh reports that on the voyage westward across the Bay of Bengal, Mukunda prophesied: "One day I will go to a very far country on a big ship." Fourteen years later, he would do exactly that.

CHAPTER 3

A TEENAGER IN THE METROPOLIS

In the early years of the 20th century, Calcutta was to India what New York and Washington, D.C., together were to America. A major seaport, it was the most populous city in the country, traditional in many ways but also modern and sophisticated, a hub of industry, commerce, trade, culture, education, and the arts. It was also the administrative capital of the British colonial government, and the Brits made sure the city was up to date by introducing automobiles, telephones, electricity, public tram lines, and, in the better homes, running water.

Despite the heavy hand of imperialism, the city had, over the course of nearly a century, been the center of a cultural and spiritual flowering that earned comparison with the Florence of the Medicis. The so-called Bengal Renaissance produced a parade of celebrated intellectuals, artists, scientists, and writers, two of whom Yogananda would meet as a young man and devote reverential chapters to in his autobiography: the scientist Jagadish Chandra Bose and the world-renowned author, poet, and educator Rabindranath Tagore.

The religious corollary to this cultural transformation was known as the Hindu Renaissance, and the man considered the father of that movement was Ram Mohan Roy. The organization Roy founded in the early 19th century, the Brahmo Samaj, revitalized the Vedantic principles embodied in the Upanishads while rejecting rites and customs they regarded as antiquated and tangential. While adamantly opposed to British rule, the Brahmos admired the West's embrace of reason, science, and social reform, and their ties to the Unitarian Universalists introduced New Englanders like Ralph Waldo Emerson to Hindu philosophy. Partly to earn respect for India's native religion, which most Europeans viewed as heathen and primitive, and partly because they felt that spiritual reform would revitalize the populace, Roy and other activist thinkers—including Rabindranath Tagore's father, Debendranath, an esteemed theologian—interpreted Hinduism in modern terms and sought to implant the mother lode of Vedic wisdom into everyday life.

Among the many Calcutta youths who were strongly influenced by the Brahmo Samaj was Narendranath Datta, who would become a national hero as Swami Vivekananda. Born in 1863, Vivekananda was a disciple of the legendary saint Sri Ramakrishna Paramahamsa, who had presided as resident priest at the Kali temple in Dakshineswar, about 12 kilometers upriver from where Yogananda's family would settle.[1] Ramakrishna passed away in 1886, and Vivekananda in 1902 at age 39. But the two spiritual giants remained a palpable presence in Bengal.

To spiritual aspirants in both East and West, Ramakrishna has always exemplified a certain kind of Indian holy man: a single-minded lover of God from humble origins, unschooled, independent, unconventional, nonconformist, who rises to the heights of realization and, by dint of his authenticity and irresistible persona, inspires an enduring spiritual lineage. By famously experimenting with Christian and Muslim practices and declaring that they led to the same inner depths as traditional Hindu methods, he also personified the Vedic maxim that all paths can culminate in Divine union, a precept that Yogananda would do as much as anyone to further in pluralistic America.[2]

Swami Vivekananda became a revered figure throughout India thanks in large part to his triumph at Chicago's World's Parliament of Religions in 1893 (nine months after Yogananda's birth) and his subsequent success implanting Vedanta in the West. In 1897, he and the order of monks he created founded the Ramakrishna Mission in Calcutta. About a year and a half later, they established Belur Math, the society's monastic and administrative headquarters to this day, across the Ganges from Dakshineswar. The organization became a leading aspirational voice throughout India, as Vivekananda's frequent invocation of a passage from the Upanishads, "Arise, awake, and stop not until the goal is reached," acquired sociopolitical connotations on top of its spiritual meaning. After his passing, his achievements were solidified by his brother swamis, Ramakrishna's spiritual wife Sarada Devi (known to devotees as Holy Mother), and the indomitable Margaret Noble, an American disciple revered by Indians as Sister Nivedita. The lineage is lauded for rendering Vedanta and yoga in rational, pragmatic terms; raising the self-respect of Indians demoralized by colonialism; making social service a central feature of the monastic order; prioritizing spiritual experience over ritual and superstition; and making traditional teachings accessible to everyone regardless of caste.

The Ramakrishna-Vivekananda legacy had a major influence on Mukunda's spiritual development, and when his life's mission came into focus, Vivekananda's success in America would serve as a kind of lodestar.

When the Ghosh family arrived in the capital city on July 2, 1906, Mukunda was a skinny kid of 13 and a half whose dark eyes revealed a depth beyond his years. Like Calcutta itself, he was playful but tough-minded, lackadaisical in some ways and disciplined in others, fiercely independent but constrained by circumstance—for him, youth; for Calcutta, colonial rulers—and aflame with a passionate yearning for freedom. Not just the usual adolescent desire for autonomy, but the ultimate freedom of *moksha*, the liberation of consciousness in yogic union.

The Ghoshes lodged for a short period at Bhagabati's sister's home on Sitaram Ghosh Street, then rented a house in Champatala, more than 40 kilometers away. A year later, they returned to the city, leasing a two-story house for 40 rupees a month at 4 Garpar Road (Mr. Ghosh purchased the home in 1919 for 17,000 rupees). A curved, leafy street, Garpar Road was then a narrow lane. As automobiles and trucks replaced horse-drawn carriages, bullock carts, and rickshaws, the asphalt strip was expanded and sidewalks were added. Now, when the windows are open at number 4 one can hear the clamor of horns and engines from the broad thoroughfare that crosses at the nearby corner. A century ago, I was told, ponds and coconut groves stood where the jungle of buildings and roads has since encroached.

The house has been occupied by Ghoshes ever since, with modern amenities added as they became available and a third story appended to the pale yellow structure with the sculpted metal balcony rail and green shutters and trimming. On the wall next to the front door is a plaque reading, "Here lived Paramahansa Yogananda, founder Yogoda Satsanga Society of India and Self-Realization Fellowship in America."[3]

In a sense, the area in which Mukunda spent his teenage years was the Greenwich Village of Calcutta: tree-lined residential streets; boulevards with shops and public transportation; top-notch educational institutions; creative thinkers, scientists, and artists; religious, social, and political reformers; freedom fighters and revolutionaries. The Ghoshes' home was about a 15-minute walk from the spacious residence where Vivekananda had been born and raised, a 30-minute walk from the Tagore estate, and a few seconds' stroll down the other side of the street from the dwelling of Sukumar Ray, a popular author of children's verse whose son Satyajit (born in 1921) would grow up to direct the *Apu Trilogy* and other cinematic masterpieces.[4] It was also about a 20-minute walk from Calcutta University, where many luminaries had studied and where future scientists, scholars, artists, and politicians were being groomed. Mukunda attended, rather indifferently, the all-boys Hindu School in the same neighborhood; its high-quality curriculum, designed by the British to westernize the natives' minds, no doubt helped him adjust to life in America.

It was a time of rising national identity and pride.[5] Mukunda imbibed Calcutta's spirit of independence and personal and national strength and was no doubt inspired by his distant relative, Aurobindo Ghose, who was imprisoned for sedition in Calcutta, underwent a spiritual transformation while in solitary confinement, and, in 1910 (when Mukunda graduated high school), fled to Pondicherry in South India and became the philosopher-saint Sri Aurobindo. As a spiritual leader, Yogananda would speak up for Indian independence and speak out against injustice, but from the start his gaze was primarily on a form of liberation that runs deeper than politics to the very core of being. What thrilled Mukunda most about Calcutta was the opportunity to pick the fruits of a veritable orchard of ashrams, temples, and holy men.

The Ghosh home on Garpar Road was spacious but clamorous. In addition to Mukunda and his father, it housed Ananta and his bride, the four youngest siblings (sisters Nalini and Purnamoyee, brothers Sananda and Bishnu), plus an uncle, a maidservant, and a cook. This made all the more crucial Mukunda's habit of staking out a sanctuary as soon as the family moved into a new home. He claimed a small enclosure on the rooftop level, which had probably been meant for storage. Little more than two meters in length and width, it had enough room for Mukunda to meditate, do pujas at an altar, and even squeeze in a few fellow devotees. His father's austere spirituality continued to be an inspiration. While he could easily have afforded a car and driver, the widower commuted to and from his office, about 22 kilometers and more than an hour each way, on a series of public conveyances. After the family supper, he retired to his room for nightly sadhana.

For all his spiritual ardor and otherworldly pursuits, Mukunda was an energetic adolescent who made friends easily, participated enthusiastically in sports and games, and organized both good deeds and mischief. Accounts of his teen years portray him as a natural leader, charismatic and strong-willed, athletically gifted and intellectually curious although disinterested in formal education. He was also a passionate, albeit untrained, singer of traditional *bhajans* (religiously themed songs) and *kirtan* (communal chanting).[6] Drawn primarily to songs addressed to Divine Mother, he was also fond of Rabindranath Tagore compositions, which are rich in philosophical and spiritual meaning (one is the Indian national anthem). He also sang songs by Swami Rama Tirtha, whose books enriched Mukunda's spiritual education and whose two years of teaching in America made him a role model second only to Vivekananda.[7] Reports of Mukunda's musical talent at that time portray him as either a gifted singer and instrumentalist or a mediocre one who made up for his lack of skill with feeling.

Today's students of Yogananda would not be surprised by his youthful passion for music. In his teaching years he composed numerous devotional songs, translated others' work (including that of Tagore and Rama Tirtha), led collective chants with gusto, and played several Indian instruments. What might come as a surprise is his love of sport, and his talent for it. It's easy to see the asceticism of the monk's way of life as incompatible with the physicality of sports, not to mention the challenges of pride and ego that come with competition. But Yogananda always taught the importance of a strong and healthy body, and even as a middle-aged yogi in America he enjoyed the occasional game of tennis and delighted in challenging people to race him (many were shocked by his proficiency). It's also true that the release from ordinary thought that comes with meditation and chanting is mirrored by what athletes call "being in the zone." Conceivably, Mukunda had such ego-dissolving experiences while running, and perhaps he was charmed by the sense of abandon, flight, and mastery that sports can generate.

In the Calcutta of his youth, physical fitness had become a virtue among young men, inspired in large part by Vivekananda's call for national vigor. Mukunda obviously stayed in shape. We learn in *Mejda* that he was a dues-paying member of the YMCA and competed in races with great success. Sananda Ghosh recalls the day his upstart brother prevailed over more experienced runners in both the 440-yard and half-mile races, despite competing barefoot with his dhoti raised above his knees while others wore shorts and sneakers.[8] He adds that Mukunda's prowess inspired him and youngest brother Bishnu to work out as well, and Bishnu went on to become a renowned fitness and Hatha Yoga expert.[9]

Mukunda was also something of an organizer and a coach, perhaps foreshadowing his skill set as Yogananda. In pastoral Greer Park,[10] he would put his brother and friends through their paces. He arranged competitions and, according to *Mejda*, "worked to create an atmosphere of impartiality that fostered fairness and the spirit of true sportsmanship."[11] He also became attracted to wrestling. He and Sananda would watch training sessions at a "wrestling gymnasium" up the street, and sometimes Mukunda would offer astute advice to the wrestlers, who thanked him with sweets. The athletes were shocked to learn that their informal coach had never himself wrestled. His ideas apparently arose from observation and intuition. Eventually, the brothers did learn to wrestle, and Mukunda apparently got quite good at it.

One site of athletic activity was the Calcutta Deaf and Dumb School, which was located directly across the street from 4 Garpar Road. From the second floor of their home, the Ghosh kids could watch the students on the playing field and in the bathing pond. They managed to gain access to both. Of much greater significance, the school provided Mukunda with a cherished friend.

Manomohan Mazumdar was the son of Mohini Mohan Mazumdar, one of the founders of the Deaf and Dumb School. He and his family lived on the school's grounds. The boys met in 1906. Although Manomohan was two years younger than Mukunda—usually a formidable gap at 11 and 13—the two became inseparable companions in both sporting and spiritual activities. Later, they would be brother disciples of the same guru, Sri Yukteswar, and colleagues in the advancement of Kriya Yoga. Manomohan became Swami Satyananda, who, among other accomplishments, penned a short memoir about his famous friend.[12] As a fringe benefit, Manomohan's father aided the boys' spiritual projects and their sporting life, with moral support and access to facilities.

But Mukunda's priorities were always spiritual. He gathered insights, meditative techniques, and yogic methodologies from every authoritative source he could find. Swami Satyananda wrote that Mukunda would run to meet every yogi or holy man he heard of if he thought he might learn something from them. In those days, Satyananda was still Manomohan, the junior companion to his older friend, who was a classic teenage instigator—the kid who thinks up schemes, prods his buddies into tagging along, and leads the way to new experiences and daring adventures. Only Mukunda's escapades were spiritual, not the naughty and rowdy exploits typical of teenage ringleaders. He stalked God like Sherlock Holmes stalked criminals, and Manomohan was the first of his several Watsons.

Mukunda's spirituality was practical, meditative, and method oriented. But he was a well-rounded yogi and would always remain so. Like Sri Ramakrishna, he knew the Divine to be formless and yet manifest in infinite forms. He read sacred texts, contemplated spiritual conundrums, and sought to discern the infinite Self from the finite self. He engaged in the devotional practices of Bhakti Yoga with ardor and regularity. Satyananda notes that Mukunda had "devotional inclinations" toward Krishna and Shiva, and that sometimes on their way to school they would bow at the door of the Radha Krishna Temple on Harrison Road.[13] His primary devotional bent, however, remained Kali. He would create icons of the deity for use in pujas and prayer, often aided by brother Sananda.

To some extent, young Mukunda was also a karma yogi, one whose path to the Divine is through selfless service. Like the adult Yogananda, he understood the benefit of helping others without attachment to results, and he initiated opportunities for *seva* (selfless service). In *Mejda*, Sananda describes the time Mukunda led an effort to raise money for the poor and distribute the funds at a festival by the Ganges. Afterward, he insisted on giving their tram fare to lepers, even though it meant walking 10 kilometers home. On another occasion, a cold winter night, Mukunda arrived at home wearing only a dhoti and shoes, to his father's consternation. He had given his shirt and coat to a homeless man who'd been shivering in worn-out rags.

While he was building the foundation of a fruitful spiritual life in the big city, Mukunda remained restless. His dream of Himalayan purity was never far from his mind. In 1908, when he was 15, he concocted a plan that would take him to the mountains where, he was certain, the guru whose face had often appeared to him awaited. The adventure that ensued occupies an entire chapter of his autobiography.

Having saved up his rupees, he and two accomplices, a high school classmate named Amar Mitter and his cousin Jotinda (full name Jotin Ghosh), chose for their time of escape the afternoon of a school day. The day dawned with what Yogananda would call "inauspicious rain."[14] Mukunda stayed home that day, feigning a minor illness. He spent the morning in his meditation room, where he bundled into a blanket what he thought an ascetic would need: sandals, a pair of loincloths, prayer beads, a photo of Lahiri Mahasaya, and a copy of the *Bhagavad Gita*. The plan called for Amar to duck out of school, engage a horse-drawn carriage, and meet his comrade, undetected, at a predetermined point close to the Ghosh residence. When the time came, Mukunda tossed his sack out the window into the alley that ran alongside the house. At the front door, he unexpectedly ran into his uncle, but he kept going without stopping for niceties. He retrieved the bundle and dashed to the getaway vehicle.

Part of the plan was to dress in European garb, thereby avoiding detection by authorities who would surely be alerted when the boys were discovered to be missing. They stopped at a market, purchased three suits, and proceeded to pick up Jotin. After stopping to buy canvas shoes, because animal products like leather were too unholy for such an auspicious venture, they arrived at the cavernous Howrah Station. There they boarded a train for the first leg of the multi-legged journey that would take more than 26 hours even today. While they were changing trains in Burdwan (now Bardhaman), Jotin disappeared. Mukunda and

Amar searched the station and made inquiries, and finally determined that their companion had chickened out.

The next morning, while changing trains at Mughalsarai, they were stopped by a station agent holding a telegram. Back in Calcutta, brother Ananta had been doing some detective work. On the first afternoon, he learned at Mukunda's school that Amar had also gone missing. At Amar's home, he found a railway schedule marked with station stops between Calcutta and the Himalayan gateway city of Haridwar. The coachman who drove Amar's father to work added details he'd gleaned from a fellow driver: Amar and two companions, dressed as Europeans, had gifted him with three pairs of leather shoes en route to the train station. Armed with these clues, Ananta wired the stations on the boys' itinerary. Jotin's confession upon his return yielded additional information.

Because the officer at Mughalsarai asked if he had run away from home in anger, Mukunda, who had vowed not to lie, was able to get by with the truth. He was, after all, an aspiring pilgrim, not some embittered runaway. Amar had no such compunctions. When asked their names, he came up with "Thomas" and "Thompson." That, plus their European clothing and the fact that there were only two boys, not the three described in the bulletin, enabled them not only to catch the next train, but to be placed in a higher-grade compartment reserved for Europeans.

One can imagine the exhilaration Mukunda must have felt, not only as a determined seeker on his way to the Himalayas, but as a 15-year-old having a grand adventure with a good friend, in clever disguise no less, and putting one over on the colonists who had imposed a discriminatory seating arrangement on the conquered natives. Still, the pilgrims knew they'd been found out and were forced to modify their plan. When they arrived in Haridwar after another overnight ride, they ran directly to a market and replaced their telltale costumes with regular Indian clothing.

The final train ride was to take them to the sacred city of Rishikesh, which had been known for centuries as the abode of yogis and saints and would become globally famous half a century later thanks to the Beatles. But their journey ended in a Haridwar police station. They were apprehended and held for three days, housed in a policeman's home, waiting for Ananta and Amar's brother.

Ananta insisted on returning to Calcutta via Benares. He had cooked up a two-pronged scheme to persuade Mukunda to give up what he and his father considered a misguided and, at his tender age, dangerous renunciation fantasy. The idea was to find Mukunda a suitable guru closer to home. The candidate he had in mind was a presumably enlightened master in Benares who was regarded by followers as an incarnation of God. Amid the ceremonial trappings and the crush of disciples trying to get as close to the holy presence as possible, Ananta managed to bring Mukunda to the guru's attention. Mukunda was not impressed; he saw in the man's demeanor a giant ego.

Ananta had had a good idea, but he chose the wrong guru. He then drew the second card up his sleeve. He had colluded with a father-son team of learned Benares pandits and, as planned, brought his brother to their home. In the courtyard, the junior pandit, having established his reputation for psychic ability, disclosed this revelation: Mukunda was not meant to be a *sannyasi* (an ascetic renunciate); indeed, he would not find God in this lifetime unless he worked off his past karma through action in the world.

Mukunda would have none of it. He countered with a passage from the *Bhagavad Gita* (Chapter 9, Verses 30–31), which states that any sincere devotee who ceaselessly meditates on God can rise above the residue of karma. The coup de grâce was delivered by a sadhu who had overheard the conversation. He assured Mukunda that he was destined for monkhood. Ananta was out of cards to play.

In its entirety, the story of the aborted escape reiterates certain traits that Yogananda would exhibit his entire life, and that made his mission to the West both challenging and uniquely successful: a fierce independence, astute self-awareness, enormous confidence, and a single-minded focus on his lofty goals.

He returned to Calcutta disappointed but undaunted. His father and older brother were relieved, but also undaunted. They would keep on trying to maneuver the wannabe ascetic into the normal life of an Indian householder.

CHAPTER 4

THE MAKING
OF A GURU

By the time he was 15, Mukunda's calling was as obvious as that of a math prodigy who tutors graduate students and works on unsolved theorems in his spare time. After his intercepted pilgrimage, he was a "marked boy," to use Swami Satyananda's term, and was treated differently by classmates, friends, and relatives. Predictably, he was teased by some of his peers, who tagged him with the nickname Sadhu Baba ("renunciate father"). Teasing is a burden all unusual youngsters bear, of course, but few are taunted for meditating too much or skipping fun and games to sit at the feet of swamis. Adults, on the other hand, now treated Mukunda with newfound respect, perhaps recognizing that his spiritual yearning might be a sign of a future sannyasi. This conferred two benefits, according to Satyananda's memoir. One was that he got away with minor misbehavior like classroom banter and noisemaking. The other was that he could be more open about devoting time to spiritual practice.

His reputation was such that friends would tip him off to the presence of gurus and yogis. His appetite for new spiritual disciplines and rituals was insatiable, and his inventory grew into a blend of devotional and meditative practices. He was a stalwart meditator, and, as Yogananda, he would urge his followers to be the same. He acquired methods from a variety of sources, including a neighbor who belonged to a spiritual community called "the Radha Swami group" and members of the Brahmo Samaj. He also learned some basic Kriya Yoga techniques from his father, who had learned them from Lahiri Mahasaya. As Mr. Ghosh was clearly a man of rectitude and loyalty, he must have had permission from his guru, or from a representative of Lahiri's lineage, to pass along instructions to his family. Mukunda practiced with diligence from the start. In the coming years, he would acquire from gurus the complete sequence of Kriya Yoga breathing and concentration techniques that he eventually introduced to the West.

In his writings, Yogananda does not mention having learned Hatha Yoga *asanas* (postures), whose bends and stretches are now ubiquitous. Students of his work have found this curious, and have conjectured about it, because Yogananda assiduously taught that care of the body was a crucial component of spiritual development, and he was a proponent of asana practice. It was part of the students' routine in the school he established in India, and later for his monastics in America. In the 1940s, he had young men demonstrate asanas in public and had the postures pictured and described in his organization's magazine. Because Hatha Yoga was part of the overall effort, centered in Calcutta, to raise the fitness level of Indian youth, Mukunda must have been exposed to it in one form or another.[1]

He spent long hours on inward journeys to the Infinite, and would happily have spent entire days in his attic sanctuary instead of at school. This relentless pursuit of the Divine led Mukunda to some offbeat teachers, landed him in peculiar circumstances, and attracted the curious attention of others. In an incident witnessed by his brother Sananda, he became so God-intoxicated during a morning bath in the Ganges that he remained there, immersed to the neck, ecstatically voicing devotional songs and prayers as the sun rose to its apex and began its descent in the western sky. He not only lost track of time, but also of his clothing. In today's Kolkata, the route back to Garpar Road would be along concrete and asphalt, with a soundtrack of the traffic's roar. Back then, there were open spaces, and greenery, and the songbirds Mukunda loved to listen to. He kept up his own singing as he walked, naked, oblivious to passersby, who may have been used to seeing unclothed mendicants (*naga sadhus*) along the sacred river. He snapped out of it when one of his aunts spotted him and cuffed him on the ear, calling him an "evil boy" and a disgrace to his family. He calmly informed her that the evil was in her mind and strolled back to the river to retrieve his garments.

It was not the only time Mukunda got so absorbed in the Eternal that he was oblivious to the finite realm. Sananda recalls one of many occasions when he and others accompanied Mukunda to the Dakshineswar Kali Temple for a long day's journey into God. Mukunda topped off the activities with an extended meditation outdoors under a banyan tree—part of a sacred five-tree grouping known collectively as the *Panchavati*, which had been planted by Sri Ramakrishna. When Mukunda's friends went to retrieve him for evening *aarti*[2] at the temple, they found him sitting perfectly still with one snake wrapped around his neck like a scarf and another resting in his lap like a pet cat. It took some effort to get his attention. According to Sananda in *Mejda*, he clapped his hands and the snakes slithered meekly away.

One of Mukunda's more provocative experiments was with esoteric tantric practices. In the Western mind, the word *tantra* is associated almost exclusively with prolonged, ritualized sex, but it actually consists of a huge body of texts and spiritual disciplines that range far afield. Much of tantra has mixed easily with yoga and Vedanta, and some of the meditative practices common today—particularly those involving mantras—have tantric origins. A central feature of the tradition is its attempt to make sacred the ordinary aspects of material life.[3]

Some tantric practices utilize death as a vivid symbol of impermanence, with the aim of realizing the eternal reality that transcends birth and death. In India, such disciplines might be practiced in crematory grounds, and for a while Mukunda would go—sometimes when he should have been at school and sometimes late at night—to the riverbank where the bodies of the recently departed were ritually burned. "Human inadequacy becomes clear in the gloomy abode of miscellaneous bones," Yogananda would write in the *AY*.[4] His brother Sananda and his friend Manomohan both joined his crematory sadhana, only to be so spooked by the bones and corpses that they couldn't continue.

During this period, Mukunda became intrigued by a *sadhu* from a tantric sect whom his brother describes as wearing dark red and having a frightening visage. The sadhu would accompany Mukunda to his attic meditation cell and presumably instruct him. One night, when Sananda entered the room after his brother and the sadhu had left, he was shocked to find an actual skull and crossbones. He squealed to Mr. Ghosh, who put an end to the sadhu's visits. Subsequently, Mukunda advised others to stay away from the occult aspects of tantra, but the higher teachings seem to have endured, as the tantric ideal of sanctifying the mundane and perceiving each slice of creation as Divine was an integral aspect of Yogananda's teaching.

This phase of his life also saw a furthering of Mukunda's interest in the power of the mind and its capacity to affect both material objects and other minds. What we in the West think of as hypnosis traces its origins to the 18th century, when the Austrian physician Franz Mesmer explained the skill scientifically and developed a consistent method for employing it. In India, yogis and siddhas had cultivated similar practices for centuries. It is not clear whether Mukunda drew only upon the yogic tradition or also learned from Western hypnosis— which was surely accessible in colonial Calcutta—or if he was entirely self-taught, as Swami Satyananda contends. In any event, Mukunda began demonstrating hypnosis and mediumship, sometimes for show and sometimes for practical ends, like solving petty crimes and ridding his sister of a demon. On occasion, he would use Sananda as a medium. To track down a boy who stole a coat, for instance, he induced in Sananda a receptive state of relaxation and applied hypnosis to obtain information psychically. On another occasion, he got his hypnotized brother to "read," without using his eyes, the page of a book he opened at random. And once, after commanding Sananda to place his hand on a wall, he rendered him unable to pull it away. He also contacted the souls of the dead through his brother, on one occasion speaking to their late mother.

Through these experiments, he was no doubt learning how to harness the dormant abilities of consciousness that yogis had extolled for millennia. He was also becoming aware of his own innate powers, which were, by any standard, exceptional. At the same time, he needed to learn firsthand about the dangers of the occult. In one instance, he reportedly coaxed a spirit to enter his hypnotized sister Thamu, and to use her voice to reveal the location of a stolen object. It worked, only the spirit didn't want to leave. It took some hard negotiating on Mukunda's part (his trump card was brandishing a photo of Lahiri Mahasaya) and a lot of effort to bring Thamu back to consciousness and full strength.

Eventually, as with the tantric sadhu, his father persuaded Mukunda that hypnosis and spirit contact could cause real harm. In his years in the West, Yogananda, like countless yoga masters, warned against becoming overly enamored of, and distracted by, occult powers. At the same time, he explained their operation rationally and demonstrated them to awaken interest in the more profound benefits of yogic discipline.

Mukunda's exploration was not entirely solitary. He is described by his brother and Satyananda as eager to arouse in others the passion for God that came naturally to him. As a result, he acquired something of an entourage. Throughout his mid-teens, he would round up members of his movable sangha for sadhana and satsangs, much as he had gathered athletes for games. He led his companions to sacred sites and solitary places, and orchestrated rituals and worship celebrations. They rode by carriage or boat to Dakshineswar. They meditated inside temples and on temple grounds, in gardens and in the bushes alongside playing fields, in Mukunda's rooftop cell and in the Ghoshes' parlor.

At Mukunda's urging, some of his friends agreed to become vegetarians, observe traditional behavioral codes like right speech and nonviolence, and rise at dawn to do sadhana at home. At times Mukunda coaxed them into marathon meditation sessions. Satyananda describes nights when he would sneak

out of his house and into Mukunda's, and the two would meditate until it was time to creep back home before his absence was
discovered. Escapades like that caused the parents of Mukunda's fellow *sadhaks* (spiritual practitioners) to worry that spiritual zealotry would take precedence over schoolwork—and it
often did.

Mukunda's discipline was extraordinary even by the standards of adult sannyasis, and while his brethren couldn't always
keep up with him, he stretched them like a coach stretches athletes. By all indications they were grateful.

In a talk to Los Angeles disciples on Christmas Day, 1949,
Yogananda waxed nostalgic: "Our Self Realization work started in
a little hut in India for twenty-five cents a month as rent. Father
used to call me back every night: 'Stay in the day, but don't stay
at night.' But I said, 'In this little hive there is honey, and the bees
will be coming.' So when our honey of God gathered in that little
hive, bees of devotees began to come from far and near."[5]

That one-room hut—essentially, Yogananda's first ashram—
was acquired in 1908, when Mukunda was 15, because the
Ghosh home was too clamorous for satsangs. Located for the
group by a boy named Pulin, who would go on to become a
swami, the small thatched-roof structure with adobe walls was
located a couple of kilometers east of Garpar Road. Mukunda
named it Sadhana Mandir. As *mandir* is usually translated as
"temple," it was, therefore, a temple devoted to spiritual practice.
The young yogis met there regularly; Mukunda led them in
scriptural reading, kirtan chanting, and meditation. He seems to
have made the place his personal responsibility. In his memoir,
Satyananda wrote that Mukunda devoted an extraordinary
amount of time and energy to fixing up the ashram, sometimes
laboring through the night. Once, when cementing the floor, his
hands bled. When he pulled all-nighters, his sister Thamu, then
around seven, would let him into their home in the morning
before their elders awakened.

As he would when he was a grown-up guru, he relied on
benefactors to keep his operation going. One was his sister

Nalini. Affluent thanks to her marriage to a physician, she would secretly stash rupees in the carrying case of her harmonium and Mukunda would borrow the instrument when he needed money for his spiritual efforts.

After making do with the minuscule hut for about a year, Mukunda prayed for the arrival of a friend who could provide a larger, more convenient location. As the story goes, he had a vision of a young man whose family would help. He soon saw that very boy sitting on a bench in Greer Park, a popular gathering place for sports. It was in May 1909, and the boy's name was Tulsi Narayan Bose. He was slightly older than Mukunda and had never seen him before, even though he lived on Pitambar Bhattacharya Lane, a few minutes' stroll from Garpar Road.

Mukunda proposed a race. Tulsi, an accomplished athlete, accepted. To his surprise, he proceeded to lose, twice, to the younger upstart with the unorthodox running style. He accepted Mukunda's invitation to visit him that evening. Tulsi later told relatives that he and his new friend sat on the floor in lotus posture. Mukunda touched Tulsi's forehead to quiet his mind. He then taught him to meditate (with which method is not known), and they meditated all night.

The young men quickly grew close to one another and to their families. Tulsi's father, Hari Narayan Bose, was the headmaster of an art school and formerly a college classmate of Narendranath Datta, who became Swami Vivekananda. Mr. Bose encouraged the young men's spiritual pursuits and eventually purchased a plot of land adjacent to his home, adding enough cash to build a three-room structure on the property.[6] Sadhana Mandir had a new and larger home, virtually in Mukunda's backyard.

The new location was big enough to accommodate another of Mukunda's dreams. He acquired books and periodicals, hauled over chairs and a table from home, and opened the Saraswati Library (Saraswati is the deity associated with knowledge). The founding date, according to Sananda, was January 10, 1910, five days after Mukunda's 17th birthday. Later, a rift erupted over the policies and content of the library, with Mukunda on one side and Tulsi and a youngster named Prokas Chandra Das on the

THE LIFE OF YOGANANDA

other. Mukunda obtained a new location, in the sitting room of a private home, and when his opponents refused to let him take the reading material, he went door to door and gathered up books for a new collection.

There is no indication that the incident damaged Mukunda's friendships or his ongoing spiritual work. However, it is hard to resist the observation that the juvenile library schism, in its own small way, foreshadowed more calamitous ruptures between Yogananda and some of his colleagues in America. Both sets of circumstances have at least one thing in common: a certain ambiguity about the relationships.

Mukunda's crew of adolescent yogis were his friends, but also, in meaningful ways, his students. They were buddies, but also followers. On the one hand, Mukunda was their peer; on the other hand, he had the knowledge, passion, and personality to assume a leadership position—not just the leadership of, say, a cricket team, but in the holiest aspects of Hindu life. Satyananda acknowledged this ambiguity: "Mukunda became a friend-teacher and the charioteer of life's chariot in my heart. However, I have always related with him as a friend."[7] On some occasions, he adds, "there was too much of a feeling of authority" and "sometimes slightly unpleasant situations would come about."[8] But Mukunda's spiritual leadership does not seem to have diminished the joys of boyhood camaraderie. For the most part, he led without violating the norms of friendship.

At one point, Mukunda was emboldened to do what only gurus, or those authorized by gurus, traditionally did: he transmitted meditation methods to others. The turning point occurred one early evening when a twilight cloudscape in the western sky captured the boys' attention. For Mukunda, the clouds evoked snowcapped mountains. Animated by the image, he implored Manomohan to join him in emulating the path of the Himalayan sadhus, and he offered to teach him two practices he had recently learned, presumably from his father. One involved inwardly hearing the primordial sound of "OM," and the other was to "see" the Divine Light within. Mukunda instructed Manomohan the next day.

At least one critic of Yogananda[9] has called this an early sign of self-importance and a tendency to deviate from tradition. Based on conversations I had in India, other traditionalists have, much less harshly, expressed disapproval of a teenager teaching yogic methods without authorization. At the same time, many see the action as the justifiable self-confidence of an exceptional human being who recognized his gifts and his life's purpose at an early age. The latter perspective would place Mukunda squarely within India's history of spiritual prodigies. Over the course of Hinduism's measureless history, young gurus have arisen, sometimes out of nowhere and sometimes, like Yogananda, with links to established lineages, and attracted followers by dint of their own realization, knowledge, and charisma. Around some of those "godmen" (and a handful of notable "godwomen"), durable institutions have blossomed; others wafted away like the smoke from evening aarti.

Mukunda started teaching at a precocious age, all by himself, but he felt connected to the Vedic heritage, and to Lahiri Mahasaya in particular. In a few years' time, he would become Swami Yogananda, and those ties would be formalized. He would always maintain strong links to lineage while doing his own thing, just as he did at age 15.

Photos of the teenage Mukunda reveal a slim lad, with shoulder-length hair as black as a raven's feathers, sporting in some shots a mustache and a wispy beard and able to pose for the camera in full lotus position without evident strain. What stands out most are the eyes: dark, intense, penetrating, somehow both present and otherworldly. One wants to know what's behind those serious eyes and why the young man they belong to appears to be special. They are the eyes of someone who knows deep secrets and can't wait to know more.

Perhaps it was those commanding eyes that opened doors for Mukunda as he eagerly pursued the company of swamis, saints, and other notables. For while he rehearsed for his eventual role as a global guru, he also humbly assumed the receptive attitude of a novice at the feet of spiritual authorities. Five consecutive chapters of the *AY*, plus parts of others, are devoted to encounters that clearly had a lasting impact on him.

One of the more important of his teachers and role models was Sri Ashutosh Chatterji. A scholar of Sanskrit and Hindu scriptures, he was known by the respectful sobriquet Shastri Mahasaya (sacred texts are called *shastras*). He was hired by Bhagabati Ghosh as a tutor for Mukunda after his thwarted Himalayan escape. The idea was to avert future flights by satisfying close to home his son's fervent quest for knowledge. Like other family interventions, it backfired. "My new teacher, far from offering intellectual aridities, fanned the embers of my God-aspiration," said Yogananda in the *AY*.[10]

Unbeknownst to Mr. Ghosh, Shastri Mahasaya, who would later take monastic vows as Swami Kebalananda, was a fellow disciple of Lahiri Mahasaya. Yogananda described his new teacher, who was in his mid-40s at the time, as handsome, guileless, gentle, and loving. His own progress in Sanskrit he called "unnoteworthy."[11] He was not terribly interested in scholarly erudition. What he loved was discussing yoga with his tutor, absorbing subtle interpretations of ancient Hindu tales, meditating for long hours at a time, and hearing about sages and gurus, especially Lahiri Mahasaya. Shastri Mahasaya also taught Mukunda additional Kriya Yoga methods. Yogananda concludes his tribute to the masterful teacher this way: "I never became a Sanskrit scholar; Kebalananda taught me a diviner syntax."[12]

Another luminary whose company Mukunda sought was the eminent physicist and botanist J. C. (Jagadish Chandra) Bose. Dr. Bose performed pioneering work on electromagnetism and demonstrated that plants respond to stimuli with the equivalent of human responses such as love and hate, pleasure and pain. Yogananda praised Bose for revealing the unity of life. As a teenager, Mukunda visited the scientist at his home. Years later, as Swami Yogananda, he attended the opening of the Bose Institute,[13] and was deeply moved by Bose's speech on that occasion. It is easy to see why. His own life was dedicated, in large part, to bringing together East and West and religion and science; he saw Bose doing the same from the platform of empirical research. He must have loved hearing the scientist say that his institute was as much a temple as a lab. Evident throughout the chapter is Yogananda's profound pride in India. Tears came to his eyes, he said, when Bose extolled "the burning Indian imagination." It is not hard to imagine that Bose strengthened Yogananda's conviction that he would be greeted by receptive minds when he sailed west bearing India's treasures.

Two other exceptional people Mukunda met during those impressionable years were holy men with rarified powers. One was "the Perfume Saint," so called because he could, allegedly, manifest through the power of mind the fragrance of any flower he chose. Mukunda was clearly impressed by this skill, but as Yogananda, he asserted that such ostentatious displays were entertaining but fruitless digressions from the deep purpose of the spiritual pursuit.

Another brief encounter was with "Tiger Swami," a muscular sannyasi who had, in earlier days, gained fame by wrestling and taming tigers. Mukunda's key takeaway from the swami's story was the need to tame the beasts of ignorance that prowl the human mind.

The truly important figures in Mukunda's life during that period were not tricksters but advanced yogis and wise teachers with whom he forged ongoing relationships. One was Nagendra Nath Bhaduri, aka "the Levitating Saint." Then in his 70s, he dwelled in a three-story ashram on Upper Circular Road, near Mukunda's home, and he had earned his nickname by hovering in the air as if seated on an invisible cloud. Yogananda implies that he witnessed this feat, as had his brother Sananda. In the *AY*, the conquest of gravity is treated matter-of-factly: "A yogi's body loses its grossness after use of certain pranayamas [breathing practices]. Then it will levitate or hop about like a leaping frog."[14] He described watching the Levitating Saint perform a pranayama exercise called *bhastrika*, whose robust exhalations can sometimes be observed in today's yoga studios. Once again, we see Yogananda's pattern of calling attention to superpowers, almost to the point of sensationalism, and then putting them into perspective as fringe benefits of a spiritual life whose real purpose is the soul's liberation.

Mukunda dropped by Bhaduri Mahasaya's abode often and was "vastly entertained by the wit in his wisdom."[15] That wit would cause Mukunda to break out in conspicuous laughter, triggering a dynamic commonly observed in the presence of holy figures: earnest disciples disdain the merriment, but the revered one himself rather enjoys it. The Levitating Saint's role in Mukunda's life was not to entertain or to demonstrate yogic powers, however. He was a spiritual mentor, and his philosophical discourses and the personal counsel he tendered in private moments were gratefully absorbed by the young sadhak. Yogananda's description of a key statement the guru uttered is now displayed in the Levitating Saint's bedroom, which has been preserved as a shrine:[16] "You go often into the silence, but have you developed *anubhava* [personal experience of the Supreme]? Do not mistake the technique for the Goal." The lesson, said Yogananda, was "to love God more than meditation."

Yogananda realized in retrospect that long before he dreamed of going to the West, Bhaduri Mahasaya foresaw his future mission. He told him as a teenager that nascent yogis in America were waiting for instruction, and his parting words in 1920, before Yogananda set sail on his historic journey, are also displayed in the bedroom shrine, under an always-garlanded photo of Yogananda: "Son, go to America. Take the dignity of hoary India for your shield. Victory is written on your brow; the noble distant people will well receive you."

In a twist of karma that would probably be rejected as over the top in a Hollywood screenplay, the four-story building in which Mukunda suffered the most grievous loss of his life, the death of his mother, became the source of sublime spiritual transmissions just a few years later. Fifty Amherst Street was turned into a high school by a saintly educator named Mahendra Nath Gupta.[17] Known as Master Mahasaya, Mr. Gupta was no ordinary educator. Then in his mid-50s with a full white beard, he had been a close disciple of the illustrious Sri Ramakrishna. For the last four years of the holy man's life (1882 to 1886), Gupta took every opportunity to sit with him at Dakshineswar and record his every word in a diary. That stenographic record was published in the West as *The Gospel of Sri Ramakrishna*.[18] As a pen name, the humble author chose simply M.

When Mukunda met Master Mahasaya on the top floor of that house of pain, he was still in the grip of what he called "an indescribable torture" caused by the separation from both his human mother and the supreme goddess. He begged for intercession. That night, after a long meditation in his attic room, he said, Divine Mother appeared to him. She stayed only long enough to give him this healing message: "Always have I loved thee! Ever shall I love thee!"[19]

Mukunda returned to Amherst Street frequently to be with the humble teacher he held in the highest esteem. The relationship was a turning point in his spiritual development. "From him I learned the sweetness of God in the aspect of Mother, or Divine Mercy," he wrote.[20] The lessons came not only in Master Mahasaya's simple room in the school building, but on numerous outings to Dakshineswar, where the sage imparted the teachings of Sri Ramakrishna, and also in Calcutta locations where some of the *AY*'s miraculous events took place. In *Mejda*, Sananda Ghosh says that he and Mukunda once asked Master Mahasaya to summon their mother from the astral plane. He refused at first but eventually acquiesced. The brothers sat behind the guru for two full hours as he meditated. Then he bid them to turn around and behold the figure in the doorway. It was, of course, their beloved *amma*.

They asked if she remembered them. She said she watches over them at all times and that they are under Divine Mother's protection. Then she was gone. When the boys told their father what had happened, he admonished them, not because he thought they had made up a tall tale, but out of compassion for his departed wife. He did not want her soul to be troubled by demands from the earthly plane.[21]

Master Mahasaya may have been Mukunda's most significant *upaguru*, a term applied to virtually anyone who teaches something of value. But he was not his *satguru*, the master whose role is to guide the disciple to ultimate realization. Master Mahasaya told Mukunda early on that his true guru would come to him at a later time. That long-awaited meeting, yearned for unceasingly, would take place in Benares in 1910.

CHAPTER 5

THE MASTER COMETH

The list of high school underachievers who go on to accomplish extraordinary things is long, but the subset of indifferent students who were confident that God would intervene to help them graduate is no doubt small. Mukunda Lal Ghosh was one of them. His sights were set on becoming a sannyasi, a vocation for which a diploma was not a prerequisite. If anything, as he approached the end of his high school years, he had become even more detached from worldly duties. He favored secluded places near the river to classrooms, and late nights at the cremation grounds to academic study, and he led his sangha comrades in rehearsals for a future of austerities. "We practiced sleeping on benches," wrote Swami Satyananda, "sometimes lying on the bare floor, walking barefoot, being spartan in clothing and eating, restricting speech, traveling far distances on foot and such other things."[1]

With the approach of the weeklong final exams, anxiety soared in the homes of students throughout India, as passing was a ticket for entry to university. Mukunda did not share that anxiety, since he had a different kind of higher education in mind. But he was not entirely without concern. He had promised his father he would complete high school. That presented a problem, and that's where God came in. Mukunda was certain that the Almighty would step in and "extricate" him.[2]

Sure enough, the cosmic delivery system dropped off two karmic gifts just in the nick of time. First, he ran into a smart and studious classmate named Nantu, who volunteered to tutor him. Nantu drilled Mukunda late into the night. They had time to cover every key subject but one, Sanskrit. Yogananda describes his solution to this problem: "Fervently I reminded God of the oversight."[3]

Deliverance came the next morning. Mukunda took a fortuitous—or divinely guided—detour through a vacant lot, where, amid the weeds and rubble, he stumbled upon some discarded pages of Sanskrit verse. He recruited a scholar to interpret the material. The Sanskritist did as requested but opined that a poetry translation would be of no help on the exam. He was wrong. Mukunda passed Sanskrit just as he passed the other subjects, by the skin of his teeth. He graduated in June 1909.

Having fulfilled his obligation to his father, Mukunda thought he was free to pursue the path of renunciation. Mr. Ghosh had other ideas. He got his son to enroll in Sabour Agricultural College, in the state of Bihar, agriculture having been a passing interest of Mukunda's. He did not stay long. According to brother Sananda, his only takeaway from his foray into agriculture was the big cabbage he brought home with him. Next stop, Metropolitan Institution,[4] a mere 15-minute walk from Garpar Road. It was chosen because Mukunda contemplated becoming a physician, a career plan that lasted about as long as it took to purchase medical reference books and get rid of them.

In the summer of 1910, Mukunda bonded with a young visiting guru named Swami Dayananda, who was holding forth at a nearby ashram. He hatched a plan with his friend Jitendra Nath Mazumdar to leave home and join Swami Dayananda's ashram, Bharat Dharma Mahamandal, in Benares.[5]

His father, of course, tried to talk him out of it, but Mukunda was resolute. His own heart, however, put up an unexpected roadblock, albeit a temporary one. In a memorable passage in his autobiography—one of many moving moments in which he displays a vulnerable side—Yogananda recalls being overwhelmed by love for his family and the thought of leaving them. He says his affection for his family had grown since his mother's passing, and he felt especially warm toward his younger siblings. He retreated to his meditation den to wrestle with a conflict that plays out in the hearts and minds of dedicated seekers everywhere, between the known joys of capricious human bonds and the longing for the infinite bliss of Divine union.

He wept for two hours and emerged "singularly transformed," purified of a strong, binding attachment—the final attachment, perhaps, that stood in the way of unadulterated renunciation. There was no longer even a sliver of space—no Achilles' heel, as it were—in which Mr. Ghosh's pleas could take hold. And plead he did; his son, after all, was only 16. Mukunda responded by proclaiming his mammoth love for his father, but added, "Even greater is my love for the Heavenly Father, who has given me the gift of a perfect father on earth."[6] Reluctant though it may have been, the parental blessing he sought was now his.

In October, Mukunda arrived in Benares, the eternal city where devout Hindus hope to die and spiritual aspirants go to learn from the wise, worship in timeless temples, perform sacred rituals along Ma Ganga (as the river Ganges is called), and soak up thousands of years of holy vibrations. He was welcomed to the Mahamandal Hermitage by Swami Dayananda, joining his friend Jitendra, who had gone on ahead. (Curiously, Yogananda doesn't mention this, but the hermitage was in the same neighborhood as Lahiri Mahasaya's family home, where the master had presided as an esteemed householder guru for decades.[7]) He would remain there for the next eight or nine months, although he was not always a happy camper.

There are many types of ashrams in India, with different spiritual orientations, different requirements, different management styles, and different rules. Mukunda might have been better off at one that emphasized sadhana. That was, by miles, his top priority. He had access to an attic where he could meditate early in the morning. It wasn't enough for him, but it was apparently too much for his fellow devotees. They saw him as overeager and made remarks such as "Don't try to catch God so soon!" Catching God quickly was, of course, precisely why Mukunda was in an ashram. In the afternoons, he performed his office duties, but the others worked longer and expected him to do so as well.

Swami Dayananda seems to have been a saintly man and a patient teacher, although not destined to be Mukunda's satguru. When the newcomer expressed his hunger for Divine perception and said he was confused about what was expected of him at the ashram, the swami told other disciples not to bother him. He was sure that Mukunda would eventually learn the ways of the community, but he never did. The ashram ethos was evidently one of Karma Yoga, a path whose emphasis on service, work, and discipline is meant to subordinate the ego and attune the disciple to the consciousness of the guru and, through him, Divine Intelligence. Mukunda was more aligned with the meditative accent of Raja Yoga and the devotion of Bhakti Yoga.

The tension would eventually become intolerable. Making matters worse, he was forced to stop receiving spending money from his father and to adapt to the ashram's spartan menu and meal schedule, which deprived him of the ample breakfast he was used to. He did, however, learn a great deal from Dayananda, and one of the lessons he valued was his attachment to "food consciousness." "Gone was an age-old delusion by which bodily imperatives outwit the soul," he said. "There and then I tasted the Spirit's all-sufficiency."[8]

Yogananda chose to remain at the hermitage through the winter and early spring. Presumably, the rewards of life with Dayananda outweighed the animosity of his fellow residents. In retrospect, he would surely say the hand of God was holding him in place until all necessary conditions were aligned for the life-changing event that occurred sometime in the late spring or early summer of 1910.

Much of the world was in turmoil at the time, with social upheavals in far-flung places like Mexico, Korea, Egypt, Portugal, and the Balkans. The United States witnessed heated labor unrest in several cities and the beginning of the Great Migration of African Americans from the former slave states to the north. In India, agitation against the partition of Bengal intensified. And in the brand-new dominion called the Union of South Africa, Mohandas K. Gandhi established Tolstoy Farm as the command center of the passive resistance strategy he later applied to his homeland. Mukunda was probably oblivious to all of this in the rigorous routine of the ashram and the timeless beats of life in the byways of ancient Kashi,[9] as Benares had been known since the era of the *Rig Veda*.

Today, most of what is called Varanasi is a sprawl of dense, dirty, deafening streets far too slim to accommodate the massive population explosion and the influx of motorized vehicles. Yet magic is still conjured on the banks of Ma Ganga and in the narrow lanes that circulate like blood vessels, at seemingly random angles, immediately inland from the *ghats* (steps leading down to a river). In Yogananda's day, when humans had to compete for space only with bicycles, rickshaws, bullock carts, dogs, and cows, those pathways were quiet, making even more room for magic.

So it was late one morning when the trajectory of Mukunda's life changed radically. He may have been on the alert for an auspicious day since, not long before, he had discovered that the amulet given to his mother by the mysterious sadhu was gone. He had kept it in a sealed envelope inside a locked box hidden in his ashram room, but the last time he checked, the box was still locked and the envelope was still sealed but the trinket was not inside. This day began as quite the opposite of auspicious. He awakened at dawn, distraught over the worsening discord between him and the other ashramites. He climbed to the attic and began praying intensely, desperate for guidance or intervention from on high. After a few hours of what he called "sobbing pleas," everything changed. His consciousness ascended to a celestial realm. He heard, from some nonlocal and unlocatable place, the sweet sound of a feminine voice. It said, no doubt in formal Bengali, "Thy Master cometh today!"[10]

His bliss was interrupted by the shout of his name. He was being summoned to run an errand. He roused himself, and soon was walking with a fellow ashramite named Habu. They wound through the warren of winding lanes to a bustling marketplace to purchase necessary items. On the way back to the hermitage, Mukunda saw, at the intersection of two narrow streets, a stately swami dressed in the traditional yellow-orange color usually called ochre. He is described in the *AY* as leonine, and the description is apt; photos show a handsome face regally framed by thick wavy hair, either dark or snow white depending on his age at the time, with a beard to match. Yogananda also applied to him a descriptor he favored for the saintliest of people: "Christlike."

The sight of the swami registered on Mukunda, but he was not sure why. Dismissing the feeling as a mistaken association with someone he may have known, he walked on. Ten minutes later, he says, his feet grew numb; then they turned as heavy as stone. He could walk no further. The thought occurred that he was being pulled like an iron filing to the magnet of the swami he had just seen. He handed the packages he was carrying to the bewildered Habu and sped back to the nondescript corner, maybe 60 meters from the Ganges, that Yogananda devotees now mark as the spot where their guru met his own beloved guru, Sri Yukteswar Giri.

In Yogananda's account, Sri Yukteswar hadn't budged. He found him gazing in his direction as he rushed toward him, now recognizing his face as the very one that had come to him in visions all his life. He was soon at the swami's feet, he says, uttering "Gurudeva" (divine teacher). He quotes Sri Yukteswar's first words[11] to him: "O my own, you have come to me! How many years I have waited for you!" Spoken, Yogananda wrote, in a voice "tremulous with joy," the words are known to thousands upon thousands of devotees.[12]

It must be noted that the number of seekers whose minds have been blown by Indian ascetics who looked into their eyes and said, "I have been waiting for you," is legion. In this case, however, the guru was no charlatan but a master of impeccable dignity and abundant knowledge whose reputation has only been burnished by time. He was, in short, the real deal, and the one Mukunda always knew he would find.

Sri Yukteswar took Mukunda's hand and led him—either along the Ganges or through the winding streets—to a house in the Rana Mahal district that served as an ashram, his mother's residence, and his base of operations when he came to that part of India. Yogananda describes the 55-year-old guru's walk as "firm" and "vigorous" and his stature as "tall," "erect," and "athletic." Sitting on a balcony overlooking the river, they talked until dark. During that time, among other things, Sri Yukteswar pledged to him his unconditional love, and asked for his in return.

On several occasions, including a talk to devotees on his birthday sometime in the late 1940s,[13] Yogananda said that during that initial meeting, Sri Yukteswar revealed that he, Mukunda, was destined to take the wisdom of India to the West. In his autobiography, he appears to say that the information was revealed to him during his *second* meeting with his guru.[14] Be that as it may, the first meeting contained another revelation that stunned him: Sri Yukteswar's main ashram/residence was in Serampore, only about 24 kilometers upriver from the Ghosh home in Calcutta, not in the remote Himalayas where he expected to find his preceptor. This made him wonder about the way God plays with devotees.

Sri Yukteswar had some crafty play of his own—the sort gurus often use to test disciples' commitment, rupture their egotism, and stretch their minds. He told Mukunda it was time for a change; his prescription was to go home to Calcutta. On hearing that, Mukunda's independent streaked kicked into gear. He informed Sri Yukteswar that he would follow him anywhere but he would not be going home. This is not the attitude a guru expects from a *chela* (disciple). Sri Yukteswar grew stern, and not for the last time by a long shot. He said Mukunda was to come to him in four weeks' time—more of a prediction than an instruction—and added that, having disobeyed his wishes right off the bat, he would not easily be granted discipleship but would have to prove himself worthy. Mukunda stiffened his back. Needless to say, he would soon change his mind.

Mukunda ended the historic meeting with the appropriate bow of reverence, and then walked back to the hermitage in the dark wondering why the momentous first encounter with his destined guru had taken such a contentious turn.

Things only got worse at the hermitage. The other residents now accused Mukunda of being a parasite who took more from the ashram than he contributed. He had finally had enough. One day while Swami Dayananda was away, he decided to depart. Jitendra left with him.

Geographically, their plan was odd: go first to Agra, about 600 kilometers northwest of Benares, then to Calcutta, even farther in the opposite direction, and connect to Serampore and Sri Yukteswar's ashram. But 17-year-old adventurers don't bother with such trifles, especially if one of their parents can supply railroad passes. Agra held two attractions: the Taj Mahal and Mukunda's older brother Ananta who had recently moved to that city.

The two brothers had moved further along their respective paths in life, and for all their love and the commonality of their genes and upbringing, those paths could not have been more different. Each was following his personal *dharma*. The word is most often translated as "duty" but that doesn't do justice to its complexity. It derives from a root form meaning to uphold or sustain. Something that is *dharmic* upholds that which is positive, righteous, and conducive to the well-being of all who are affected. Ananta was following the dharmic tradition of his family and caste. He had married in the proper way and had, like his father, embarked on a career as an accountant in a government agency.[15]

Mukunda had discerned a different dharma, and he met with understandable family resistance. They did not want to lose a beloved son and brother to remote caves and forests, and they did not want him to make a premature choice that could impair his future happiness. They had tried to arrange a marriage for him on three separate occasions, only to be rebuffed. Mukunda knew his dharma at an uncommonly early age, and defended it in the spirit of the *Bhagavad Gita*: "Better it is to die in *svadharma* [one's own dharma]; *paradharma* [other than one's own] is fraught with fear and danger."[16]

When Mukunda and Jitendra visited Ananta, now 27, they found him as cynical as ever about his brother's spiritual obsessions. As a test of Mukunda's adamant statement that God always provides for the needs of a faithful servant, he proposed that the boys take a day trip to Brindaban (usually spelled Vrindavan),[17] the most sacred locale for devotees of Lord Krishna, who was born and spent his youth in the area. Ananta's conditions were: they must leave with no money, they could not beg, they could not speak about their situation, and they could not get stuck in Brindaban. If they returned by midnight the same day having broken none of the rules, Ananta would ask his younger brother to initiate him as a disciple—a risky proposition for an elder brother, whose authority was considered second only to the father's. He bought two one-way train tickets for Brindaban, about a two-hour ride, and left the boys at the station with empty pockets.

"For the faithful, the patient, the hermetically pure," wrote J. D. Salinger, "all the important things in this world—not life and death perhaps, which are merely words; but the important things—work out rather beautifully."[18] It is hard to imagine a teenager more faithful, patient, and pure than Mukunda Lal Ghosh. Jitendra, like the worrywart partner of the confident leading man in a road movie, harbored doubt and fear. The combination made for entertaining banter in Yogananda's narrative, and in the end things worked out rather beautifully—proof positive, Yogananda would say, that divinely attuned souls attract the benign forces of nature.

The Hindu maxim "the guest is God" is taken quite seriously by the average Indian, especially at pilgrimage sites like Brindaban. But some of what occurred that day, in Yogananda's telling, goes beyond hospitality into the territory of Grace. First, without being asked, a man seated in their train compartment took the boys directly to an ashram and had the staff feed his young friends. Fed they were. As it happened, the kitchen had prepared a feast for some visiting dignitaries. The honored guests could not make it, so the boys were treated to a lavish spread, which they consumed voraciously.

It was, by then, late spring or early summer, when tempera-tures in that flat, inland part of India can surpass 40 degrees Celsius (100 Fahrenheit). After lunch, the two stuffed youngsters sat in the shade of a tree. Jitendra was fretting over their lack of money to get through the day when a young man approached them. Krishna had come to him in a vision, he said, and had shown him the two boys sitting under that very tree. He had seen one of the faces before, in previous visions and dreams, and he knew it to be the visage of his spiritual teacher. That would be Mukunda, despite his tender age.

The supplicant must have made a big impression because, when writing about the incident some three decades later, Yoga-nanda remembered his name: Pratap Chatterji. Pratap hired a horse carriage to ferry his guests to Brindaban's many temples and shrines. He treated them to sweets, purchased their train tickets back to Agra, and handed them a fistful of rupee notes. At the station, Mukunda rewarded his generosity with initiation into Kriya Yoga. The boys made it to Ananta's home before the midnight deadline. Ananta acknowledged his defeat, but hap-pily, like someone relieved to have his doubts dispelled. "The law of demand and supply reaches into subtler realms than I had supposed," said the accountant.[19] Despite the lateness of the hour, he insisted that his brother fulfill the terms of their wager then and there—a gesture not to be taken lightly in the Hindu context.

So it was that Mukunda stepped into his destiny with not one but two unanticipated initiations in one day. It could be said that the twin events marked the beginning of Yogananda's career ("mission" might be a better term) as a Kriya Yoga guru. He had taught meditation techniques before, but, in his memoir at least, this was the first time he used the word *diksha* (initiation). For traditionalists, a 17-year-old performing diksha would have been regarded as a kind of spiritual juvenile delinquency—a presumptuous act by a boy who had not been properly authorized. Then again, others would have seen it as a sign of spiritual genius, or the moment an avatar assumed his incarnational duties. From those perspectives, age, custom, and rules have no meaning. It is a good bet that Pratap Chatterji, had he ever testified, would have concurred.

The train from Agra to Calcutta takes anywhere from 20 to 31 hours on today's railway lines. We can only imagine what thoughts and feelings floated across Mukunda's mind on that long journey, and what he and Jitendra spoke about. What reflections? What insights? What lessons learned in what we would call their gap year experience? What expectations and uncertainties about the future before them? We know only that Jitendra decided to see his family in Calcutta rather than go straight to Serampore. As for Mukunda, so eager was he to begin his life as a sannyasi that he would not delay reuiniting with Sri Yukteswar even by a day to see the family he once had been heartsick over leaving. It was exactly 28 days from the time Sri Yukteswar said he would return to him in four weeks.

CHAPTER 6

HIGHER EDUCATION

Sri Yukteswar Giri was born Priya Nath Karar on May 10, 1855, in Serampore.[1] As an only child, it was left to him to manage his late father's affairs and provide for others—the same responsibility, curiously enough, that fell to both Bhagabati Ghosh and Lahiri Mahasaya. He married and had a daughter. Wife and child both died tragically young, the latter not long after giving birth herself. When his granddaughter came of age and married, Priya Nath considered his householder duties fulfilled and stepped up his ravenous pursuit of spiritual knowledge. In 1884, he landed at the feet of Lahiri Mahasaya. For the next 11 years, until Lahiri's passing, he traveled frequently to Benares to be with his guru. Along the way, he reportedly had a rare and auspicious encounter with the same Mahavatar Babaji who had charged Lahiri with reviving Kriya Yoga. Among other things, Babaji promised to send him an ideal disciple whom he would train to bring India's timeless wisdom to the West.

Priya Nath was soon initiated as Swami Sri Yukteswar Giri.[2] He established an organization called Sadhu Sabha and converted his family home in Serampore, a handsome two-story structure with a lush garden, into an ashram called Priyadham.[3] That was Mukunda's destination when he boarded a steam train at Howrah Station after the long journey from Agra. One can imagine his young body fending off fatigue with adrenaline as he anticipated seeing Sri Yukteswar a month after their momentous first encounter. When he arrived at the hermitage on Rai Ghat Lane, his heart was pounding, he said. He took the stairs to the guru's sitting room. He knelt to touch the master's feet, and told him he had come to follow him.

Sri Yukteswar responded skeptically. Recalling the young man's refusal to obey his instructions in Benares, he challenged his sincerity. Mukunda was contrite. He pledged his fealty and his obedience. Sri Yukteswar was satisfied. The conditions of the guru-disciple bond were established. Then he told Mukunda to go home and enroll in college.

This was not what Mukunda expected to hear, and certainly not what he *wanted* to hear. Sri Yukteswar was hardly the first or last guru to order a young disciple to complete his or her education. But his rationale may have been unique. Mukunda was destined to represent India's spiritual heritage in the West, and a foreigner preaching a foreign message would be more readily accepted if he had a degree. (This was a time when fewer than 5 percent of Americans attended college.) He may also have understood that studying in an institution sanctioned by their British overlords would give the future emissary a facility with the English language and knowledge of the values, customs, ideas, and history that had shaped the West.

Mukunda knew that his task at that moment was to demonstrate the disciple's proper deference. But his inner rascal could not be suppressed entirely. He attached a condition to his pledge to attend college: that Sri Yukteswar promise to show him God. They debated for an hour, Yogananda recalled in his memoir. One assumes the dialogue was conducted in the spirit of the *Bhagavad Gita's* advice to seekers: to approach sages "with reverence, thorough inquiry, and humble service."[4] In the end, he was given the master's assurance. The promise cleansed his heart of what he called "a lifelong shadow."[5]

Then came another pleasant surprise. He noticed on a wall a garlanded photo of a familiar face: Lahiri Mahasaya. Somehow, the fact that Sri Yukteswar was a disciple of the very guru who had initiated his parents, blessed him as an infant, and served him as a spiritual touchstone had not previously been mentioned. Now, Lahiri was his paramguru, his guru's guru, and Yogananda would pay homage to that lineage the rest of his life. Many holy personages from India are venerated in the West despite never having been there in the flesh.[6] But perhaps none is more widely known than the trio of Babaji, Lahiri Mahasaya, and Sri Yukteswar. Their faces, along with Yogananda's, are not only on altars throughout the world; they can even be spotted on what is surely the most iconic album cover in music history: The Beatles' *Sgt. Pepper's Lonely Hearts Club Band*.[7]

Mukunda slept at the ashram that night, on a slim cot. The next morning, he received formal Kriya Yoga diksha from Sri Yukteswar. He had already learned the basic techniques in the Kriya Yoga sequence from his father and Shastri Mahasaya (Swami Kebalananda), and he had already taught some to others. But the formal initiation was something special. Yogananda does not portray the ceremony itself, but Brother Chidananda, the President of the Self-Realization Fellowship (SRF), described Lahiri Mahasaya's initiations in an e-mail exchange: "There is a *homa* fire in front of the altar, and the initiate offers fruit and flowers as symbolic offerings. The initiator imparts the guru's blessing by a touch of the hand and places the *tilak* mark on the forehead of the devotee, during which time the initiator transmits the divine current to awaken the devotee's spiritual eye." There are other elements to the ceremony, as well as transmission of the core Kriya Yoga technique.

Phenomena such as *darshan*—literally "viewing" but connoting the benign effect of being in the presence of an adept or a deity—and *shaktipat*, the transmission of subtle energy from a guru, have been described since ancient times. For Yogananda, this energy made the experience of diksha more than a commemorative experience. In the *AY* he described the impact of Sri Yukteswar's transformational touch memorably: "[A] great light broke upon my being, like the glory of countless suns blazing together. A flood of ineffable bliss overwhelmed my heart to an innermost core."[8]

When Mukunda boarded the train for Calcutta the following afternoon, he quite likely knew that he would ride those rails back and forth scores of times in the coming years. And his father, then 57, could not have been happier to see him. The child he feared losing to a faraway search for God would, instead, be safe and well cared for under his own roof, studying at a reputable college and fulfilling his desire for a spiritual guide a short distance away with, to top it all off, a fellow disciple of Lahiri Mahasaya.

Mukunda enrolled at Scottish Church College. The institution was founded in 1830 by Dr. Alexander Duff, a young missionary from Scotland. It started with five students in a private home and eventually took root at Urquhart Square, 10 or 15 minutes from home for a brisk walker like Mukunda Lal Ghosh. Missionary schools have always been controversial in India. Some deplored them as tools for the subjugation and conversion of the native population; others, often reluctantly, welcomed them as a modernizing influence and a doorway to occupations for which speaking English and understanding British customs were necessary. Scottish Church earned a reputation for its quality education and its respect for India and its people. It excelled in biblical studies—which appealed to many Bengalis as a way to better understand the imperialists—while remaining nonaggressive about conversion.[9]

In every respect, Scottish Church was the perfect choice for Mukunda, except for one thing: he could not have cared less.

Mukunda's college years spanned a period of great unrest in India and in the homeland of its imperial rulers. In 1911, Bengal was reunited, a move that placated Hindus and infuriated Muslims. When the British moved their Indian capital from Calcutta to Delhi, a lethal bomb blast at the ceremonies led to a stepped-up effort to destroy the freedom movement centered in Calcutta. At the same time, tensions in Europe were building toward the First World War, and India figured into the combatants' strategies. When war erupted in the summer of 1914, just after Mukunda's junior year, Germany stepped up its clandestine aid to Indian nationalists on the theory that the enemy of one's enemy—in this case Britain—is one's friend. Americans watched these portents unfold at a distance, consumed mainly with domestic events such as the *Titanic* tragedy, Henry Ford's assembly-line rollout of the Model T, the passage of the 16th and 17th Amendments,[10] and the 1912 presidential campaign won by Woodrow Wilson. Mukunda was just as detached from the world's affairs, and even from his own as a student. Now that he had found his guru, his quest for enlightenment was more single-minded than ever. Because he favored Sri Yukteswar's ashram over the classroom, he may have walked to campus less often than he shuttled between Calcutta and Serampore, at first by train and later by motorcycle.

The bike was Sri Yukteswar's idea, in response to his disciple's complaints about the time he wasted on the train. Mukunda asked his father to fund the new mode of transportation. In typical fashion, Mr. Ghosh at first refused, invoking his own hardscrabble youth just as the frugal parents of American Baby Boomers cited the Great Depression. Mukunda prevailed. The Triumph motorcycle enabled him to speed past autos, cows, and carts on the pastoral road between ashram and home. As a fringe benefit, according to *Mejda*, Sri Yukteswar really enjoyed riding in the sidecar.

Mukunda could not be in Serampore all the time, of course, so he created an ashram of sorts at home. According to brother Sananda, at times he would meditate for as long as two straight days. He clearly was making spiritual progress, if anecdotes can be used as evidence. One instance foreshadowed two traits Yogananda would display in America: a playful trickster quality and a penchant for demonstrating the power of a yoga-trained mind. At lunch one afternoon, after having been sequestered for two full days, he nibbled in silence and then abruptly fell over backward. As he lay there, unmoving and apparently unconscious, the family panicked. They summoned a doctor, who examined him and immediately turned grim. There were no signs of life. After much weeping and lamenting and praying aloud by his loved ones, Mukunda opened his eyes, sat bolt upright, and laughed. He was learning, he told Sananda, to use yogic methods to control bodily functions.

Mukunda also resumed leadership of his youthful sangha, only more authoritatively now that he had spent the better part of a year in a Benares ashram and had taken as his preceptor a swami of high stature. Manomohan, the future Swami Satyananda, said the group was "strung together on the same thread" and "Mukunda was its centerpiece jewel, operator, instructor, advisor and heart-friend."[11] The markings of someone destined to lead a large-scale spiritual enterprise were clearly visible.

Mukunda's limited attendance at college produced a new friend who would remain an integral part of his life and work for almost 20 years. His name was Basu Kumar Bagchi, and he was almost exactly two years Mukunda's junior. In *Mejda*, Basu is described as "talented, intelligent, and religious-minded."[12] He and his brahmin family were devotees of Bhaduri Mahasaya, the Levitating Saint, and he, at Mukunda's suggestion, was initiated into Kriya Yoga by Swami Kebalananda. Basu and Mukunda became so inseparable that at one point, Basu lived clandestinely at 4 Garpar Road because he could not find enough privacy at home to meditate properly. Years later, as Swami Dhirananda, he would serve as Yogananda's collaborator and chief lieutenant, until their bond suffered a heartbreaking rupture.

As in high school, Mukunda barely managed to scrape by in his coursework. His heart—and, to the greatest extent possible, the rest of him as well—was in Serampore. His rebellious spirit gradually adapted to the imperatives of discipleship, something that could not have occurred with a different kind of guru. The traditional guru-disciple relationship is as difficult for outsiders to comprehend as modern marriage would be to a visitor from a polygamous tribe. Concepts like obedience, surrender, and devotion to another human being understandably raise red flags. The dangers of hero worship, dependency, and submission are all too familiar, and we are quick to pick up the scent of abuse or exploitation. Those hazards are not to be taken lightly and they surface frequently when naïve seekers attach themselves to authority figures who turn out to be frauds, or merely incompetent. It is for good reason that

Tibetan Buddhists compare gurus to fire: Stay too far away and you can't get warm; get too close and you might get burned. Self-aware and discerning devotees, however, are fireproof, provided the guru is advanced spiritually, free of selfish motives, and in tune with the individual. As in a marriage, when the pair are well matched, the result is magic, or Grace.

Guru means dispeller of darkness (*gu* = darkness, *ru* = that which dispels), and the guru's role is to lead devotees from the shadows of ignorance to the luminous state of awakened consciousness. "In serious spiritual endeavor the blessing and guidance of the guru are essential," Yogananda wrote in his *Gita* commentary. The disciple practices the guru's sadhana instructions faithfully, and "Through this *sadhana* his guru invisibly helps him to attain the successively higher steps in the art of divine union."[13] The sincere disciple is advised to submit to the guru's guiding hand like a soldier submits to a commanding officer. Yogananda called gurus spiritual doctors, noting that patients who want results do what the doctor tells them to.

As we've seen, Mukunda was not inclined to do what he was told. But he understood that discipleship demanded trust and humility if it was to bear fruit, and he sensed that Sri Yukteswar merited the leap of faith. His guru was apparently skilled at smoothing out the rough edges of a stubborn ego, the better to let the true Self shine through, without destroying the disciple's discernment or smothering his uniqueness. He urged Mukunda, and presumably other disciples, not to forsake the evidence of the senses or of reason but to add to those faculties the higher faculty of wisdom.

Yogananda's deeply felt descriptions of his guru are like a son's remembrance of a father who was both stern and lenient, knowing and humble, serious and playful, stationed on a higher plane and implacably grounded. He was a tough taskmaster who balanced ego-busting discipline, which Yogananda compared to having teeth extracted, with patience, kindness, and love. He was also a compelling conversationalist with a sharp wit and what Yogananda called a "rollicking laugh."[14] Yogananda would be described in similar ways by his own disciples.

Sri Yutkeswar has also been depicted as a yogic adept with extraordinary powers—routinely clairvoyant, if not omniscient. "My guru was not interested in what people were saying, but in what they were thinking," Yogananda said.[15] He was also portrayed as a master healer. The *AY* recounts several instances of jaw-dropping health interventions, in two of which Mukunda was the beneficiary. Once, Sri Yukteswar cured him of a lifelong battle with what he called "chronic dyspepsia."[16] On a second occasion, Sri Yukteswar perceived Mukunda's incipient Asiatic cholera, the lethal disease that had killed Mrs. Ghosh, before any physical symptoms appeared, and he healed him at the onset with no more tangible a remedy than his intent and his touch. The guru purportedly altered karmic patterns too, and at least once that Yogananda claimed to witness, appeared in two places at the same time.

As a matter of history, it seems irrefutable that Sri Yukteswar's greatest power was his ability to forge, in the smithy of his ashram, a spiritual teacher for the ages. He groomed Mukunda for the task ahead both overtly and subliminally. The disciple's inner realization was of paramount concern, beyond the lessons learned by his mind, beyond the qualities developed by his heart, and certainly beyond the chapters and verses of holy texts.

Not that textual study was neglected. Sri Yukteswar was a scholar who held that the insights of the Vedic seers were as universal as the laws of physics, and therefore to be found at the heart of all religions. Fluent in Bengali, Hindi, English, and French (with serviceable Sanskrit), he kept up with the latest developments in science and acquired a comprehensive knowledge of both Hindu texts and the Bible. What mattered to him was not book learning for its own sake, but what the scriptures said about achieving the ultimate spiritual goal. Significantly, he was as learned about the Bible as he was about Hinduism, and he wrote about their common threads in his only book, *The Holy Science*.[17] The lessons Yogananda absorbed from his guru's discourses on the Bible would prove to be indispensable to his success in Christian cultures. He probably quoted the New

Testament as often as the *Bhagavad Gita*, and the mountain of written and spoken material he left behind about both texts was eventually assembled into a pair of massive works.[18]

Because Sri Yukteswar had been a householder before taking sannyasi vows in middle age, he was an ideal trainer for someone tasked with making esoteric knowledge relevant to pragmatic, materialistic Americans. He had run a business, bought and sold properties, managed employees; he had married, raised a child, and loved a grandchild; he had grieved and mourned. As Yogananda put it, "His feet were firm on the earth, his head in the haven of heaven."[19] He saw this as modeling a munificent blend of East and West, and must have learned a great deal watching his master run an organization and a residential facility, manage personalities, supervise workers, and pay the bills.

Satyananda, who was often present at the Serampore ashram, said that Sri Yukteswar groomed Mukunda by giving him certain responsibilities to hone his managerial skills. He would reprimand him at times, and gesture for him to lighten up if he went overboard in exerting authority over fellow disciples. Mukunda even learned to cook from his guru. A vegetarian after taking his swami vows, Sri Yukteswar ate simply and sparingly, but he did not insist on austere diets for his followers, and he delighted in preparing meals and coordinating banquets, feasts, and festivals. Yogananda would do the same in America. One thing Yogananda would not be able to emulate was his guru's enviable financial independence. Sri Yukteswar had maintained control of his inherited properties and fended off would-be usurpers. As a result, he was spared the degrading struggle that turns many mission-driven gurus into perpetual fund-raisers. As he scraped to make ends meet in America, Yogananda may have wished he'd absorbed more of his guru's money karma.

Early in Mukunda's freshman year, feeling restless and perhaps bored by classes and work in the ashram, he took off once again for the Himalayas, determined to achieve God-Consciousness. Sri Yukteswar, whom he'd known for only six months at the time, told him that "Wisdom is better sought from a man of realization than from an inert mountain."[20] But he did not issue a decisive prohibition, and that, in Mukunda's mind, amounted to permission.

As before, he did not get close to his snowcapped destination. His first stop was Tarakeswar, a pilgrimage site for Shiva devotees 53 kilometers by train from Calcutta. From there, he headed on foot toward a nearby village where he was told he could find an adept named Ram Gopal Muzumdar. A disciple of Lahiri Mahasaya, the yogi was called the Sleepless Saint because he had conquered that mundane need. He had purportedly achieved enlightenment the way Mukunda hoped to, by practicing Kriya Yoga for years—45, he said—in secluded caves. Mukunda wanted the saint to bless his journey. After getting lost and wandering through forests and rice paddies in the midday sun and the frigid night, he finally found the Sleepless Saint.

Instead of blessing Mukunda's odyssey, the yogi reiterated Sri Yukteswar's rebuke that mountains are not gurus. When, upon questioning, Mukunda admitted that he had a room at home where he could be alone as much as he wished, the recluse said, "That is your cave. That is your sacred mountain. That is where you will find the kingdom of God."[21]

One of Mukunda's lingering delusions was shattered. He said his obsession with the Himalayas ended there. Not entirely, however. He did retain a tourist's desire to gaze upon the majestic peaks, and tried for three years to get Sri Yukteswar to approve a trip to Kashmir before finally succeeding. His sumptuous description of Kashmir's splendor in the *AY* inspired many a reader to visit "the Switzerland of India," now tragically the center of a tense India-Pakistan border dispute.

The chastened Mukunda returned to Serampore convinced that Sri Yukteswar, not the Himalayas, was his ticket to spiritual liberation. Upon greeting him, the guru was comforting, not reproachful, and his gaze, Yogananda said, was "unfathomable." The master touched the disciple's chest just above the heart. The breath was sucked from his chest. This is, in part, how Yogananda described what followed in his autobiography: "Soul and mind instantly lost their physical bondage and streamed out like a fluid piercing light from my every pore. The flesh was as though dead, yet in my intense awareness, I knew that I had never been so fully alive. My sense of identity was no longer narrowly confined to a body but embraced the circumambient atoms."[22]

When it ended, Sri Yukteswar helped Mukunda to his feet and warned him not to get "overdrunk with ecstasy." Then, like a classic Zen master, he brought the intoxicated disciple back to earth: "Come, let us sweep the balcony floor."

Another tutorial remained, this one theological. Sometime after his sublime experience, Mukunda asked his guru when he would find God. Sri Yukteswar said he already had. Mukunda begged to differ. The guru said he hoped Mukunda wasn't looking for an ancient figure seated on a throne somewhere in the cosmos—or, he added, looking for extraordinary yogic powers as proof. Only the depth of bliss in meditation, he said, is an adequate measure of spiritual development. It was a key lesson for Mukunda and, it should be noted, for millions of Yogananda's followers and readers of his books.

Once again, Mukunda's indifference to schoolwork led right to the brink of do-or-die exams for which he was ill-prepared, and once again he barely scraped by. He received his two-year diploma in 1913. He hoped that spelled the end of his academic career, but both father and guru insisted he go for the four-year bachelor's degree. He was through with Calcutta and Scottish Church College, though. With the help of Sri Yukteswar—either on a subtle plane or in the concrete realm of fund-raising, or both—Serampore College, which had been a two-year school, obtained the needed funds to offer four-year degrees as an affiliate of Calcutta University. Now Mukunda could satisfy the wishes of his elders a short, pleasant walk from the hermitage where he would spend every waking moment if he could. He was one of the first to enroll in the new program.

In Serampore, he lived for a while with his uncle, then moved to a student boarding house called the Panthi, where no one minded if he came home late—or not at all—after attending a long Sri Yukteswar discourse.[23] He remained an indifferent student—"a last-minute crammer," his guru called him—and his classmates considered him so "over-drunk with religion" that they called him Mad Monk.[24] The professors basically ignored him, assuming he'd just flunk the big exams at the end of his two years, if he didn't drop out before then. But he was as fervent a seeker of higher-than-higher education as ever. In those two years he drew ever closer to Sri Yukteswar, both in terms of human affection and the subtle attunement of a disciple's mind to his master's.

The time of academic reckoning arrived with spring in 1915. With a little trickery—not putting his name on an exam paper so his hostile professor would not know it was his—and coaching from his cousin, Prabhas Chandra Ghosh, Mukunda passed his final classroom exams, barely. Now came the more formidable A.B. examinations formulated by Calcutta University. Late one night—in one account, five days before the exams commenced, and two days before in another[25]—Sri Yukteswar asked Mukunda if he was prepared. He was so *un*prepared that he was planning not to show up for the exams. The guru wouldn't have it. In an interview with the scholar Wendell Thomas for his 1930 book *Hinduism Invades America*, Yogananda said that of all the miracles and wonders he had seen, "I shall declare to the world that I secured my A.B. degree through his [Sri Yukteswar's] miraculous power." He said that when he told his guru he was not going to take his exams, the adamant reply was "Then all my relations with you cease this instant."[26]

He told Mukunda to consult with his friend Romesh Chandra Dutt, a fellow resident of the Panthi, every morning during the exam period. As it turned out, Yogananda told Thomas, everything Romesh had him study was in the examinations.[27] The easiest part of the process was writing an essay about the person who inspired him the most. Needless to say, he wrote voluminously about Sri Yukteswar. Once again, he passed by the proverbial skin of his teeth.

Mukunda had fulfilled the wishes of the two most import-ant figures in his life. His guru was pleased but not surprised; his father celebrated by hosting a grand feast at the family home. Now, like all college graduates, he had to make decisions about his future. There really wasn't much to think about in his case; he knew exactly what he wanted to do. It remained to be seen whether Sri Yukteswar had other ideas.

CHAPTER 7

IN THE WORLD, NOT OF IT

Bhagabati Ghosh was a deeply spiritual man and a disciplined yogi. He was also a practical man who loved his family and wanted the best for his children. It was hard for him to accept what should have been obvious by 1915: his second oldest son, then 22, not only wanted to become a monk but was destined to be one. In a last-ditch effort to entice Mukunda to take up the customary life of a householder, he arranged for a job that most recent college grads would covet: Assistant Traffic Superintendent at the Bengal Nagpur Railway, a position normally reserved for Englishmen. Mukunda's response was a more polite version of "Thanks, but no thanks."

A suitable marriage was also arranged. For the third time, Mukunda's older sisters identified an appropriate bride. Her family agreed to the match. Mukunda did not. In *Mejda*, he is quoted as telling his father, "I will never be happy in marriage. No one knows this better than you."[1] In his autobiography, Yogananda said he had seen married sadhaks relegate spiritual practice to a low priority. He would not be one of them: "To allot the Lord a secondary place in life was, to me, inconceivable."[2]

Mr. Ghosh realized the game was over. The job offer was retracted; the marriage was canceled. Both stayed in the family, however. Mukunda's cousin Prabhas, who had helped him pass his final exams, took the job and married the betrothed.[3]

Mukunda could now fulfill his lifelong dream of becoming, officially and by traditional means, a sannyasi. He had done his best to emulate the renunciate way. He had even taken sannyasi-like vows with the core members of his sangha. Perhaps inspired by Swami Vivekananda and eight fellow disciples, who privately took sannyasi vows after Sri Ramakrishna passed away, Mukunda had gathered Basu, Manomohan, and another companion, Shishir Kumar Ganguly, for a week of austerities leading up to *Janmashtami*, the celebration of Krishna's birthday. That entire week was spent, according to Satyananda, "being barefoot, eliminating any indulgence, practicing self-sufficiency, and practicing control and discipline in many different ways."[4] On the holy day they fasted, performed sacred rites in Mukunda's attic room, and ceremoniously donned ochre-dyed garments. Before witnesses, the aspiring monks, led by Mukunda, vowed to live as renunciates. At least three of them became swamis (Shashir may have been the only exception).

That solemn occasion could be considered a dress rehearsal. Now Mukunda asked Sri Yukteswar to initiate him into the swami order. He had made the same request more than once before, only to be refused. This time, the guru assented immediately and praised his persistence. Mukunda had passed every test; he left no room for doubt that his desire to renounce was sincere, and not a youthful whim.

On a Thursday in July 1915, at the Serampore ashram, Mukunda Lal Ghosh became Swami Yogananda Giri. "Giri" indicates that the swami has taken vows in the mountain branch[5] of the order established at least 12 centuries ago (some argue twice as far back) by Shankara, the great philosopher, saint, and revivalist known as Adi Shankaracharya (Adi means first; Shankaracharya is the title given to the heads of the four monasteries that preserve the tradition).

Because Sri Yukteswar was not a fan of pomp, he chose a simple initiation over the usual elaborate rites. He personally dyed a stretch of white silk the traditional ochre color and draped it over the initiate's shoulders. He chose silk instead of the customary cotton because he knew Yogananda would be going to the West, and he understood that Westerners would react more favorably to silk. He also allowed the initiate to choose his own monastic name instead of giving him one, as was normally done. From the start, Yogananda was an exceptional swami.

As people familiar with Hindu customs know, most swamis' names end in *ananda*, which means supreme bliss. The first part of the name, Yogananda explains in the *AY*, "signifies his aspiration to attain emancipation through a particular path, state, or divine quality—love, wisdom, discrimination, devotion, service, yoga." Typically, a prefix that suits the initiate's personality or aspiration is chosen. Yogananda defined the name he selected as "bliss (ananda) through divine union (yoga)."[6] I don't think he would have minded if it was also interpreted as attaining the bliss of Self-realization through the systematic methods of yoga.

An expert in branding could not have dreamed up a better name for a swami bringing to the West a practical pathway to God. As Yogananda toured America, speaking to larger and larger crowds, every time his name was mentioned or appeared in print, "yoga" became further legitimized in the public mind. This, by itself, helped move the term and the concepts it embod ies into the vocabularies and worldviews of an unprecedented number of people.

The formal swami vows, including nonattachment to personal possessions, celibacy, and obedience to the authority of his lineage, did not represent a radical departure for Yogananda; he had lived by such strictures as best he could for some time. Now that calling was sanctified. He said he overflowed with gratitude when Sri Yukteswar spoke his new name for the first time as he knelt before his guru. He sang a verse from Shankara's *Nirvana Shatakam*.[7] It essentially summarizes the philosophy of Advaita Vedanta, proclaiming that our ultimate identity is neither mind, nor intellect, nor ego, nor anything other than formless, eternal Brahman. The verse features this repeated refrain: "I am He, I am He, Blessed Spirit, I am He!"[8] That is the realization swamis aspire to achieve in all its luminous, blissful fullness.

Sri Yukteswar made it clear that Swami Yogananda Giri was to be an active monk who would serve the greater good without concern for personal reward. One who rejects the responsibilities of family life, he told the newly minted swami, must assume responsibility for the larger human family. As a result, the push-and-pull between detachment and worldly engagement that Yogananda said he felt even in the womb would remain with him for the rest of his life. Exactly what form his service would take did not become clear for a while. Then again, the whole world lacked clarity in 1915.

Europe—and, by extension, India and the rest of the British Empire—was embroiled in the Great War. One-sixth of all British forces, more than a million strong, were Indian conscripts. About 115,000 would be killed or wounded in the hostilities, and an estimated 370 million tons of supplies would be diverted from India's use. Many in the Indian independence movement took to aiding the German forces in order to weaken the Raj, while others, notably Rabindranath Tagore and Sri Aurobindo, saw Germany as an even greater potential evil than the imperialists they sought to expel from the homeland.

Turmoil reigned in those years. The Russian Revolution exploded early in 1917. A few months later, America entered the war. Around the same time, Jews and Arabs were going at it in Palestine. In 1918, the Spanish Flu began to spread, quickly becoming the lethal World Influenza Pandemic. And in 1919, tragedy added impetus to the Indian freedom movement. The infamous Jallianwala Bagh Massacre in Amritsar, in the Punjab, began with a peaceful protest and ended with British troops killing more than a thousand people. Independence fervor gained momentum from Gandhi's campaign and the work of two unlikely activists, the Irish-born Annie Besant, who headed up the Theosophical Society of India, and Sister Nivedita, an American disciple of Swami Vivekananda. In 1917, Besant became the first president of the Indian National Congress, the party that would eventually win India's independence and dominate its politics for decades.

It would not be fair to say that Yogananda was oblivious to the turbulence; more likely, he understood that his role was to move humanity to higher ground from the inside out. Some of his college friends urged him to help them obtain arms from German ships to use against the British. He says he told them that it would do India no good to kill Englishmen, and he predicted that the homeland's freedom would come through spiritual, not military, force. The friends ended up in jail, and some later joined Gandhi's nonviolent movement.

The war in Europe did affect Yogananda in a peculiar but profound way. One morning, while meditating, he reflected on the conflict's tragic toll. Suddenly, his consciousness "transferred" to the body of a battleship commander in the middle of combat. The ship blew up. He dove into the water along with other sailors. On shore, a bullet struck the captain in the chest. As he was losing consciousness in the sea, he suddenly reappeared in his Calcutta room, as Yogananda, sitting in lotus position. Confusion reigned as his soul ricocheted back to the captain's dead body, and then a field of light arose and filled his vision.

Battlefield horror continued to alternate with celestial light and messages from a divine voice. The experience was transformative, said Yogananda, because it showed him vividly that we are all light, and that this eternal light has little to do with what we call life and death.

The records are muddled about where Yogananda spent his time, and what he did, in the months following his entrance into swamihood. Mention is made of him being in Calcutta and Serampore, but also in Benares, perhaps to coincide with one of Sri Yukteswar's residencies in the city. Sananda Ghosh said his brother considered studying for a Ph.D. in America—an odd idea for someone with a strong aversion to academia, unless Sri Yukteswar proposed it. Satyananda's memoir has Yogananda enrolling in a local master's degree program in philosophy. If that is true, he clearly did not last long.

By Satyananda's reckoning, his friend loved discussing philosophy with professors, but the books he purchased for his courses were "somewhat decorative."[9]

The first major post-initiation event Yogananda describes was a shattering family tragedy. Monks in his lineage were not required to cut ties with their birth families, as many renunciates do. Consequently, he was yanked back into the world of familial duty, sickness and death, heartache and grief. In 1916, his brother Ananta, then 33, became seriously ill. Yogananda and his father went to Gorakhpur, the city of his birth, where Ananta was then living. As he sat in silent meditation one morning, the thought arose that his brother did not have long to live. By his own account, he reacted so strongly to that message that he couldn't bear staying a moment longer: "Amidst uncomprehending criticism from my relatives, I left India on the first available boat."[10]

As Gorakhpur is landlocked, he probably took a train to Calcutta, some 775 kilometers away, to catch that boat. It sailed south on the Bay of Bengal, along the coasts of Burma and Thailand (then Siam), and northward up the South China Sea to Japan. As described in the *AY*, the journey sounds like an impulsive effort to escape the horror of watching a loved one die. In *Mejda*, and in Satyananda's book, the trip was more purposeful, and Japan was not just the destination of the first available ship. Sananda Ghosh says that Yogananda thought he might be able to get a visa in Japan to travel to the West. In Satyananda's recollection, his friend had been selected to study Japanese farming as part of a program that sent Bengali youngsters to foreign lands.

Whatever the reason for the voyage to Japan, Yogananda's heart no doubt ached for his family as he viewed for the first time the world beyond the Indian subcontinent. He set foot on land in several exotic ports before arriving in the Land of the Rising Sun. He did not tarry long. His brother says he found Japan "too restless and too much directed toward outer material accomplishments."[11] Yogananda himself said only that his heart was "too heavy for sight-seeing."[12]

At a port stop in Shanghai on the way home, he shopped for gifts. He selected a carved bamboo chest for Ananta. When the salesman handed him the chest, Yogananda was stricken by a revelation so upsetting that the gift item fell from his hands and cracked. He sensed that Ananta's soul had just departed his body. When he arrived at 4 Garpar Road, he saw his father cry for the first time. Evidently, the timing of Ananta's death matched the time of the intuition in Shanghai. The official cause was typhoid fever. It was the second time Yogananda was not present at the death of a loved one, his mother being the first. It would not be the last.

To his dismay, he learned that a second sibling's health crisis had erupted in his absence. This one had a happier ending, thanks to him. His sister Nalini, two years his junior, had come down with typhoid fever, and on the heels of that dreaded disease developed blood dysentery. When Yogananda arrived at her home, she was in a coma. Her distraught husband, Panchanon Bose, was a physician, and he had exhausted all promising treatments.

Yogananda waged a war on his sister's afflictions with intense prayer and yogic healing techniques. Nalini recovered from the dysentery, but her legs were paralyzed. Yogananda turned to Sri Yukteswar. The details of his intervention (and of the siblings' relationship) can be found in Chapter 25 of the *AY*. Suffice it to say that Nalini was back to normal in a month. Sri Yukteswar added a bonus: he told Yogananda that his sister, who had been judged medically incapable of pregnancy, would bear two daughters. She did, and she lived until 1946, the year *Autobiography of a Yogi* was published. However, another sister, Uma, would die in 1919, at age 29, adding another tragic note to what was otherwise an ebullient and transformative period in Yogananda's life.

During the war years, Calcutta was rife with intrigue, tension, agitation, and pathos. But Yogananda and his comrades were focused on spirituality, and by 1916 it was time to step up their efforts. He was, after all, a swami with a mandate from his guru to serve, and by now his second in command, Basu Kumar Bagchi, had earned a master's degree in psychology. The group set out to fix up their ashram on Pitambar Bhattacharya Lane, the property that belonged to Tulsi Bose's family.

Led by Yogananda, the young men renovated the building and landscaped the grounds. Sananda Ghosh describes their activities in *Mejda*: "Meetings were held regularly, with scripture readings, devotional songs and kirtans, spiritual discourses, and *Kriya Yoga* meditation. At the end of the meetings, fruits and sweets were distributed to all."[13] Those sweets usually included rice pudding, at Yogananda's insistence. The ashram also housed two young boys who became catalysts for the educational enterprise that captured Yogananda's passion.

One child, Nirmal, was from a poor Calcutta family that was about to yank him from seventh grade to work in a printing plant. Yogananda offered to provide for his housing and schooling. The second was Sushodhan, an orphan who was working for a tea vendor on a Calcutta street when Yogananda and Basu took a liking to him. In return for room and board and classwork at the Athenaeum Institution, the pair maintained the ashram. Yogananda and his team added exercise and music programs to their offerings. Older students started coming around. Energy and enthusiasm grew, and at some point an educational mission came into focus.

It may seem ironic that a young man who had little use for school would be driven to start one of his own. But not when one considers *why* he disliked the schools he attended. They bored him, and they neglected the interior dimension of life. Students emerged well prepared for employment, he saw, but not for living fulfilled and meaningful lives. As Wendell Thomas put it in *Hinduism Invades America*, Yogananda "was impressed by the ideal of popular education along the lines laid down centuries ago by Hindu saints and *risis*, or wise men."[14] He appreciated what education *could* be, and he set out to create an institution that would develop youngsters into complete persons.

The idea was to establish a modern version of a *gurukulam*, a residential school where students had close contact with a guru. In this case, yogic practices would be employed to culture the mind and body and enhance receptivity to learning; traditional spiritual teachings would be transmitted by learned instructors; and modern academic subjects would be taught by qualified teachers. In this regard, Yogananda had much in common with Rabindranath Tagore. He had met the revered poet briefly in 1913, shortly after Tagore became the first non-European to win the Nobel Prize for Literature.[15] Later, he paid a visit to Santiniketan ("abode of peace"), the iconoclastic school Tagore created in 1901 based on the understanding that "the highest education is that which does not merely give us information but makes our life in harmony with all existence."[16] A brief chapter in the *AY* is devoted to the meeting, in which Tagore, then in his mid-50s, and the young swami compared notes on educational philosophy.

The educational enterprise was a group endeavor, with Yogananda as the acknowledged leader and Basu and Manomohan as his right and left hands.[17] When the idea of establishing a proper school arose, Yogananda, with all the audacity of youth, thought of requesting funds from a Maharaja who was visiting Calcutta for a religious festival. Manindra Chandra Nandi Bahadur, the Maharaja of Kasimbazar—located about 200 kilometers directly north of Calcutta—was known for his unpretentious ways, his concern for education, and his philanthropy. Yogananda and Basu worked into the night to formulate a proposal. When they were ready, they woke up Manomohan and dictated their ideas for him to write down.

Basu carried the petition to the Maharaja. The prince was intrigued and asked for a more detailed plan. Yogananda and the others outlined their educational objectives and the methods they would use to achieve them. The Maharaja accepted their invitation to visit the ashram. They scrubbed the place clean and decorated it, and assembled the seven students who had been studying there informally (one was Yogananda's baby brother Bishnu). The presentation worked. The Maharaja offered to house the new school in a bungalow he owned on the Damodar River in the village of Dihika. He would cover all expenses. Based on Sri Yukteswar's astrological advice, Brahmavidyalaya (School of Divinity) was inaugurated on March 22, 1917, in sync with the spring equinox.[18] It was a week after Czar Nicholas II of Russia abdicated his throne, paving the way for the Bolsheviks, and two weeks before the United States declared war on Germany.

The school was set on a hill in a picturesque landscape, with a winding river, forests, fields, and waterfalls close by; below was a small railway station that served the village. In his book, Swami Satyananda[19] calls it a "dream-world," and the lifestyle he paints is idyllic.[20] He describes a routine of sadhana, singing, recitation of sacred texts, spiritual discourses, and forays in the natural setting to trek or picnic or swim in the river. Classes were held outdoors when appropriate, and the indoor classrooms had floor mats and low desks instead of chairs and tables. Meals were vegetarian, and Yogananda took a hand in creating new recipes—an enjoyment he would carry with him to America. He would reprimand slackers, Satyananda reported, but at times he would mischievously violate his own directives, as when meals were delayed because of his kitchen experiments. "Rules are made for us and not we for the rules," he would say (in Bengali), a maxim that speaks to his often ambiguous and flexible relationship to custom, tradition, and orthodoxy.[21]

The school's reputation grew. New students enrolled. Teachers were hired, including a Hatha Yoga instructor, a young scholar who was a Ramakrishna devotee, and, to head up the spiritual curriculum and sadhana, Swami Kebalananda (formerly Shastri Mahasaya). Sri Yukteswar visited and gave the school his much-valued imprimatur.

But growth has its challenges, as Yogananda would find out in spades in America. More space was needed. About a year after its founding, the school's materials and inhabitants moved to the Maharaja's refurbished mansion in Kasimbazar. Almost immediately, virtually everyone took ill with what may have been malaria. Medical treatment was mobilized, but the fear of further outbreaks was intense. As it happened, the Maharaja also had a splendid 25-acre summer palace in Ranchi, about 300 kilometers west of Calcutta. The school moved there in 1918; a century later, the property remains an educational and organizational hub for the Yogoda Satsanga Society (YSS) of India.

CHAPTER 8

GO WEST, YOUNG MAN

In August 1918, with the conflagration called "the war to end all wars" grinding to a conclusion that would total 9 million dead and 21 million wounded, Yogananda relocated his school to the Maharaja of Kasimbazar's tranquil acreage in what he called "one of the most healthful climates in India."[1] Perhaps that climate helped the population at his school evade the Spanish Flu, which caused up to 50 million deaths, including 17 million in India. That there is no mention of the pandemic in anything written by or about Yogananda suggests that the Ranchi residents were as removed from that scourge as they were from the battlefields of Gallipoli and Verdun.

What had been a summer palace was now the main building of the newly renamed Yogoda Satsanga Brahmacharya Vidyalaya, and the royal patron pledged 2,000 rupees a month to cover expenses. The land, at an altitude of about 600 meters, was blessed with hundreds of fruit trees, under which classes were held; fertile soil for growing vegetables and herbs; songbirds, monkeys, peacocks, and deer, one of which, a Disneyesque fawn, became Yogananda's personal pet; and a large pond for sport and relief on hot days.[2]

Yogananda and Basu Kumar Bagchi were busy from the outset, only by now Basu had become Swami Dhirananda. He had taken initiation as a sannyasi from Yogananda, who, as a swami, was authorized by tradition to ordain others. The leadership became a triumvirate when Manomohan joined the team. After graduating with honors from City College of Calcutta, he became Swami Satyananda Giri in a ceremony conducted by Sri Yukteswar. As was noted earlier, Yogananda called Satyananda his left hand and Dhirananda his right hand. More noble nicknames were used around campus: Yogananda was Bara Swamiji (top or elder swami), Dhirananda was Meja (middle) Swamiji, and Satyananda was Chota (younger) Swamiji.[3] In light of what they accomplished, it is remarkable to note that when the Ranchi school opened its doors, they were 25, 23, and 21 respectively.

As per the custom of the era, Brahmacharya Vidyalaya was an all-boys' school (in time, classes for girls were conducted nearby). To fill academic needs, teachers were hired, among them Ananda Mohan Lahiri, who was a grandson of Lahiri Mahasaya and an advanced Kriya Yogi in his own right. Sadhana and spiritual knowledge were tended to mainly by Yogananda and Swami Kebalananda, who was known on campus as Guru Maharaj.[4] Competitive sports and vigorous exercise were encouraged. The discipline was firm but kind. The routine was clocklike. The students were instructed in ethical principles, yoga asanas, and basic meditation techniques. Those who were qualified were initiated into Kriya Yoga by Yogananda.

Developing sound minds in healthy bodies was a guiding principle, and, to that end, the Ranchi students were among the first beneficiaries of what Yogananda called "a unique system of health and physical development." Based on principles he said he discovered in 1916, the system he named Yogoda involves directing energy to specific body parts with concentration, will, breath, and the tensing and relaxing of muscles. Here is how Yogananda describes it in the *AY*: "As no action of any kind is possible without willing, man may avail himself of the prime mover, will, to renew his strength without burdensome apparatus or mechanical exercises. By the simple Yogoda techniques, one may consciously and instantly recharge his life force (centered in the medulla oblongata) from the unlimited supply of cosmic energy."[5]

The use of the anatomical term medulla oblongata is an interesting example of Yogananda's ongoing effort to integrate East and West, ancient and modern, esoteric and scientific. He claimed that the cosmic life force known as *prana* enters the body at the base of the skull, through the medulla oblongata. Ancient yogis used different terminology, of course, but they considered that part of the body, which Yogananda called "the mouth of God," of great significance with respect to the regulation of breathing rhythms and its proximity to the *ajna chakra*, the subtle energy center associated with wisdom and intuitive knowing. Located behind the space between the eyebrows, *ajna chakra* is known as the "third eye" and is a focal point of Kriya Yoga practices.

What did Yogananda mean when he said he "discovered" the principles of Yogoda? Some devotees believe the system came to him as a divine revelation, or as a cognition arising from knowledge carried over from a past life. Others say the discovery was a product of information gleaned from multiple sources, coupled with imagination, creativity, and intuition. Based on my research, both are correct. We know that some of the Yogoda principles mirror those in the yoga tradition, particularly the hatha and tantric branches that were well represented in Bengal at the time. We also know that certain European approaches to physical culture were popular then, as Indians responded to Vivekananda's entreaties to develop physical vitality as a component of national strength.

Perhaps the best known of the physical culture exponents was a German bodybuilder named Eugen Sandow. Born Friedrich Wilhelm Müller, the Prussian showman toured the world giving demonstrations and became known as "the father of modern bodybuilding." According to yoga teacher and author Mas Vidal, Sandow toured India in the early 20th century, drawing thousands to his exhibitions, and was in Calcutta before the Ghosh family moved there. Vidal quotes this passage from a Bengali newspaper: "The essence of his system [is] to concentrate the mind upon the physical effort, so that mind and body may both work together to produce muscular development."[6] It is not known whether Yogananda read that article, but he referred to Sandow in talks and in the SRF Lessons.[7]

Yogananda may also have been exposed to the work of another European bodybuilder, one Maxick. Born Max Sick in Austria, he parlayed his chiseled five-feet-four body into a noteworthy career performing feats of strength. He does not seem to have visited India, but he was a sensation in England, and he published an influential book, *Muscle Control*, in 1910, the year Yogananda finished high school. Controlling the muscles strengthens the mind, he said, and mental willpower can strengthen the body.

However much Yogananda was influenced by hatha yogis and European bodybuilders, his insight and creativity led to a unique system of exercise that proved to be of great benefit, first to the students at Ranchi and eventually to practitioners around the world. His unique contribution, Brother Chidananda, president of SRF, explained in a private exchange, was "the application of will power to connect the body's energy with cosmic energy and draw it in through the medulla, and then direct it consciously, through the act of tension and relaxation, to charge specific body parts with life force." Modified from time to time over the decades, and called by various names—"Recharging Exercises," "Rejuvenation Exercises," and, most commonly now, "Energization Exercises"—the routine remains a fundamental element of the practices taught in Yogananda's name.

Yogananda presided over the Ranchi school like, in his words, a "father-mother."[8] And, if reports are accurate, like a friend and an uncle as well—kind, caring, playful, and available. He engaged in sports with the students; organized outings and joined in; sang, chanted, and played music; concocted pranks and told jokes; and, as he did in Dihika, cooked up meals and experimented with ingredients. In another preview of things to come, he would combine various nuts, grains, and spices to mimic the taste of fish and fowl. Flash forward about three decades to the opening of SRF cafes in Southern California, with vegetarian menus featuring Yogananda's mushroom burger recipe.[9]

In *Mejda*, Sananda Ghosh extolled his brother's leadership virtues: "[H]is manner was so charming, and his heart so loving, that no one felt rejected or uncomfortable. His sweet smile was always present; and in the warmth of that glow, all hearts and minds were caught." Then he added, "On the other hand, when Mejda decided to get to the bottom of a matter or to make it a point of issue, there was no avoiding the sharpness of his perception. His testing was severe indeed."[10] Satyananda concurred (as would American disciples in later years): "Sometimes he would become upset and unmercifully deride someone." But, he added, immediately afterward Yogananda "would break down with his gentle heart, become outwardly pained, and try to heal that person's hurt." There were, to be sure, reasons to get upset. Despite the Maharaja's generosity, the school ran into financial troubles, and of course, people misbehaved, made mistakes, and failed to measure up in competence, dedication, or loyalty. Yogananda once called organizations hornets' nests, and the Ranchi school offered a taste of bigger stings to come.

Yogananda would sometimes leave campus to raise funds, meet with influential people, attend festivals, and work on behalf of Sri Yukteswar's Sadhu Sabha, of which he would be named vice president. In another portent of things to come, he put Swami Dhirananda in charge in his absence. In their two years at Ranchi, the Yogananda-Dhirananda collaboration produced a landmark book in addition to a school. On the voyage home from Japan in 1915, Yogananda had met an American couple with whom he spoke about the nature and substance of religion. The couple encouraged him to write down his ideas. In Ranchi, his notes turned into *Dharmavijnana* (Wisdom of Dharma). Initially published in India, it was later edited and retitled *The Science of Religion*, which was also the title of Yogananda's first lecture in America.

Exactly how much Dhirananda contributed to the book has been debated for decades. He was, as Yogananda freely admitted, the more scholarly of the two and, at that time, more facile with English. That leads some critics of Yogananda to contend (in online discussions and in e-mails to me) that Dhirananda did the bulk of the writing and contributed key ideas and information. Others say he served merely as an editor or a ghostwriter, helping Yogananda shape his ideas into coherent form. Yogananda himself said that Dhirananda only edited for grammar.[11] The title page of the first American edition, published in 1924, lists "Swami Yogananda, BA" as principal author (the copyright is in his name), followed by several lines of credentials. Below that is "Swami Dhirananda, MA," with "Associate" beneath the name. In a note of acknowledgment inside the book, Yogananda thanks Dhirananda, Satyananda, and Tulsi Narayan Bose "for various forms of help I have received from them."

Dhirananda's name has been absent from the book for decades now. The ongoing, and surely irreconcilable, debate over who contributed what is a reflection of bigger controversies surrounding the demise of the friendship a decade later. But at Ranchi between 1918 and 1920, all was well and the duo made for a highly successful team. After their first year of operation, Yogananda wrote, 2,000 students applied for admission. The facility could hold only a hundred.[12] Day students would soon be admitted, and branch campuses would be added. One was at Sri Yukteswar's ashram in Puri, a seal of approval that Yogananda no doubt welcomed as much as any accolades he'd ever received. Other satisfactions for a job well done came from the Maharaja's continued support, commendations from people of stature, visits from spiritual and secular dignitaries, and respect from admired people such as Rabindranath Tagore.

With the exception of Sri Yukteswar, two honored visitors no doubt rose above the rest in Yogananda's heart. One was Swami Pranabananda, the bilocating saint who blew his mind in Benares as a boy. The other was his father. Watching his son preside over his successful school was a healing tonic for Mr. Ghosh. He now understood that Yogananda could never have been happy in a career like his own, confined to an office as a small spoke in the wheel of a vast railway bureaucracy. Sadly, another of his son's life choices was about to break his heart again.

In the middle of the Ranchi property was a stone cabin where rice and other food items were stored. Because it was cool and quiet inside, Yogananda would sometimes seclude himself in the storeroom to meditate.[13] One morning, in the summer of 1920, he entered what he described as "a deep state of ecstasy." A vision came to him of a "panorama of Western faces."[14] He took it as a sign that it was time to fulfill his guru's prophecy and go to America. He would later say that he recognized the faces that appeared to him that day as those of American devotees.[15]

When he returned to waking consciousness, he saw one of the students sitting nearby. Yogananda told him that God had just said he should go to America. It did not take long for the word to spread throughout the 25 acres, and probably beyond. Some were skeptical. In those days, journeys to America seemed a remote possibility, especially since travel had been severely restricted because of the war and the influenza pandemic. Furthermore, such a journey would require a good deal of money, and neither Yogananda nor the school had any. "I was starting out for America like the fellow who polished his whip even though he had no horse to ride," he would one day remark.[16]

Undaunted, he displayed a sense of conviction that some would call mad and others divinely inspired. He decided to take the 3 o'clock train that afternoon so he could arrive in Calcutta early the next morning. When he left, placing the school in the hands of the trusted Dhirananda and Satyananda, there was weeping among the students, and no doubt consternation among the teachers and staff—and at least one animal. Yogananda's pet monkey broke its chain and ran away.

A series of obstacles was about to stand in his way like strong-armed sentinels guarding the gates to the future. These would be dispensed with one by one, as if deftly nudged aside by some cosmic jujitsu.[17] His father was deeply disturbed by the news; Ranchi was about as far away as he wished his now-eldest son to be. Since Yogananda had no idea how he would get to the United States, or when he might go, or under what auspices if any, Mr. Ghosh had reason to hope that the barriers to travel would prove insurmountable. Ironically, someone in his own home helped remove those barriers.

A family friend, a teacher at Calcutta City College, happened to be visiting that day. He told Yogananda that, coincidentally, the principal of his college was also planning a trip to America. Thinking that the principal, Haramba Maitra, might be helpful, he arranged a meeting. Professor Maitra, a leader in the Brahmo Samaj, was on the council of the Congress of Religious Liberals in Boston. The congress, which was run under the auspices of the American Unitarian Association, was scheduled to meet in September. Professor Maitra was to be India's only representative, and it turned out that he couldn't make it. Impressed by the young swami's educational initiative, he suggested that Yogananda take his place. He wrote accordingly to the congress in Boston.

Just like that, Yogananda had a specific destination, a credible purpose for going, and Americans to welcome him. The next day he went to Serampore to seek his guru's blessing and counsel. Sri Yukteswar, of course, had been anticipating this moment. He said that all doors were open to him and he should seize the moment. Yogananda expressed concern about his inexperience and his uncertain command of English. "English or no English," said the master, "your words on yoga shall be heard in the West."[18]

Now all he had to do was get to America on time for the congress and find a way to pay for the trip—no small feat. At the shipping office, where sea voyages were ticketed, he learned that the first passenger ship to sail from India to America since the start of the war was slated for departure in about a month. Even better, the SS *City of Sparta* would be sailing directly to Boston. Then came the bad news: the ship had been completely booked for six months. Yogananda told the English clerk he intended to be on board nonetheless. The man got angry. Not only were no berths available, he told the impertinent swami, but it took three to six months to process passport applications.

With the war recently ended and the independence movement heating up, the British government saw all Indians as potential saboteurs and revolutionaries. Yogananda insisted that the clerk write down his name in case there was a cancellation. Probably just to get rid of him, the functionary did so, on his shirt cuff. Years later, Yogananda joked that he caused the disagreeable man to ruin a good shirt.

Shortly after that incident, Mr. Ghosh asked him to run an errand to one of their relatives. In telling the story years later, Yogananda said he almost refused—a prompting from Satan, he called the impulse—but he did not. The relative, a deputy magistrate, verified that obtaining a passport on time was a serious impediment. Then again, another relative, a distant uncle, happened to be in the next room, and he was very well connected. A week later, Yogananda had his passport.

He returned to the shipping office. The same clerk greeted him with contempt. Probably in an attempt to torment Yogananda, he revealed that a reservation for a first-class cabin had been canceled. But you can't afford that, he sneered, and you don't have a passport. Yogananda showed him the passport. The man was incredulous. But there was still the matter of coming up with enough cash to secure the booking before someone else grabbed it.

When Mr. Ghosh learned what was going on, he reacted like . . . well, like a father: "What is this nonsense?" and "Who is going to finance you?"

Yogananda answered like a monk. "God," he said.

"I am not going to give it to you."

"I never asked," said Yogananda. Then he added, like the son of an affluent and generous man, "You never can tell. You may change your mind."

"Never!" declared Mr. Ghosh.

But he did change his mind, although change of heart would be more accurate. The next day, admitting he was wrong to react as he did, he wrote a check to cover the cost of first-class passage. Yogananda handed it back. He couldn't accept it, he said, if his father had been coerced by his words. Mr. Ghosh insisted. He had been adamant about not giving him the money because he just didn't want him to go. He had, after all, lost his first-born son already, and at 67, the thought of losing a second to a mission halfway around the world was hard to bear.

"Don't take it from your father," he said of the money, "but from a student of Lahiri Mahasaya." Then he cried. "When are you coming back?" he asked.

"In three months—if the Americans don't need me."[19]

They needed him. The three months became three decades, although father and son had one last reunion halfway through that span of time.

Now the only remaining obstacle was Yogananda's own trepidation. He needed a sign from God. It came in the form of his guru's guru's guru, the fabled Mahavatar Babaji.

At this pivotal moment in Yogananda's life, legend collides with history, faith with reason, personal testimony with the known laws of science. Readers will choose for themselves whether the story was imagined or fictionalized by Yogananda, or whether they should heed Hamlet's assertion to Horatio that there are more things in heaven and earth than are dreamt of in their philosophy.

On July 25, 1920, Yogananda said, the ageless Babaji showed up at 4 Garpar Road to put an end to his wavering. Early that morning, Yogananda began to pray, determined to keep at it until he heard from God. By noon, he said, "my head was reeling under the pressure of my agonies." His entreaties had yielded no heavenly response. Then there was a knock at the front door. He opened it to find a radiant ascetic who reminded him of the young Lahiri Mahasaya. In the house, speaking in Hindi, the sadhu responded to Yogananda's unspoken thought: he was, indeed, Babaji, and he had a message from the Almighty: Go to America, as your guru told you to, and have no fear because you are under protection. He added, after a pause, "You are the one I have chosen to spread the message of Kriya Yoga in the West."[20] Yogananda prostrated before the holy presence. Babaji helped him up and proceeded to issue instructions and prophecies that Yogananda never revealed.[21]

He was now satisfied that his mission was divinely sanctioned. It was further blessed by Nagendra Nath Bhaduri. Yogananda went to see the Levitating Saint, who was about 74 at the time, and knelt before him. "Take the dignity of hoary India for your shield," his former mentor told him. "Victory is written on your brow; the noble distant people will well receive you."[22] Those words are framed and displayed beneath a large garlanded photo of Yogananda next to the Levitating Saint's bed in the ashram maintained by his devotees.

The final benediction, so to speak, was left for Sri Yukteswar. On the night before his disciple departed, the guru dispensed this advice: "Forget you were born among Hindus, and don't adopt all the ways of the Americans. Take the best of both peoples."[23] In the coming years Yogananda lived up to that prescription as well as anyone could. Sri Yukteswar was present, and no doubt proud and gratified, at the Kidderpore dock the next day to see him off. So were most of Yogananda's family, and the students and faculty of the Ranchi school. One of those students, when he was in America as Swami Premananda, recalled an incident from that day. Yogananda was with him and others at the ship's rail when the captain ordered him, gruffly, to go to his cabin or else leave the boat. Yogananda met the captain's gaze and said, "Sir, a gentleman does not speak in that manner." According to Premananda, "the humbled English captain withdrew with bowed head, speechless." Americans who looked down upon the "heathens" of Asia were also about to be humbled by Yogananda's dignity and erudition.

The *City of Sparta* left Calcutta on August 2 with a cargo of mostly jute and tea, plus 61 passengers, including 11 Indians (Yogananda plus 10 students bound for American colleges), some returning missionaries, businessmen and tourists, and two refugees from the Armenian massacre in Turkey. On the ship's manifest, under Family Name, was written "Mukunda Lal Ghosh"; under Given Name was "Swami Yoganandageri" (sic). His age was listed as 25, although he was actually 27 and a half.

Under Calling or Occupation were the typed words "Brahim in charge." That was no doubt meant to be *Brahmin*, although Yogananda was not that, but the confusion was allayed with a handwritten "Professor." He was listed as an English-speaker traveling as a British subject. Under Race or People, the typed "Bengali" was crossed out and replaced with "E. Indian." It was stamped "Legal Entry for Arranged Residence Verified." And, written in script, these curious notations, one under the other: "Political opinions. Not raising funds. Not liberal, except on religion."[24] He was good to go.

One can only imagine the multitude of feelings that washed over him as the smoke billowed from the ship's chimneys and he watched his loved ones fade from view: apprehension, no doubt; melancholy, for sure; excitement, to say the least; and, as he put it, "aloneness." He must have known that his life was poised for a radical shift. Surely he was inspired by the magnitude of the mission articulated by Babaji to Sri Yukteswar years earlier: "India has much to learn from the West in material development; in return, India can teach the universal methods by which the West will be able to base its religious beliefs on the unshakable foundations of yogic science."[25] And he was no doubt strengthened by his guru's last words to him the night before: "Your lot to attract sincere souls is very good. Everywhere you go, even in a wilderness, you will find friends."[26] He would, indeed, find many friends.

CHAPTER 9

BOSTON BRAHMAN

Before dawn on Sunday, September 19, 1920, the *City of Sparta* floated into the C-shaped natural harbor where the Boston Tea Party had erupted and Hindu and Buddhist texts had arrived on sailing ships, eventually to wend their way to Ralph Waldo Emerson and Henry David Thoreau. Aboard the vessel, Swami Yogananda watched America draw closer. He felt alone and forlorn for a spell, but his mood was lifted by a vision similar to the one he had in Ranchi, of American faces he called "sleeping memories of friends once more to be."[1]

In his 48 days at sea, he was the proverbial sore thumb in his ochre robe and turban and his long hair, beard, and mustache.[2] Speculation and rumors about him spread. One wonders if this thought occurred to him: since most of the passengers had boarded the ship in Calcutta (it made one stop, in Port Said, Egypt), they had presumably seen Indians, and even swamis, before; if they found him odd, what might he expect from Bostonians who had never laid eyes on someone like him? He was accustomed to being different, having been teased throughout his youth for his spiritual zealotry, but now his mere appearance could invite ridicule, torment, and perhaps even abuse.

Despite Sri Yukteswar's assurances, Yogananda remained insecure about his facility with English. His skill was put to the test when he was urged to give a talk to his fellow passengers. The topic chosen for him was "The Battle of Life and How to Fight It." When the captain introduced him to the audience, he was struck mute. He said that his mind went blank and he remained silent for a full ten minutes. Some in the audience chuckled. Then the voice of his guru came to him: "You *can*! Speak!" He did, of course, and he described the lecture the way musicians describe their best performances, as flowing from some unknown source beyond their own volition.

The success of that maiden voyage into English oratory did more than boost his confidence. A number of listeners gave him their cards and suggested he speak at their various associations.

When he walked down the gangplank at Pier 3 in East Boston, late in the morning of that last day of summer, Yogananda was greeted by weather more pleasant than what he was accustomed to that time of year. The sky was clear and temperatures hovered around 70 degrees Fahrenheit (21 Celsius). It would not be surprising if one of the New Englanders he'd met told him to enjoy the weather while he could.

A *Boston Globe* photographer with an eye for photogenic arrivals had the exotic visitor pose for a picture that would appear on page 7 of the next day's paper, in a black-and-white tableaux with three other images: a comely young woman, an adorable child, and the Armenian refugee sisters Nashooshay and Zaroohy Gueevjian, decked out in matching coats and feathered hats. Yogananda is pictured head to toe, in his turban and shin-length tunic with a white collar that looks like what we now call mock turtleneck, dark puttees (cloth strips wound around the lower leg), and Western-style shoes. Staring at the camera with a pleasant half-smile, he is as clean shaven as a baby, and he would remain so for the rest of his days, even earning a reputation for never looking like he needed a shave. Some friendly shipmates had convinced him it was wise to get rid of the beard. It was the first of many times he modified or abandoned an Indian custom in America, but he adamantly refused to cut his hair. The accompanying article identified him as "Swami Yoganadageri (sic), a Hindu of Ranchi, India," and said he'd shocked reporters when he "bid them good morning in perfectly good English."[3]

He stepped into an America whose can-do spirit was birthing the Roaring Twenties.[4] The Great War had ended in victory; the country was nine months into the Prohibition era and one month into a new electoral era, with women having just won the right to vote. Woodrow Wilson, severely limited by a stroke that had been kept secret, was in the final stretch of his presidency. The first female voters would help determine his replacement: the Republican ticket of Warren G. Harding and Calvin Coolidge or the Democrats' James M. Cox and Franklin D. Roosevelt. (In November, the Republican victory would be announced on the world's first radio station.) On the streets and saloons of Beantown, the talk was about the Irish War of Independence and the Red Sox. The team's fans were reeling from the first signs of the Curse of the Bambino: Babe Ruth, having been sold to the archrival Yankees, was about to end the season with more home runs (54) than the entire Red Sox team.

The newcomer from India knew little of all that, of course, although one wonders what he might have thought about the Irish rebellion against British rule. As his legs adjusted to walking on land again, he was led by some of his new friends down a long stairway. The next thing he knew, he was boarding a train that "shot away like lightning." Back in India, it seems, he had been advised to ride the "suboy" in America, as taxis were expensive. He now found out the proper pronunciation was subway, and that Boston's 23-year-old system had been the very first built in the U.S. He marveled that one could ride a speedy train 60 feet beneath the ground. Other marvels awaited him.

He was deposited at the Greater Boston YMCA at 316 Huntington Avenue, a short walk to Symphony Hall where he would one day speak to capacity crowds. A strange-looking nobody in unfamiliar surroundings, he settled into his simple room. He had never seen a drinking fountain like the one in the Y, and it took him a while to figure out its use. Then he had to learn about food. He waited for room service that never arrived. Fortunately, he had learned the virtues of fasting. Eventually, another guest took him downstairs to the dining room. He waited to be served. No one came, not because he was being ignored but because it was a self-service cafeteria. When he saw how others were obtaining their meals, he joined the line. All he would risk eating was milk and bread; he feared that the unfamiliar dishes might contain meat.

He soon moved to Unity House, where the congress was being held and other delegates were lodged. Located at 7 Park Square, it was a far more convenient and congenial location. He could stroll across the street to Boston Public Garden and the adjacent Boston Common; the Charles River was as close as the Ganges was to his home in Calcutta; the State House, Beacon Hill, and major historic sites were nearby. Coming from an ancient land, he might have found it amusing that "historic" in America meant 200 or 300 years old. If he wanted to read up on something, the Boston Public Library was four blocks away. If he craved fresh fruits and vegetables, he could call on the pushcart vendors at nearby Haymarket Square.

Bostonians have always been a strange mix of progressives and conservatives, and many at the time had trouble adjusting to the East European Jews and Irish and Italian Catholics who had swarmed into the city in the preceding decades, much less foreigners with dark complexions and bizarre clothing. Yogananda's stature was that of an average American male: five-feet-eight on official documents, but two inches shorter by the estimates of some who knew him, and about 150 pounds. But he was longhaired and orange-robed nearly half a century before hippies and Hare Krishnas pranced in the Commons, and he was brown skinned in a city whose baseball team would be the last one to integrate. He endured sneers, glares, stone throwing, and name-calling ("snake charmer" was one), but, he said, he maintained his dignity.

Some of his culture shock moments were humorous. Seeing signs for hot dogs, he was horrified that God would send him to a land where people ate canine flesh. People seeing only his lustrous shoulder-length hair directed him to the ladies' room, and on at least one occasion he walked in. Out of politeness, he drank coffee when it was served, only to discover one day that he craved it—and therefore never drank a drop again. An ardent opponent of habits that interfered with the use of one's free will, he did the same with another beverage he took a liking to: ginger ale. He never touched alcohol except the one time he dipped his finger into a beer and tasted it to placate a friend (he didn't like it). And he got at least one person drunk when, at a dinner party, he surreptitiously poured his wine into the man's glass each time his was refilled.

Like all newcomers, he gradually adjusted. But in a sense, the enculturation process continued throughout his 32 years in the U.S., and so did the irritating reactions to his appearance. In a talk recorded in the late 1940s, he tells about the time he sat opposite a man on a long train ride who stared at him with disgust. Ironically, the fellow passenger was Warner Oland, a Swedish-American movie actor known for playing Asians like Charlie Chan and Dr. Fu Manchu. Yogananda asked why he was looking at him that way.

"None of your business," said the actor.

"Of course it's my business, because every time I look ahead I have to see your face."

That broke the ice. We are all a little crazy, Yogananda pointed out, only "I know about your craziness, but you don't know what kind of craziness I have." He made an offer: they would have a constructive discussion, and whoever lost would follow the other. They conversed for two hours, and, Yogananda said, "He lost and I won, and I was saved from being a movie actor."[5]

Needless to say, he could not lighten his complexion or lose his accent, but he did attempt to attract less attention. At one point, he started wearing Western clothing when out and about, favoring brown, gray, and navy blue suits with a white shirt, sometimes with a clerical collar, and a white scarf whose folds he usually pinned together at the chest. He always wore an overcoat, one of his close disciples, Durga Mata, asserted, because it was like wearing a robe. He wore a real swami's robe when he lectured, taught, conducted services, performed rituals, and spoke to interviewers—cotton at first, as is worn in India, and silk after he realized that Sri Yukteswar had been right and he was viewed less favorably when he wore cotton. He let his hair flow naturally when he wore robes but at other times would pull it back and tuck it under his scarf, or fasten it with a bobby pin under his hat. In some photos, wearing a fedora and an overcoat, he looks like a Hollywood version of a dapper Latino. Once, Durga Mata wrote, Sri Yukteswar saw one of those photos and remarked, disapprovingly, that his disciple had been so Americanized that he cut his hair. When he got wind of that, Yogananda immediately had a portrait taken and mailed to India to show his guru he had kept his hair traditional swami length.

In an anecdote described in her useful book, Durga Mata describes the guru standing in a crowded Boston streetcar when a gaggle of young girls begin teasing him and tugging at his hair. "So these are the American girls I heard so much about in India," he said. The mortified girls quickly apologized. It was Halloween season, and they thought he was in costume. They showed him the way to his destination.[6]

The thick, wavy hair was also a haven for the era's ubiquitous cigarette smoke. He would air out his hair and brush it to get rid of the foul odor and toxic fumes. Characteristically, he turned the experience on its ear with mind power and used it as a teaching tool. In a letter to a disciple, he said that once he realized that Divine Spirit was smoke and light, tobacco smoke stopped irritating him.[7]

Aside from a few anecdotes, little is known about how Yogananda spent the two weeks between getting settled in Boston and his inaugural speech. We know he spent time at the nearby office of the American Unitarian Association. We know that he and other delegates were taken to Plymouth Rock to commemorate the 300th year since the Pilgrims' arrival.[8] One hopes that he got to other sites in America's most historic region, and was perhaps driven to the countryside to see pumpkin patches and fall foliage. One thing he did comment on was his initial sense of unease. He was uncertain what to do after his congress lecture was over. He prayed for a sign.

On the morning of October 6, the Congress of Religious Liberals convened at Unity House. A page 12 article in that afternoon's *Boston Globe*[9] reported that the morning's theme was "Interdenominational Fellowship" and the speakers included Protestant ministers, a rabbi, scholars, and laypersons. It was a celebration of religious freedom. Yogananda's talk on "The Science of Religion" offered a distinctly Vedic vision of spiritual unity amid religious diversity. It was, by all accounts, a triumph. There is no record of the actual speech, but the book of the same title is said to be an expanded version of it. Containing the essence of what Yogananda would teach for the remainder of his life, it advocates a systematic, experiential approach to the life of the spirit that transcends doctrine and theological differences and all the categories the West has assigned to religion. The message would have been thoroughly understood and deeply appreciated by the Transcendentalists who dwelled in Concord, 25 miles from the site of the congress, about half a century earlier.

The lecture also stands as a textbook illustration of how teachers and interpreters have adapted India's metaphysical teachings to a secular and scientific era. Like Vivekananda before him and a parade of gurus after him, Yogananda asserted that he had not brought a creed or a dogma, but rather a set of universal principles that could be seen as "a science of soul." In the book version, he states: "If by religion we understand only practices, particular tenets, dogmas, customs, and conventions, then there may be grounds for the existence of so many religions. But if religion means primarily God-Consciousness, or the realization of God both within and without, and secondarily a body of beliefs, tenets, and dogmas, then, strictly speaking, there is but one religion in the world, for there is but one God. In reality, God and man are one, and the separation is only apparent."[10]

That is as clear a summary of Hindu philosophy as can be found, and its unifying distinction between what scholar of religion Huston Smith called the esoteric and exoteric (internal and external) aspects of religion is one that would ring refreshingly true to many Westerners today, while at the same time sound threatening to others.

If *The Science of Religion* reflects the speech of the same name, Yogananda went on to explain the pragmatic dimension of classical yoga: "As the sun's true image cannot be perceived in the surface of moving water, so the true blissful nature of the spiritual Self—the reflection of the Universal Spirit—cannot be understood, owing to the waves of disquietude that arise from identification of the self with the changing states of the body and mind." Stressing that "there is no distinction here of caste or creed, sect or faith, dress or clime, age or sex, profession or position," he introduced the scientific approach of his lineage. It consists, he said, "of magnetizing the spinal column and the brain, which contain the seven main centers, with the result that the distributed life electricity is drawn back to the original centers of discharge and is experienced in the form of light." This, he explained, frees up the "spiritual Self" from physical and mental distractions. He also invoked the Bible, quoting Saint Paul and claiming that the "seven stars" in the Book of Revelation were actually the seven energy centers—what even Westerners now refer to as *chakras*.[11] This combination of scientific rationality and respect for the Judeo-Christian tradition would become hallmarks of Yogananda's teaching, and a key to his success.

Evidently, his concerns about his command of English were misguided. In its official account of the congress, the American Unitarian Association noted that Yogananda spoke "in fluent English and a forcible delivery."[12] Curiously, the speech was not reviewed in the local papers. The *Boston Post* mentioned that Yogananda was one of the speakers, representing "the Brahmins of India," but was more interested in the theme of Christianity in Japan addressed by others. It did note that the delegates attended a reception afterward at the Unitarian Laymen's League. Wouldn't it be wonderful to know how Yogananda experienced his first American party—the food, the drink, the company of Unitarians, many of whom would have known about the amicable relations between their New England ancestors and Yogananda's antecedents in Bengal?

He remained at Unity House after the conference, hoping for that sign. His lodging and other expenses were covered by the money his father had given him. He thought of establishing a center in Boston, but none of the promised help materialized. Finally, the sign he had been waiting for arrived. A minister he referred to as Mr. Foster invited him to his church in West Somerville, just north of Cambridge, on the following Sunday.[13] "His invitation made me so happy!" Yogananda said.[14]

For a man with his mission, there could be no better place to begin life in America than the place where America's life as a nation began. In the 18th century, British reign solidified in India as it disintegrated in its New World colonies and exploded with the "shot heard round the world." Vessels sailed from Boston Harbor to Calcutta and Bombay in increasing numbers, and by the early 1800s their return cargo included translations of India's sacred texts, the writings of religious modernizers like Ram Mohan Roy, and commentaries that shifted the Western image of Hindus as idol-worshipping heathen in a more sympathetic, and accurate, direction. It was in Boston that Rev. William Emerson published articles about India and its philosophies in the *Monthly Anthology*, and where his son, Ralph Waldo, absorbed Eastern ideas that changed the course of his, and America's, future. In and around Boston, the New Thought movement of Theosophists, Christian Scientists, and other metaphysical explorers set the tone for the uniquely American spirituality that the scholar Frederic Spiegelberg called "the religion of no religion." In Cambridge, America's first Sanskrit scholars took root at Harvard, and William James wrote *The Varieties of Religious Experience* and befriended Vivekananda, who lectured on campus. One of the swami's followers, the socialite Sara Bull, gathered the intellectual and creative elite to her Cambridge Conferences in the late 1890s, and another Ramakrishna monk, Swami Paramananda, founded the Vedanta Society of Boston only 10 years before Yogananda arrived.

That history of free-thinking spiritual exploration, combined with old-fashioned Yankee pragmatism, made Boston a natural launching pad. When he entered the Somerville church, no doubt turning some heads, he was given a choice seat. As he surveyed the room, he noticed a woman enter, set up a bouquet of flowers, and take a front-row seat. An inner voice told him that she would be the one to start his Boston center.

Midway through the service, he was shocked to hear himself introduced as a guest speaker. His mind went blank, as it had on the ocean voyage. Again he stood in silence as the audience waited. Again he called on his guru, and again he was told he could do it. He did, of course, although the content of his talk is unknown. Afterward, the woman with the flowers went up to speak to him. Her name was Alice Hasey, and not only would she help him start his center, she would aid him in other important ways and eventually become Sister Yogmata, the first American ordained by Swami Yogananda.

Accounts of the events that followed that fall are chronologically fuzzy and, in some ways, contradictory. We don't know how he managed the New England chill, or what he thought of Halloween, or how he spent Thanksgiving. Chances are he spent much of his time outlining speeches and working out the lessons he would teach the students he expected to gather around him. Invitations to speak at clubs, churches, and associations came his way. "The Roslindale Unitarian parish house was filled last evening . . . when Swami Yogananda Giri of Calcutta, India, delivered a most interesting address," reported *The Boston Globe* on October 19, adding that "Miss Hazel Morris and Edward Orchard sang, accompanied by Alfred New." He spoke to small groups in living rooms, like the 15 or 20 metaphysically inclined women at Mrs. Hasey's home.[15] By the time he turned 28 on January 5, 1921, he had his first American disciples, supporters, patrons and, not incidentally, loyal friends.

One Sunday night he attended a lecture at the Rosicrucian Society in Boston. Who spoke on what topic is unknown. The matter of importance is whom he met afterward: a Rosicrucian member named Mildred Lewis, who had come by streetcar and subway from Somerville with a friend. When introduced to the visiting swami, she later said, she was too awestruck to speak. She mentioned the encounter repeatedly to her husband,

Dr. Minott Lewis, a dentist and an ardent seeker of spiritual truth. As it happened, the Lewises were close friends with Alice Hasey, who told Dr. Lewis he absolutely *had* to meet Yogananda. Dr. Lewis was skeptical; he had learned to be wary of religious charlatans. But he agreed to call and introduce himself.[16]

The eventful meeting of Dr. Lewis and Yogananda took place on Christmas Eve, 1920, at Unity House. Why Yogananda, a great lover of Jesus who would become known for treating Christmas with more reverence than most Christians do, would not have spent that night at any of a thousand Boston churches is a mystery.[17] Also a mystery is why Dr. Lewis would risk getting home late and spoiling the family tradition of decorating the tree and preparing the gifts with his wife while their son and daughter slept. Perhaps it was, astrologically, the perfect time for a first guru-chela meeting—or perhaps, a reunion of two souls with business left over from previous lives. Dr. Lewis would become the first American to be formally initiated into Kriya Yoga by Yogananda.

The dentist was guarded when he entered Yogananda's room, wary of being taken advantage of.[18] The two men spoke at length. At one point, Dr. Lewis shared his frustration with religious leaders whose answers to his metaphysical queries had been unsatisfactory. He singled out one enigmatic passage from the New Testament: "If thine eye be single, thy whole body shall be full of light."[19] What did it mean, and how can one see that light, and why had no authority been able to answer those questions? Yogananda impressed his inquisitor by citing another biblical passage in response: "Can the blind lead the blind?" He placed a tiger skin on the floor and asked Dr. Lewis to sit opposite him, cross-legged. He then asked something that would stun anyone unfamiliar with the guru-disciple dynamic, much less a man of science: "Doctor, will you always love me as I love you?"

Dr. Lewis said he would. He probably surprised himself with that reply, but he later explained that he had looked into Yogananda's eyes and had seen something he'd never seen before. As Sri Yukteswar had once said to him, Yogananda told his new disciple that he would take charge of his life.

Dr. Lewis did not know what that meant, but, he later recalled, "at least I felt it was all right, so I acquiesced." Yogananda leaned forward and placed his forehead on Dr. Lewis's. The student's mind quieted. Then, he reports, "He told me to lift my eyes and to look at the point between the eyebrows"—an internal gaze at the ajna chakra. "There appeared the great spiritual light of the spiritual eye." The experience persisted, deepened, brightened, and finally Dr. Lewis saw "the little silver star in the center, the epitome of Christ Consciousness," and then, after a pause, "the great light of the thousand-rayed lotus—the most exquisite thing that can be seen." Understandably, the longtime seeker was overwhelmed.

Yogananda promised more of the same if Dr. Lewis followed his prescriptions and made one promise: "that you will never avoid me." Dr. Lewis agreed. "Little did I realize how difficult it would be," he said, but he did his best to keep the commitment, and happily so.[20]

Students of religious history would recognize in Dr. Lewis an archetypal American seeker: independent, restless, inquisitive, fed up with dogma and superstition, hungry for inner transformation and a taste of the Transcendent: in short, precisely the type of person who was eager to imbibe what ambassadors from the East had to offer. As for Mrs. Lewis, it took her a while to forgive her husband for coming home after 2 A.M. on Christmas Eve, but she came around eventually, and she too became a loyal disciple for the rest of her life.

As Yogananda's earliest American students, supporters, workers, and friends, the Lewises—and, in a more limited way, Alice Hasey/Sister Yogmata—earned a special place of honor in his movement. Later followers regarded them with a certain awe because they had known the master when he was young and unknown, had hung out with him, sheltered him, fed him, opened doors for him, and written checks for him. The Lewises' accounts of their experiences with their unique guest—the cooking sessions, the weekend getaways in their Stanley Steamer—are as charming as their spiritual experiences at his hand are profound, and their descriptions of Yogananda's clairvoyance and healing powers are as jaw-dropping as his adjustment to American amenities like showers in bathtubs are humorous. They shared meals and recreation and transportation and housing, and, for Dr. Lewis on one occasion, a bed. That last item might sound shocking to Westerners, although far less so than the alternative phrase, "slept together," would be. As it happens, sleeping beside the guru—to absorb the higher vibrations of an advanced yogi's energy—is considered a rare and mighty privilege among Hindus, one that was conferred on Yogananda by Sri Yukteswar and mentioned in the *AY* as if it were about as provocative as taking a walk together.

Yogananda's relationship with the Lewises, captured in their daughter Brenda Lewis Rosser's book, *Treasures Against Time*, illustrates one of his American challenges, balancing four sometimes conflicting roles: the guru guiding the spiritual progress of disciples, the organizational leader commanding workers and volunteers, the supplicant needing financial help, and the pal who cared about his friends and enjoyed their company. We also see in their correspondence the early signs of annoyance with the business end of his mission. The time will come, he says in one letter, "when I shall not be a slave to any organization."[21] It turned out to be more of a plaintive hope than an accurate prediction.

Now began the formidable task of translating the wisdom of the Himalayan rishis into the American idiom and the American ethos, with its breezy informality, its egalitarianism, its antiauthority brass, its manic striving, its spunk, and all that jazz. It started small. Only a handful of people came to his earliest satsangs. The numbers grew slowly, through word of mouth, and then accelerated with the help of American know-how. One student suggested he offer free public lectures, followed by classes for which a fee would be charged. Yogananda was hesitant, but he was a practical man and he understood that his work could not proceed without funds. He also embraced advertising. Followers placed ads for his events in the classified pages of newspapers, arranged an appearance on the newfangled medium of radio, and displayed posters in trolley cars. I was told by several sources in India that such marketing tactics did not sit well with some traditionalists in India who heard about them, but had he eschewed the advice Yogananda might have returned to his homeland boasting only a handful of American devotees.

He rested his head at night in different places over the next three years. The Haseys and the Lewises set aside rooms for him in their West Somerville homes on Lester Terrace and Electric Avenue respectively. For a while, he took a room in a boarding house near Harvard Square, where Indian students served up home cooking. He may have relished Cambridge's youthful energy and wondered if Emerson, whom he admired, or William James and Vivekananda had walked on the same cobblestone streets. At one point he rented space in Boston, in a six-story office building at 30 Huntington Avenue called Huntington Chambers.[22] Located near Copley Square on a busy street with trolley tracks and automobile lanes, the space served as both living quarters and the office of Sat-Sanga (later Yogoda Sat-Sanga), as his maiden organization was called.[23]

His first free public lecture was at Jordan Hall in the venerable New England Conservatory of Music. The date was Friday, March 4, 1921; the time was 8:00 P.M.; the topic was "The Analysis of Man's Inner Life, and its Ideal as Taught in India." The five-line classified ad in *The Boston Globe* identified the speaker as Swami Yogananda Giri, "Famous Psychologist and Educator of Calcutta." The ad was listed under Amusements, along with movies (silent in those days), theatrical productions (*Uncle Tom's Cabin*, *Kismet*), burlesque, vaudeville, and concerts. It seems that Yogananda had some stiff competition that night: a block away, at Symphony Hall, the legendary conductor Arturo Toscanini was leading the La Scala Orchestra. Curiously, the ad also says that Amelita Galli-Curci would be performing that Sunday afternoon. Perhaps the famed coloratura soprano met Yogananda at that time, or maybe soon thereafter in New York, because by mid-1926, she would be cheerfully singing high notes of praise for the guru and his teachings. There is no record of his maiden speech, or of how many of the thousand seats were filled, but the mind can conjure his robust voice and formal locutions reverberating through a concert hall renowned for its acoustics. It was, at the very least, the start of something big.

In the following months, small classified ads promoted Yogananda's weekly events under the banner SAT-SANGA. They took place on Saturdays at 7:45 at Huntington Chambers or at the Pierce Building up the street. The title changed each week: "The Holy War Within," "The Inner Meanings of the Bible and Their Connections to Yoga," "How to Control Life Force," "The Law of Karma and Fate," "Pain, Pleasure and Bliss," "Why We Seek God." "Practical lessons" were available by appointment.

In 1922, Thursday and Friday events were added. That spring, Yogananda had built up enough of a following to host special events, such as the "Grand Sat-Sanga Festival" at Faelton Hall, with two Christians and a Bahai joining Yogananda on the platform. At a subsequent festival, the guest speaker was a prominent new devotee who would open doors for Yogananda in the coming months: Jessie Eldridge Southwick, who, with her husband, Henry, ran the Emerson College of Oratory. Yogananda, learning about American priorities, spoke on "Psychology of Success." The year culminated with a festival on December 23, when Yogananda's topic was "Spiritual Christmas"—no doubt a rather different take on that subject than Americans were accustomed to.

Invitations to speak at clubs, churches, civic associations, and educational institutions increasingly came his way: the Boston Metaphysical Club, the Professional Women's Club, the League of Neighbors, the Boston Masonic Club. At a luncheon sponsored by the Liberal Club at Harvard, his topic was "India and Internationalism." A headline in the next day's *Harvard Crimson* read: "Gandhi Held as Second Christ by all India, Says Swami Yogananda. His Aim is to Conquer India through Ideals, Says Noted Speaker . . ."[24] For this he was reportedly placed under surveillance by the U.S. government, which was on the lookout for potential subversives. He went on record as a Gandhi supporter on other occasions as well, when American liberals rallied to the cause of Indian independence—on March

17, 1922, at Boston's Steinert Hall, and a year later at historic Park Street Church, from whose pulpits leading abolitionists had called for an end to slavery. Reporting on that occasion, the *Boston Post* said: "Swami Yoganda [sic] of India said that any league of nations must be based upon a league of hearts, that when the heart of the individual becomes imbued with a strong desire for peace, world peace will follow as a matter of course."

With the growth of his following and attendance at his events, Yogananda let it be known that he'd like to have an ashram where he and his students could meditate in rustic silence. In the spring of 1922, with the financial help of Alice Hasey, a simple cement-block building was erected on Hardy Pond in Waltham, about nine miles from Somerville.[25] A group assembled there each Sunday for a Yogananda discourse followed by a curry dinner. How they managed those meetings without a bathroom is left to the imagination. Many hours of meditation were logged beside the tranquil pond, and sometimes Yogananda camped there alone in a tent. The mini-hermitage came to be known as the Sat-Sanga summer school (it was useless in the colder months).

With his prospects brightening, Yogananda heard the call of the road. There was a continent to conquer. Soon it would be time to emulate Adi Shankaracharya and other storied figures from India's past, who wandered from place to place like spiritual Johnny Appleseeds, planting wisdom trees wherever they stopped. He also understood the importance of securing the one foothold he had established in America, and he could not count on students who were new to his teachings and busy with worldly responsibilities. He decided to summon reinforcements from India. Reportedly, his first choice was Swami Satyananda, but his schoolboy friend from Garpar Road demurred. Swami Dhirananda did not. He made arrangements to sail to America while Satyananda, who had been serving Sri Yukteswar at his Puri ashram, took over the Ranchi school (he would run it for the next 20 years). It is alleged that Sri Yukteswar said, ominously, that he felt something inauspicious in Dhirananda's departure to the West.

He arrived on August 19, 1922, on a ship called the *City of Salem*. It must have been a grand reunion; he and Yogananda hadn't seen one another in two years. The wonder of these two young men, not yet 30, sailing halfway around the world from an oppressed and downtrodden British colony to enlighten the affluent, sophisticated citizens of a former British colony could not have been lost on them. As in their formative years at home, they made a good team. They lived together most of the time, at Hardy Pond and on Huntington Avenue, and they divvied up the duties of teaching and organizing. Sat-Sanga's progress ramped up a notch. The lectures, classes, private lessons, and Grand Festivals continued apace, but now there could be more sessions for more students. Most important, with Dhirananda handling the Boston homefront, Yogananda was free to range farther afield.

On February 18, 1923, the *Boston Post* ran a half-page article about Yogananda ("personal representative of the Maharaja of Kasimbazar, the richest native prince of India") and the Yogoda method.[26] Saying it will "revolutionize all systems of exercise," take off fat at will, and perhaps eliminate the need for drugs, the piece illustrates a phenomenon familiar to anyone following the history of yoga in the West: physicality, health, and fitness attract more ink, and more eyes, than the deeper, higher, spiritual aspects of the perennial teachings.

The writer, Oliver Light, calls Yogananda "the man who exercises without exercising" and describes him using willpower to cause his biceps to "do a shimmy without moving his forearms." Yogananda is pictured three times. In one photo he sits on a tiger skin, looking directly into the camera with his deep dark eyes, bending forward with his hands grasping his toes. In another, he is wearing a one-shoulder leopard skin, his beefy arms and chest exposed, sitting comfortably in lotus position. The third shot is a straight-on portrait with an amused smile and his chin resting on the head of a tiger. Readers must have been taken by the exotic image of a pleasant-looking young man with bronze skin, a wrestler's body, and a woman's hairdo, decked out in jungle accessories.

The article acknowledges that Yogananda, "a philosopher and mystic," did not come to America to teach physical fitness, and that he lectures on religion and philosophy. But it's almost all about the body. Yogananda tells the reporter that "I soon found that my message to America, to be complete, must include something of physical development as well," hence the demonstrations of muscle control and the Yogoda system that combines "the basic laws of the ancient yogis with modern physiological science." He had once been rail thin, Yogananda says, and Dhirananda had been fat, before willpower transformed them both. "And there was no question," the writer concedes, "but that the speaker was inclined to stoutness, while his associate Swami had the lithe lines of a swimmer."

Significantly, Yogananda is dubbed "the Coué of gymnastics." Never mind that "gymnastics" is hardly the word for a system in which the performer doesn't budge from his location; it was in many ways an apt comparison, and one that would have produced a favorable image in the minds of readers. Émile Coué, a Frenchman who had just been to Boston on a well-publicized speaking tour, had achieved international fame with the therapeutic self-improvement method described in his best-selling book, *Self Mastery Through Conscious Autosuggestion*. His ritual application of the mantra-like phrase "Every day, in every way, I'm getting better and better" had caught on with the masses and would influence self-improvement gurus from Norman Vincent Peale to myriad seminar leaders today.[27] In fact, Yogananda may have been influenced to some degree by the Coué phenomenon; he later used the term autosuggestion himself, and made extensive use of affirmations in his teaching. This is not to suggest that he borrowed anything more than terminology and perhaps presentation style; regulating mental content and reframing negative thoughts had been part of the yogic repertoire for centuries, and Yogananda had employed such methods before coming to the West.

The falling of leaves in 1923 marked the beginning of expansion. In November, Yogananda lectured on "Concentration and the Cure for Nervousness" for the Applied Psychology Club[28] in Worcester, about 40 miles west of Boston. Admission was $.50. "Psychology is the hide that covers the body of the elephant of truth," he told the audience. "The 'isms' and 'ogies' that have been put forth in the hopes of discovering the real truths of life are merely parts of the whole, from which we see nothing."

He then delivered three lectures, on consecutive nights, in Lynn, a North Shore town about halfway between Boston and Salem (of the infamous witch trials). The topics were: "Mastering the Sub-Conscious Mind and Human Efficiency," "Science of Concentration and Success," and "Highest Health Perfection Through 'Yogoda' or 'Muscle-Will System.'" These nearby forays were just the beginning. The Big Time beckoned. He envisioned a lecture series in New York, and according to Mildred Lewis asked her husband for $1,000 (more than $14,000 now). "I was completely upset by this," said the young mother of two small children.[29] Evidently, Yogananda got most, if not all, of the money he requested.

With additional help from Alice Hasey and the well-connected Jessie Eldridge Southwick, the series was arranged. Prominent New Yorkers showed up on November 24 for his Gotham debut, a free lecture at prestigious Town Hall, whose midtown environs were jumping with jazz and bootleg liquor. A classified ad for the event—right next to one for Al Jolson, "the world's greatest entertainer," who was pictured in blackface—shows Yogananda in a turban and says he'll be speaking on "the sensational discovery of everlasting youth." Mrs. Southwick would also speak and a violinist would perform. Tickets were $1 to $3. A spread about coming events in the *New-York Tribune* showed Yogananda walking on a city street in a long robe and turban, his wavy hair flowing over his right shoulder to his chest. With him are four Americans in unlikely garb: Indian-style flowing fabrics and head scarves for the three women, and a turban for the man in an overcoat. They are identified as Mrs. Southwick, Mr. and Mrs. J. E. Smith, and "Sister Yogomata."

The headline reads: A FAMOUS SWAMI COMES TO TOWN. It was surely an eye-catching scene, even in a city where eye-catching scenes were commonplace.[30]

In attendance at Town Hall was Margaret Woodrow Wilson, the daughter of the former President, who became Yogananda's student.[31] Also present was the manager of the Hotel Pennsylvania, who invited the visiting swami to be his guest at the upscale, four-year-old hotel. Yogananda vacated his suite at the Waldorf-Astoria and settled in at 401 Seventh Avenue, across the street from the architectural marvel of Penn Station. There, he held a four-month series of classes.[32]

When the scheduled series went on hiatus for the Christmas season, Yogananda returned to Boston for the Grand Sat-Sanga Festival at Convention Hall, a larger venue than those for previous festivals. The ad for it was bigger too, and so was the asking price: $1 ($14.25 in 2017) instead of zero. Musical entertainment was promised, as well as unspecified "Hindu refreshments" and a lecture by Yogananda on "Health thru Poetry." Why poetry? Because his "unique book of inspirational poems," *Songs of the Soul*, would be given out free to everyone in attendance.

That last item signifies another landmark in Yogananda's American campaign, and another advantage of having Dhirananda around. Sat-Sanga had started a publishing arm that would become a small income producer and, in the long run, a substantial one. In addition to the free hundred-page, clothbound book of poetry, three newly published volumes were sold at the festival: *Science of Religion* ($1.00), *Psychological Chart* "for self-analysis" ($.50), and a 20-page booklet, *Yogoda or Tissue-Will System of Physical Perfection* ($.10). The booklet explains the theory and benefits of the system now called Energization Exercises; instructions were given only in person.

The *Psychological Chart* is a remarkable product, about 14 pages long. Created for use with students at Ranchi, the chart is based on passages in the *Bhagavad Gita* that describe the personality and behavioral traits associated with the dominance of one or another of the three *gunas*, the subtle tendencies said to govern the created universe.[33] Still in use to this day, the chart comes with a thorough explanation and instructions for proper use.

The publishing operation also produced a small, two-sided Sat-Sanga handout. One side listed the December schedule of free Sunday lectures (three by Dhirananda, one by Yogananda). The swamis also offered, by appointment, "lessons in definite psycho-physical methods of spiritual concentration." And on Thursday evenings they presented an "inner interpretation" of the Bible and the *Bhagavad Gita.*

The other side of the handout is also of interest. On the top is printed "AUM," the sacred sound usually rendered "OM." Beneath that was an inverted teardrop with a five-pointed star within it, a symbol, no doubt, of the higher consciousness revealed through concentration on the ajna chakra. Under that are two banner-like flares, joined at the center, that evoke a pair of eyebrows. Inside each flare is printed a word: THE and DOOR. This is the text that follows, which can be taken as Yogananda's early mission statement:

> Sat Sanga is not a new religion or a religion which claims to unite all denominations by taking away their individual expressions. It is an organization for Good Fellowship, where men of different denominations, without relinquishing their individual characteristics, can meet and confer for mutual benefit. It teaches how fellowship with the good in all, and the Highest Good— Truth or God—is possible. Sat Sanga also aims at a better understanding between the East and the West.
>
> MEMBERSHIP
>
> Persons who find themselves in sympathy with the ideals represented by SAT SANGA and who desire to lend to it their moral support by seeking fellowship with the good in all and with the highest good, TRUTH, thus

THE LIFE OF YOGANANDA

doing away with all denominational and racial preju-
dices, may be enrolled as Associate members.

Persons who have taken the definite spiritual training and who practice the universal scientific methods
there received, for developing Higher Consciousness,
and who attend the services and classes, are known as
Enlightened Members.

Leaving New England in Dhirananda's hands, Yogananda
spent the holidays in New York. The City That Never Sleeps
would become the launching pad for the Westward Ho campaign that led to his becoming what the *Los Angeles Times* later
called "the 20th century's first superstar guru."[34]

CHAPTER 10

FROM SEA TO SHINING SEA

When Yogananda settled in for his extended stay at the Hotel Pennsylvania, the roar of the '20s was not yet full throttle but it was growing louder by the day. New York City was the center of that manic universe, a frenzy of stock market fever and materialist fantasies; speedy autos, racing pedestrians, and zooming subways; hot jazz, Charleston dancing, and bootleg booze—an oddly perfect place for an envoy of inner peace who said, "Where motion ceases, God begins." Certainly, it was a perfect place to test the efficacy of the thesis Mahavatar Babaji purportedly expressed to Sri Yukteswar: "East and West must establish a golden middle path of activity and spirituality combined."[1]

The '20s roared because Americans were letting loose after the fear, death, and deprivation of wartime. A new spirit of freedom had arisen—freedom of mobility, of lifestyle, of belief, of artistic expression, of sexuality, of personal fashion—as the restraints of the past were unfastened bit by bit, just as the mysteries of the universe were being unraveled by physicists in a series of quantum mechanical revelations and the mysteries of the unconscious were being unearthed by Freud and other mind miners. Nothing was as it appeared to be, even space and time. In a preview of the '60s, the '20s were marked by a surge of intellectual, artistic, and philosophical exploration. Conventional wisdom was being called into question from all angles, and thought became as free as the music that gave the Jazz Age its name. All of which made educated urbanites receptive to an articulate foreigner with a hopeful spiritual message that, unlike conventional Western religion, did not conflict with reason or science.

It was also a pleasure-seeking period, and an ambitious one. Ordinary Americans heard opportunity knocking, and the middle class enjoyed unprecedented leisure time, thanks to labor-saving inventions like refrigeration (not everyone had a refrigerator in 1924, but groceries and delivery trucks did), retail bakeries (housewives used to spend one full day a week baking bread), a variety of canned and packaged foods, washing machines and public laundry services, electric irons and toasters, sewing machines and vacuum cleaners. It's easy to imagine Yogananda being delighted by these products of American ingenuity and envisioning how they would one day improve the lives of people back home. It's also easy to imagine him appalled by the pandemic of avarice.

Perpetual prosperity became not only a wish and a political slogan, but a firmly held conviction of both leading economists and the dreamy masses who were buying and selling at a fever pitch. The stock market was aflame, manufacturing was booming, and consumers were consuming as never before, fueled by rising incomes and low unemployment, recent inventions like mail order and low-price chain stores, sophisticated advertising techniques, and two financial innovations: buying products on the installment plan and buying stocks on margin. All of which, of course, would lead to the crash of 1929 and the Great Depression. But for now, giddy optimism reigned and people could celebrate it by dancing to the latest tunes in speakeasies and "dry" dance halls, and in their own living rooms by spinning phonograph records or, most miraculous of all, turning a dial on a radio console and pulling in sound waves from far away.[2] Yogananda probably enjoyed radio, but he clearly saw its potential beyond mere entertainment. In future years he would use the new technology to broadcast his message to large numbers of people and also as a metaphor, comparing the power of the human mind to radio transmission.

The same kind of constituency that turned out for Yogananda in Boston was present in New York in greater numbers. In one *New York Times* classified section, under Religious Services, where ads for Yogananda's talks appeared, were 14 notices for the Theosophists and other groups in the New Thought category. In addition, fertile seeds had been planted at the New York Vedanta Society, which Vivekananda founded in 1894,[3] and by other yogic and Hindu voices. Swami Rama Tirtha had spent two years in America, mainly in the Bay Area, and left behind books and followers. Premananda Bharati, a Krishna devotee, was stateside from 1902 to 1911 and had touched base in New York. A. K. Mozumdar had come in 1903 and appealed to the New Thought community with, of all things, "Christian Yoga." A Hatha Yoga master named Shri Yogendra had taught in New York just prior to Yogananda's arrival, meeting with medical researchers in hopes of establishing scientific credibility for the system. Other Indian teachers also came and went in that era: Bhagat Singh Thind[4], Hari Rama; Rishi Singh Gherwal (author of *Kundalini: The Mother of the Universe*); Yogi Wassan, one of whose students was impeached as governor of Oklahoma partly due to their association[5]; Sant Ram Mandal; Swami Omkar; and others. Not to mention the most visible and respected Indian emissary, Rabindranath Tagore, who visited the U.S. three times and drew huge audiences and laudatory press coverage during his post-Nobel lecture tour in 1916–17.

There were even American yogis, principally one Pierre Bernard (real name Perry Arnold Baker). Dubbed The Great Oom and Oom the Omnipotent by the tabloids, Bernard taught what he called Tantrik Yoga in San Francisco in the early 1900s until he was arrested on morals charges brought by two women. He was released, but later served time on the East Coast for abduction. When Yogananda was in Manhattan, Bernard reigned over something like an ashram (it was called the Clarkstown Country Club) an hour or so up the Hudson River in Nyack, where he also established a sizable library of Indian philosophical and religious texts. The Great Oom got a lot of bad press, but his notoriety also gave many people a favorable impression of yoga.[6]

At the same time, many had a decidedly *unfavorable* impression of yogis, and of Hindus in general. As meticulously detailed in Anya P. Foxen's book on the subject,[7] the yogi had a rather complex image back then, a composite of largely erroneous ingredients. On the one hand, he was a conjurer, a sorcerer, a snake-charming, idol-worshipping charlatan, and a turbaned exhibitionist who lay on beds of nails and twisted his body into pretzel-like contortions for a buck. Yogananda himself addressed this image, defining the yogi as "one who knows the scientific psycho-physical technique of uniting the matter-bound body and soul with their source of origin, the Blessed Spirit."

On the other side of the coin was the exaggerated image of the inscrutable Oriental sage with uncanny psychic abilities, fortune-telling acumen, and access to the hidden mysteries of the ages. This caricature of a mental Superman appeared in novels, short stories, and movies, where he was invariably played by white actors with olive complexions, good suntans, or darkening makeup. The image was employed to good effect in the marketplace as well. To cite the most successful example, a healthy number of books on yoga and Eastern metaphysics were sold by one Yogi Ramacharaka, the pseudonym of an American named William Walter Atkinson, who published New Thought books under his real name. There were even instances of African Americans passing as Indian, a far safer minority group to belong to. One, Arthur Dowling, performed as Jovedah de Rajah, "The East Indian Psychic."

Whether one spoke sincerely about yogic philosophy on the lecture circuit or performed mind-body routines in vaudeville shows, the prevailing images were both opportunities to market and obstacles to overcome. Ever since Vivekananda's notoriety riled up conservative Christians, yogis had been attacked from both sides of the prevailing image: either they were frauds who were duping the ignorant or they were skilled mind controllers and black magicians who manipulated the vulnerable for money and/or sex. Lurid tabloid headlines like "American Women Going after Heathen Gods" appeared on newsstands, and a 68-page screed called *The Heathen Invasion* by Mabel Potter Daggett convinced large numbers of Americans in 1911 that yoga "leads to domestic infelicity, and insanity and death."[8]

It wasn't just those promulgating Hindu ideas and practices who were targeted. The country was only two generations removed from the Civil War, and anything could happen at any time to someone with dark skin. While Yogananda was conducting his New York classes in 1924, Congress was formulating one of the most restrictive immigration laws in U.S. history, the Johnson-Reed Act, whose stated purpose was "to preserve the ideal of American homogeneity."[9]

Yogananda would confront racial bigotry of the virulent kind a few years later in Miami. But even in New York, America's most tolerant and diverse city, he was no doubt pointed at, stared at, mocked, and perhaps discriminated against. Still, he no doubt enjoyed the Big Apple's sights and sounds. His hotel was nine blocks from Times Square (he probably would have passed on Ziegfeld Follies, but he might have enjoyed Cecil B. DeMille's silent film *The Ten Commandments*). He could walk to the Hudson River, to Carnegie Hall, to Central Park, and to the gigantic public library on Fifth Avenue. Prominent Manhattanites embraced him, studied with him, promoted his work, feted him in their well-appointed parlors, and probably invited him to concerts, museums, and fine restaurants, to the extent that he cared about such things. He did have a privileged seat at the Metropolitan Opera House on at least one occasion. A newspaper clip about a performance of *Le Roi de Lahore*, a Jules Massenet opera set in India, said: "A front-row spectator was the Swami Yogananda of India, who appeared in native dress."

The pattern Yogananda had established in Boston continued in New York: free public lectures followed by a series of classes (12, if later courses are a guide) for $25.[10] The titles of his talks resonated with both practical and metaphysical interests: for example, "The Tangible Cosmic Consciousness," "Power of Will," "Death and Immortality," and, during Easter week, "Spiritual Baptism." His message never strayed far from classical yoga philosophy, but he adapted it to the needs and wants of American moderns. He promised God to God-seekers, and for secular strivers and self-improvers he offered a vigorous body, a peaceful and powerful mind, and the potential for more effective action. And he was not above a bit of hyperbole. "I expect to live forever," he told a wire service. "My system brings everlasting youth."[11]

What did he teach in those courses? There are no transcripts or class outlines, but based on the lessons he later codified, it can safely be said that he presented the basic premises of Hindu philosophy: that our true identity is One with the omnipresent Spirit that permeates and transcends Creation; that fulfillment derives from awakening to that reality through direct experience; that contact with the Divine can be cultivated through systematic, predictable—and therefore scientific—yogic methods; that the universal, nonsectarian practices he teaches are both spiritually enriching and a boon to a better material life. He is likely to have taught the application of positive thinking; he certainly explained key yogic concepts such as karma; he surely discussed the uses of prayer and taught students nonsectarian forms of the practice; and he probably showed them how to cultivate spiritually supportive habits and overcome detrimental ones. Most important, he taught the three techniques whose consistent use has long been a prerequisite for initiation into Kriya Yoga proper. They were, in their recommended sequence of practice:[12]

- *Yogoda Exercises.* Now called Energization Exercises, this is the system Yogananda developed in 1916 and emphasized in many of his public presentations. As was mentioned earlier, they involve directing energy to different parts of the body using will, concentrated breathing, and the systematic tensing and relaxing of muscles in a definite sequence.

- *Hong-Sau Technique of Concentration.* This practice
  employs breath and a two-syllable mantra that has
  been used since ancient times, often in slightly
  varied form, such as "hamsa," or "hansa" or "so-
  ham."[13] Says the SRF website, "Through practice
  of this technique one learns to withdraw thought
  and energy from outward distractions so that
  they may be focused on any goal to be achieved
  or problem to be solved. Or one may direct that
  concentrated attention toward realizing the Divine
  Consciousness within."

- *Aum Technique of Meditation.* AUM, or OM, is said to
  be the primordial sound of creation. The technique,
  according to SRF's website, "shows one how to use
  the power of concentration in the highest way to
  discover and develop the divine qualities of one's
  own true Self."[14]

Yogananda almost certainly initiated some New Yorkers into
Kriya Yoga, as he had Bostonians. Since no required amount of
time practicing the prerequisite techniques had yet been established, he would have assessed applicants' spiritual progress, sincerity, and dedication, if not more subtle factors, just as gurus
had always done, before offering initiation (diksha). Initiation
was not just a matter of learning a new method of practice. It
was, and remains, a serious step into discipleship, wherein the
initiate commits to a spiritual path, with requisite disciplines,
under the guidance of Yogananda and his guru lineage.

As for the method itself, Yogananda explains it this way:
"The Kriya Yogi mentally directs his life energy to revolve
upward and downward, around the six spinal centers (medullary,
cervical, dorsal, lumbar, sacral, and coccygeal plexuses) . . ."[15]
Here, the language of physiology replaces the yogic terminology
for the subtle energy centers known as chakras. The technique
employs concentration and focused breath to move the primal
life force called prana up and down the subtle channels that are
said to run from the base of the spine to the "third eye" in the

forehead.[16] It is done repeatedly according to instructions given to the initiate. (Initiates can apply for advanced variations at appropriate intervals.)

It should be noted that, as scholar of religion Lola Williamson puts it in her study of what she calls Hindu-Inspired Meditation Movements, "When Yogananda brought the techniques to America, he simplified them for Westerners."[17] Swamis and other scholars have made the same point in interviews and in writing, sometimes approvingly and sometimes not. Some of a traditionalist bent have criticized Yogananda for altering the traditional teaching methods to suit American practitioners, and to reach more of them.[18] What he taught to groups, in a classroom setting for a fee, they asserted, should only have been transmitted on a one-to-one basis. The same sources also claimed that Yogananda altered certain nuances in the Kriya technique as taught by Lahiri Mahasaya. Even the relatively mundane matter of how a practitioner should sit was critiqued. Yogananda recognized that Americans could not sit in lotus position, or even cross-legged, for very long, so he broke tradition by giving instructions for practicing in a chair.

Four points should be made in this context: 1) Virtually every Eastern teacher who gained a following in the West faced similar critiques, as the line between a distortion and a responsible adaptation to a different culture is not always easy to discern, 2) the various Kriya Yoga lineages are not uniform in their teaching procedures; nuances vary, but the essential principles are the same, 3) many traditionalists, including swamis in Kriya Yoga and other lineages, not only approved of Yogananda's adaptations but applauded them,[19] and 4) Yogananda asserted many times that he was teaching the Kriya Yoga technique exactly as taught by his guru lineage. "The Kriya Yoga technique taught by Lahiri Mahasaya, Swami Sri Yukteswar, and Paramahansa Yogananda was the same technique," Brother Chidananda told me. "Naturally there were some differences in the wording used by each of these masters when giving instruction, but the technique itself and its effects are the same. Paramahansaji also innovated the giving of initiation in groups instead of one at a time, even though the sacred moment of initiation is still very much a personal, one-on-one blessing from guru to disciple."

By the spring of 1924, Yogananda had established Sat-Sanga communities in two U.S. cities with a high proportion of the nation's cultural and intellectual elite. While he was in New York, Dhirananda held down the fort in Boston and no doubt kept in close contact through telephone and mail. A letter Yogananda wrote to Dr. Lewis on January 7 reveals a managerial attention to detail that would shock most sannyasis. After thanking the doctor for a monetary contribution and a promised loan to further the work, he seeks clarity in the weeds: "I think you are right in your suggestion of printing 3000 Yogoda. But I want to know right away how long it will take to print 3000 and whether $165 would be taken from $800 plus $500 or $1300 or $300 plus $200 (already deposited in my bank)." He also asks about interest rates and terms of payment, and concludes, typically, on a motivational note, saying he is pleased with how things have gone in Boston and imploring him to move forward.[20]

His letters also bring to light the warmth of his friendship. To Mrs. Lewis, whom he addresses as Mil, he offers health advice for something that ails her: "Don't take cold or sour stuff. Eat tapioca and milk and eggs if you like. . . . Please take regular walks and try to ride with windows of your car open [it was winter in Boston]. Don't stay in bed all the time if you can possibly avoid."[21]

In some instances, the line between friend and guru was a bit blurry. In the same letter, he might thank the Lewises profusely for sending him cherries and implore them to rent, not sell, their home, and then dispense spiritual lessons, urging them to meditate regularly and to carry on the work of developing the local Sat-Sanga fearlessly. "Falter not—carry on everything with incessant labor," he writes, and references "the great joy that comes in doing God's work unselfishly."[22] He sounds proud of his New York victories and touched that a farewell dinner has been planned, with 60 students spending $6 a plate ($85 now) to send him off in style to his next campaign.

On May 1, he began his conquest of another historic American city. He would spend more than a month in Philadelphia, sponsored by the city's Applied Psychology Club. His first lecture, at a large public library, was so packed that people had to sit on windowsills and hundreds were reportedly turned away. Among City of Brotherly Love students was the renowned conductor of the Philadelphia Orchestra, Leopold Stokowski. The maestro was Yogananda's first celebrity devotee, conductors of major orchestras having something akin to rock star status in those days. A 1924 print run of the Yogoda booklet has this blurb from Stokowski, beneath one from Alvin Hunsicker, the president of Standard Textile Products: "Music is vibration, and all life is vibration. Yogananda has profound knowledge of this, and of concentration and of charging the body with vitality. I have learned much from him."

By now, Yogananda had acquired a feel for America's regional differences. Each city, he said, vibrated differently. Bostonians asked, "How much do you know?" New Yorkers, "How much have you got?" and Philadelphians, "Who are you?" When asked that last question in the pedigree-minded city, he replied, "I come from a very high family headed by the Almighty Father."

He seems also to have ranged afield a bit. According to a local newspaper report, he lectured on the afternoon of June 1 in Arden, Delaware, about 30 miles from Philadelphia. Curiously, he was joined on that occasion by Swami Dhirananda. Had he summoned his colleague from Boston to help out with an exceptionally busy schedule? Did they have to meet to discuss administrative issues? All we know is what a Delaware newspaper reported, that on the village green that day "Swami Giri Yogananda, A.B., psychologist-educator, accompanied by Swami Giri Dhirananda, A.M., associate, delivered an interesting lecture to a large group of Ardenites and visitors on the philosophy of Sat-Sanga (Fellowship with Truth), or the bringing of Will into the sphere of physical culture."

He returned to New York the second week of June. By then, the election campaign that would keep Calvin Coolidge in the White House was heating up.[23] So were Yogananda's restless nature and the passion of his American dream. Two things happened while he was in New York that helped shape the next chapter of his undertaking. "Despite some successes," he said in a speech 20 years later, "I experienced troubles of every kind and went through periods of greatest poverty. When we hadn't enough to buy food, we would fast for a few days. Then one day—it was in 1924—I knelt down and asked God and the Masters: 'Why have you brought me here to America?' I felt that I was not fully accomplishing my mission, and I asked for Their guidance. The answer came, and then a vision, in which I saw myself in Los Angeles."[24]

The second significant occurrence was his reunion with Mohammad Rashid, a young Indian man he'd met on the boat from Calcutta. Whether they met again by chance or by design—perhaps because Rashid saw Yogananda's name in the newspaper—is unknown. In any case, Rashid offered his services as secretary, tour coordinator, and all-around assistant. He turned out to have a good sense of organization and the know-how to make things happen. A plan was hatched for Rashid to accompany Yogananda on a cross-country road trip, which would include lectures and classes in several locations en route to the City of Angels. Camping out would be the preferred form of lodging, and two young men, Arthur Kometer and Ralph Lubliner, both Yogoda students, would accompany them.[25] Perhaps it was felt that a pair of American guys would provide both cultural and mechanical know-how, or that a Hindu and a Muslim might need some protection in a segregated country witnessing a Ku Klux Klan revival. Then again, perhaps the prime motivation was the obvious one: neither Yogananda nor Rashid knew how to drive or were legally allowed to in states that required licenses.[26]

The American love affair with the automobile was still in the dating stage, but it was heating up so quickly that a *Vogue* magazine cover in 1924 featured a car customized to look like a fashion accessory. Henry Ford's assembly line had made car ownership affordable to the rapidly rising middle class. In 1920, 8.1 million cars were registered in the United States; by 1924, there were 15.4 million, and 3.5 million *new* ones were built (by 1927, the total would exceed 20 million). You could pop into one of the country's 10,000 Ford dealerships and purchase a Model T, aka "Tin Lizzie," for less than $300—in any color as long as it was black, as the saying went.

But a Tin Lizzie would not do for four men with luggage and camping gear on a journey that would rack up over 5,000 miles, some of them on steep Rocky Mountain roads. "We had at that time a little money from classes I had given," Yogananda once recalled, "and we bought a Maxwell car."[27] Depending on the model, a new Maxwell might have been twice or three times as expensive as a Model T, but it would have been roomier and sturdier. The Model 25-C Touring Car, for instance, could seat five and featured a three-speed manual transmission, two-wheel mechanical drum brakes, and a four-cylinder, 34-horsepower engine that could zoom along at 50 miles per hour or more.

In recalling the events leading up to their departure, Yogananda said, "There was only enough money left to last until we reached Denver." But, as would happen often in his life, the need was quickly met. At a farewell dinner in his honor, the hostess, whom he does not name, took him aside. "I cannot do very much for you," she said, "but please accept this." She gave him a check for $7,000. Assuming he remembered the number correctly, the gift amounted to nearly $100,000 in 2017 money. "Behind it I saw the hand of God," said Yogananda. "I was so overcome, tears of gratitude flowed, and I predicted to her: 'You will see a large institution in Los Angeles as a result of this check.'"[28]

Piecing together sources, it would seem that the four men left New York on July 11, drove to Merchantville, New Jersey, which was just across the Delaware River from Philadelphia, and hit the road going west on or about July 14.[29]

To get to Colorado, where Yogananda lectured and taught for the first time on the tour, they probably would have driven straight into the sunset, following a route that is now mainly Interstates 76 and 70, only not with modern driving conditions. It was decades before writers like Jack Kerouac and John Steinbeck romanticized the open road, and even before Woody Guthrie was hopping freight cars. The automobile was just then becoming not only a convenience but a source of freedom, carefree leisure, and adventure. Five years earlier, in 1919, there were only 7,000 miles of paved road in the U.S. In 1924 there were 31,000, and three years later there would be 50,000. The federal government was attempting to connect the state road systems and make uniform a hodgepodge of local traffic laws. Private enterprise seized the moment; repair shops, filling stations, parking lots, billboards, campgrounds, diners, and tourist cabins bloomed along the roadsides.

That was the America Yogananda discovered, sleeping in a tent in designated camping sites or on the sides of roads with Arthur and Ralph and Mohammad Rashid, whom he described as "a good-hearted but impredictable fellow." We don't know much about how they passed the time, what they may have stopped to explore, or where and what they ate, except that "All of us were happy and singing all the way," in Yogananda's words.[30]

One wonders about the reaction of the locals they encountered. Rashid's skin was light enough to perhaps be taken for Latin American or Italian, and Yogananda wore American casual clothing and pulled his hair back. Nevertheless, there were an estimated 4 million Klansmen in the South and Midwest then, and buses carrying "Negro" entertainers and baseball players were refused service in many locales. There is no record of Yogananda encountering any such challenges. He did, however, recall one harrowing moment. As they were driving one night, a wheel fell off its axle and rolled away. "Several hundred pounds of luggage was scattered through the brush as we careened and jolted to a stop," he said. While either Arthur or Ralph walked up the road to find help, the others searched for, and found, the

errant wheel. Yogananda said he got it back on the axle himself, and they were back on the highway before the other driver
returned with the mechanic.

Yogananda certainly saw more of the country, and observed
a wider cross-section of America's 114 million citizens, than
he would have if he'd traveled by train. The vast landscape
impressed him, and the national soul even more. Eventually,
he would celebrate America's freedom-loving spirit by quoting
in his autobiography passages from Emerson, Walt Whitman's
hymn to America, "Thou Mother with Thy Equal Brood," and
George Washington's Farewell Address. But it was one thing to
see the amber waves of grain. When he got to purple mountain majesties his heart soared, and his vocabulary followed. As
the Maxwell chugged up the long, winding road to Pikes Peak
in Colorado, he composed a poem for the famous mountain.
He recited it at one of his Colorado talks. It began "Ne'er did I
expect to roam / On wheels four / Where thousand clouds do
soar." The published version includes these lines:

> I loved the breathless subtle air,
> So pure and clear,
> That chokes the gross
> And burns the dross
> Of those that love
> To worship Thee in breathless state, oh, far above
> The roar and din of tipsy senses.[31]

On that same scenic ride he also got a glimpse of the American psyche. In a 1947 talk on nervousness, he recalled that a
great many cars passed them on the uphill climb, and when
they arrived at the top he and his companions were the only
people watching the sunrise. Everyone else was in the restaurant. "They rushed to the top and then rushed back," he noted
in amazement, "just for the thrill of being able to say when they

got home that they had been there, and had coffee and dough-
nuts on Pikes Peak. That is what nervousness does."[32]

In their three or four weeks in Colorado, Yogananda lectured and held classes in Denver and Colorado Springs. Whether
Rashid worked with a speaker's bureau, or made haste to book
venues and advertise when they arrived in the Mile High City, or
went ahead of the others by train (as he would later in the tour)
is unknown. However he did it, he managed to book at least
three public engagements in Denver. At one of them, in the spacious Denver City Auditorium, 3,000 people showed up.[33] The
public knew about the events through ads, standing billboards,
and articles in the local newspapers, all no doubt Rashid's handiwork. But we don't know if Rashid was responsible for ads calling Yogananda "The Man Who Is Thrilling America with His
Mighty Messages," or who came up with this curious phrase:
"Under the auspices of the Christian Yogoda Sat Sanga Society."
We do know that Yogananda stayed in a good hotel, not a tent,
in Denver, and he left behind a sizable Sat-Sanga group.

In a touching letter to the Lewises that August, Yogananda
reflected on lessons learned. "I am the same Yogananda who
coaxed sixty people to listen to him and hardly he could get that
number," he wrote. "Now he talks to up to 2000 people. I am
unchanged, only I have got bigger scope to serve and work for
your countrymen." A prime factor in that evolution, he implies,
was his acceptance of the need for organization. "[E]ven Truth
has to go in an organized way," he said, "otherwise it is not only
not received but rejected, and even slighted." He adds, "I suffered, wept tears just because I did not know the law of organization and presentation of Truth."

From Denver, the Maxwell carried the troupe diagonally
northwest across Wyoming to Yellowstone National Park. The
Wild West was considerably wilder then, and Yogananda must
have relished the broad, untamed vistas on the 540-mile drive.
The Cowboy State's population was only 200,000, whereas
nearly 6 million squeezed into New York City alone. He was
awed by Yellowstone, describing its wildlife, natural beauty, and

famously punctual geysers in a colorful passage in the *AY*, which concludes: "I was disposed to say that Yellowstone deserves a special prize for uniqueness."[34]

After traversing northern Idaho and the width of Washington state, they arrived in Seattle on September 3. The plan was for Rashid to stay there and organize lectures and classes while Yogananda, always the inveterate sightseer, took a cruise to Alaska with the other men. The cruise ship sailed from Vancouver, British Columbia. In a talk given sometime in the '20s, he described what happened at the immigration office when he applied for a Canadian visa.[35] He was kept waiting an inordinate amount of time while the man in charge refused to acknowledge his presence. Yogananda finally tapped on the man's desk. He described what happened next: "The officer looked at me with scorn, his eyes fixed on my turban, and said, 'Do you gaze at crystals, tell fortunes, swallow swords? Are you a snake charmer?'" Yogananda told him he was not a fakir—a word then associated with emaciated ascetics and applied derisively to Gandhi by the British, because it sounded like "faker."

He was told to return the following day. He did, bringing with him one of his books and copies of his poems. Calling the rude immigration officer "Sir," he assured him that he never swallowed swords or tamed cobras, like India's street magicians do. As for his turban, he pointed out that he has seen many hypocritical Westerners wearing hats and dress suits, but does not associate hypocrisy with hats. "You cannot expect all Hindus to forsake turbans because some Hindus are far from exemplary," he said, "just as I do not expect all Western brothers to forsake their hats because some have practiced hypocrisy while wearing hats." Decrying the arrogance of Westerners who think Indians had to wear "swallow-tail coats and neckties to be civilized," he added, "Customs and mannerisms are nonessentials resulting from certain climatic influences. The real development of man consists of the development of his mind power." The chastened official, he says, promptly processed his visa.

The steamship cruise up the Inside Passage lasted either 10 to 12 days or 26.[36] Yogananda was delighted by the hospitality he received on the ship and in several port stops, and was more than impressed by the scenery. "If it were possible to hold a beauty contest of all Nature's grandeurs and scenes of loveliness," he gushed, "it would be difficult to choose between Alaska and her Hindu sister Kashmir for the Queen's throne."[37]

During Yogananda's Alaska idyll, Rashid seems to have made good use of what one observer called his "talent for socializing with the well-to-do." He obtained prestigious lecture halls, classroom space, and publicity in Seattle. On October 7 more than 2,000 people filled the Masonic Temple auditorium.[38] As in other locations, volunteers registered people for the classes and handed out free materials. No doubt names and addresses were collected to build what we now call a database. One young Seattleite in attendance would turn out to be particularly notable. Rex Bissett went to hear Yogananda at the urging of his mother, Edith Anne Ruth Bissett (maiden name D'Evelyn). A longtime seeker and student of Indian philosophy, she would have gone to the lecture herself but she thought that being seen at such an offbeat event might damage her husband's reputation. Clark Prescott Bissett was a prominent lawyer and the acting dean of the University of Washington Law School. Rex became Yogananda's student and reported good things to his mother. She met the swami a year later, when he returned to Seattle, and she eventually became Sister Gyanamata, one of Yogananda's more beloved and, he said, spiritually advanced disciples.

Next stop, Portland, Oregon. His 10 days in the City of Roses began on October 21 at the Multnomah Hotel. Historically, the Portland stop is notable for one new addition to Yogananda's repertoire: the collective use of healing affirmations. He would recite an affirmation aloud and have the audience repeat it, phrase by phrase. Students were also encouraged to employ affirmations on their own. Some examples:

- The healing power of Spirit is flowing through all the cells of my body. I am made of the one universal God-substance.

- Daily I will seek happiness more and more within my mind, and less and less through material pleasures.

- I possess the creative power of Spirit. The Infinite Intelligence will guide me and solve every problem.

Yogananda would assemble a collection of affirmations for the book *Scientific Healing Affirmations*. It is still in print and quite popular.

In late October, the travelers crossed San Francisco Bay on a ferry.[39] Yogananda would remain in the Bay Area for the better part of two months, teaching in Berkeley and Oakland as well as San Francisco proper. Three free public lectures kicked things off in the city on November 10, 12, and 13 at the Scottish Rite Auditorium.[40] Ads in local papers showed a turbaned and robed "Swami Yogananda, renowned lecturer, educator, psychologist and metaphysician from India." The place was packed, according to reports, as were most of the other venues he appeared in. Overall, hundreds of students (Yogananda said 1,300) enrolled in classes on both sides of the bay.

He stayed at the Palace Hotel in San Francisco, one of the grandest hotels in California, and reportedly the largest in the world when it was built in 1875 (it was subsequently rebuilt in 1909 after being destroyed in the great earthquake and fire of 1906). This is historically significant for one reason. The Palace retained a professional photographer named Hugo Schreiber, whose job was to photograph distinguished guests. One of Schreiber's shots of Yogananda came to be known as the "Standard Pose." It can be seen today on home altars and in Yogananda centers and temples around the world, not to mention on millions of bookshelves on the cover of his autobiography.[41]

Two other events of enduring significance occurred during that Bay Area sojourn. Both involved people who would figure significantly in Yogananda's life. One was Luther Burbank, the renowned botanist, horticulturist, and agricultural pioneer. Burbank met Yogananda in his hometown of Santa Rosa in Sonoma County, north of San Francisco, and he quickly came to be a beloved friend, student, and initiate. Not only is *Autobiography of a Yogi* dedicated to "the memory of Luther Burbank, an American saint," but a four-page chapter is devoted to him. The *AY* also contains Burbank's glowing endorsement of Yogananda's ideas about education and his plans for establishing How-to-Live schools. They would know each other for only two years before Burbank died in 1926. Yogananda was in New York when he got the news. He describes his grief in his memoir: "Locking myself away from secretaries and visitors, I spent the next twenty-four hours in seclusion."[42] The following day, he conducted a traditional Vedic ritual for his friend.

Another new student would prove to be consequential in a different way. Laurie Pratt was 24 at the time, a descendant of one of the founders of Mormonism and the daughter of a Berkeley professor. A seeker with an independent spirit and an inquisitive mind, she had graduated from Berkeley at a time when higher education for women was just becoming acceptable and most universities were unisex. She would become one of Yogananda's closest disciples, eventually taking monastic vows and the name Tara Mata. Most important, she was her guru's principal editor and, other than the author himself, the one most responsible for shepherding his autobiography to completion.[43]

When their business in the Bay Area was finished, the group headed inland instead of taking the coastal route to Los Angeles (Rashid may have gone on ahead to scope out LA). Yogananda wanted to see Yosemite. We don't know if he'd read John Muir's lush accounts of the area, or if he knew that Emerson had traveled across the country to see it in 1871. Ansel Adams had not yet published his iconic photographs, but paintings and earlier photos had given Yosemite a worldwide reputation for natural grandeur that Yogananda, who loved the handiwork of God, would have wanted to see even in the icy chill of the Christmas season. "At Yosemite Park in California the ancient majestic sequoias, stretching huge columns far into the sky, are green natural cathedrals designed with skill divine," he rhapsodized in the *AY*.[44]

As 1924 drew to a close, America had turned the corner on the Teapot Dome scandal that exposed corruption at the highest levels of government, and had a new president, Calvin Coolidge, who believed that the business of America was business. And business was booming so much that Americans could barely see the ominous portents elsewhere in the world. Mussolini and Stalin were consolidating power in Italy and Russia; the Nazis were on the rise in Germany; and in India the British released Gandhi after the Mahatma served only two years of a six-year term, but their divide-and-conquer strategy was fomenting Hindu-Muslim tension.

Yogananda, however, would surely have felt celebratory if he'd looked back on the year that had just passed. If he'd had any fear that his message would not be well received, or that he lacked the requisite skills to fulfill his mission, it would have been eased by the size and enthusiasm of the audiences he'd attracted, the results of the practices he'd taught, the support he'd gained from prominent citizens, and the respect with which he'd been treated by journalists and civic leaders. The future would have seemed bright as the Maxwell rolled south toward what came to be known as La La Land.

CHAPTER 11

CITY OF ANGELS

On December 13, 1924, while Yogananda was still in San Francisco, this notice appeared in the religion section of the *Los Angeles Times*: "Students of oriental religions and philosophies will be interested to learn of the coming to Los Angeles on January 2 of Swami Yogananda who will give free lectures at the Philharmonic Auditorium on the evenings of January 13, 14, 16, 21 and 22." M. Rashid had evidently done his job as advance man.

LA's reputation as either the cutting edge of the future or the end of the road for the frivolous and zany was already in place. It was Tinsel Town, where minds were said to be as superficial as a Hollywood smile, where occultists and psychics were celebrities, where any self-improvement fad could find a gullible audience and new religions popped up as predictably as orange blossoms. But the La La Land vibe that some saw as flaky, others recognized as a spirit of openness and experimentation. It was a place where people reinvented themselves and valued spiritual creativity as much as the artistic variety, where ideas that East Coast sophisticates dismissed as bizarre and heartland preachers denounced as heathen were given a shot. Yogananda must have sensed all that when he dubbed LA "The Benares of America." He perceived something in the city's character that set it apart as a destination for explorers of the soul.

It seemed like an ideal home base for someone propagating a body of knowledge that was at once venerable and brand new. Swami Vivekananda and other Eastern teachers had been warmly received in Southern California; the Hollywood Vedanta Society would not open for another four years, but a Ramakrishna monk named Swami Paramananda had founded Ananda Ashrama in 1923 (Yogananda enjoyed his company over the years). New Thought groups had acquired sizable followings; the Hindu-influenced Ernest Holmes, for instance, was increasingly popular and would soon pack them in when he published *Science of Mind* and opened the Institute of Religious Science and the School of Philosophy (it is said that Holmes and Yogananda would sometimes dine together).[1] Also headquartered in LA was the controversial and flamboyant revivalist and faith healer Aimee Semple McPherson. A forerunner of megachurch preachers and televangelists, "Sister Aimee" broadcast her fervent gospel on radio and produced huge, Barnumesque stage spectacles. Her Pentecostal theology was radically different from Yogananda's teaching, but her success may have influenced his approach, as he would become quite a good showman.

He initially lodged at the elegant Biltmore Hotel in the heart of downtown. The location was perhaps chosen by Rashid for its prestige and because it was adjacent to the Philharmonic Auditorium, where Yogananda's main public talks would be held. The largest hotel west of Chicago when it opened only 15 months earlier, the spacious Biltmore featured exquisite decorative touches—frescos, murals, chandeliers, tapestries—and up-to-date amenities like an ornate indoor pool and radios in every room. Yogananda, who appreciated man-made beauty almost as much as nature's, no doubt enjoyed those elements more than he did the hotel's nightclub, which served bootleg gin to the Hollywood crowd in open defiance of Prohibition.

On Tuesday, January 13, he kicked off two months of lectures and classes with a whopper of an opening act. The free 8:00 P.M. lecture was titled "Mastering the Subconscious Mind by Super-consciousness." An ad in the *Los Angeles Times* invited the public to "learn about the full forces of body, mind and soul" from "an inspired Emissary . . . with a flaming message of soul-stirring power." It called the speaker an "illustrious Hindu Savant and Seer, Educator, Psychologist and Metaphysician," and, because royal titles might impress Americans, a "Representative of the

Maharajah of Kasimbazar, Bengal, India." Above the speaker's name was the Standard Pose portrait. Also of significance is a note at the bottom: "The swami is sponsored in Los Angeles by a committee of 16 foremost citizens." No names are given, but they were duly listed elsewhere by reporters and gossip columnists.[2] Yogananda and Rashid had clearly found a way to lend respectability to what might have been seen as an offbeat event, even by LA standards.

According to newspaper accounts, an astonishing 6,000 people showed up, about double the auditorium's capacity. One report compared the lobby to the Times Square subway station at rush hour, with patrons dashing to their seats or to the will call booth while an equal number, having been turned away, headed in the opposite direction. While the Philharmonic series was the main attraction, Yogananda spoke elsewhere as well; for instance, a morning talk at Music-Arts Hall before "an immense crowd," according to an *LA Times* report.[3] So many enrolled in the swami's courses, the article said, "it is difficult to secure a hall large enough." No numbers are mentioned, but Yogananda, in a letter, said that he had 450 LA students, and one photo shows him in a large theater packed with perhaps that many well-dressed Angelinos.

In a surprisingly respectful and well-informed article, *LA Times* reporter L. J. Vandenberg noted a certain irony: "A Hindu invading the United States to bring God in the midst of a Christian community. A so-called heathen from a so-called heathen land preaching the essence of Christian doctrine to the millions who contribute to foreign-mission boards in order to enlighten the benighted Asiatics."[4] Vandenberg said it should not be considered strange that the message Yogananda delivered should come from India, "the land of applied spiritual philosophy," adding that "the astonishing feature of this reversion of Evangelism is that it has been so long postponed."

The reporter offered muted praise for Yogananda's speaking style—"His language and oratory are void of frills for which his manifest sincerity makes ample amends"—and contrasted his scientific approach with the exhibitionist yogis in India. In a remark that might not have sat well with mainstream clerics, he added this denouement: "This is a practical message which Christian preachers might well adopt to teach self-made happiness. For the swami teaches and demonstrates that God is within us. The seed of happiness lies within the frame of the individual. It merely needs connection of spiritual wires to bring spiritual power, snatched from the universal cosmic energy to pour into the stagnant and inactive cells of the physical body which is the image of God."

A visitor bearing gifts from a misunderstood culture could scarcely have asked for a more sympathetic review. Between that and the overflow crowds, Yogananda must have been reinforced in his conviction that LA would be the cornerstone of the spiritual edifice he was destined to build. Further evidence would soon come from new acquaintances who stepped up with know-how, connections, financial support, and, most important to the guru, spiritual commitment.

Two such devotees were Dr. Frances Buchanan, one of very few female physicians in that era, and her 19-year-old daughter, Mary Isabelle. Dr. Buchanan, who had separated from her husband seven years earlier, learned about Yogananda's first lecture from a billboard. She brought Mary along. Mary wrote in her diary that Yogananda's smile "is like the sunshine of a soul." She was not only charmed; she found answers to questions she didn't know she'd been asking. As a churchgoer she was impressed when Yogananda said, "Do not accept blindly what I say; practice and prove for yourselves from your own experience." She took the Introductory, Advanced, and Super-Advanced Yogoda classes (it is not clear how many of these her mother attended) and volunteered to serve as an usher. She practiced the guru's techniques regularly.

That fall, Frances and Mary met with Yogananda personally, backstage at the Philharmonic. Mary said she always remembered his parting advice to her on the second such occasion: "Always keep your dignity and remember your power of thought and will." Like the Lewises, mother and daughter Buchanans became Yogananda's devotees and friends. He would sometimes find quiet respite at Dr. Buchanan's homes in Santa Barbara, Manhattan Beach, and Colorado. He called Mary "Kamala," Sanskrit for lotus, and she favored the name until her death at 91.[5]

As it had been on the East Coast, and as it would always be, Yogananda's success was accompanied by annoyances, obstructions, and difficulties. In a letter to Dr. and Mrs. Lewis dated January 25, only three days after the last of his triumphant Philharmonic lectures, he wrote: "Tasks seem endless, bleeding unceasing. I have to be responsible . . . but expenses are heavy too."[6] He would never stop longing to be free of such travails, but he also would never stop pushing on despite them.

"We'll have a big place on a mountain," he told one of his early classes. One of the students, perhaps doing a quick calculation based on local economics, said, "Well, maybe if you stay here twenty years you can have a center like that." To which Yogananda replied, "Twenty years for those who think twenty years. Twenty months for those who think twenty months. Three months for those who think three months." He was in the three-month camp.

Accounts of what followed vary somewhat. In one report, when a student casually mentioned a place called Mt. Washington, "Swami's soul was strangely stirred," and he suggested they drive there the next day. In Yogananda's recollection, he was driving around with some followers when he was "inwardly directed" to take the road to the top of Mt. Washington. While other details also vary, what happened when Yogananda saw the empty structure that dominated the hilltop is clear: "I felt intuitively that this place was ours, for I recognized it as the building I had seen in vision in Kashmir, many years before, while gazing at the Shankara Temple on a hilltop overlooking Dal Lake."[7]

Mt. Washington, situated north of downtown LA, rises to 940 feet. Today, you can drive from the Biltmore Hotel to the peak in about 15 minutes. A century ago, not so fast. The land was first developed in 1909. While a winding road was being sculpted through the dry brush, a cable car, or "incline railway," was also built. Passengers could board at Avenue 43 and Marmion Way and ride straight to the pinnacle and take in a panorama that encompassed a burgeoning downtown, Pasadena and Glendale, the San Gabriel Mountains, the Puente Hills, the flatlands to the west, and even, on a clear day, the Pacific Ocean about 15 miles away. On pleasant summer Sundays, two or three thousand people might take the ride.

The centerpiece of the development, which included residential lots, was the Mount Washington Hotel. The three-story, mission-style hotel, which opened in January 1910, was designed for the hoi polloi. They came for tea in the handsome lobby, and for gala events, but only a few could lodge there. The hotel had only 18 guest rooms, each with a private bath, a rare amenity at the time. Smaller, shared-bath rooms housed the staff. The grounds were landscaped with lawns, gardens, flower beds, and a variety of trees. There were porches, balconies, shaded walking paths, a pair of tennis courts, and, at every turn, a magnificent view.

The hotel caught on with celebrities like Charlie Chaplin, who stayed there when shooting films at one of the nearby studios. Thanks to this cachet, the residential lots sold well, and the slopes of Mt. Washington became a neighborhood. But the hotel's halcyon period ended when the film industry moved to better facilities in and around Hollywood. Tourists and business travelers found the location inconvenient. It closed in the summer of 1921. The Mt. Washington Military School took over for a year, followed by the short-lived Goodrich–Mount Washington Emphysema Hospital. By the time Yogananda laid eyes on it, the building was occupied by vagrants, the grounds were weedy, and the incline railway was a relic.

"I knew this was the place God had promised me," he said, "but when the real estate man said he could sell the property to me for sixty-five thousand dollars, my blood froze." A competent team of business and legal professionals handled the negotiations and paperwork (the names that turn up include James McLachlan, a former Congressman; W. C. Bramham, a name so close to Brahman that it probably elicited double takes; and P.

Rogers). They drove the price down to $45,000, "through God's grace," in Yogananda's assessment.[8]

Word went out to Yogodans throughout America that funds were needed to secure a permanent home for the organization. The response was generous, but short of the needed amount. Yogananda was concerned, of course, but characteristically undeterred. So certain was he that Mt. Washington would be his that he obtained permission to hold an event on the grounds before the sale was finalized—a sunrise service on Easter Sunday, April 12.[9] An ad in the *LA Times* cordially invited the public to hear him offer a "spiritual interpretation" of "How Christ Ascended into Heaven."[10] Those without autos were advised to "Take the W car, get off at Ave. 43, and walk to top of hill."

While preparations for the auspicious Easter were being made, Yogananda gave a series of lectures and classes at the Blackstone Hotel in Long Beach, about 25 miles south of downtown LA. An unusually extravagant ad for the series promised "New Revelations That Will Revolutionize Your Whole Existence." The swami was billed as an "Eminent Hindu Metaphysician Psychologist and Poet-Philosopher, Whose Great Educational Work Is Endorsed by Foremost Universities and Personages of America." In smaller print, the copy added: "This inspired exponent of the super-life brings to America all the wealth of India's age-old wisdom and key to the attainment of every desire." There was more, and while the text may sound excessive and unsubtle to modern ears, it was in line with 1920s advertising customs. If it was M. Rashid's handiwork, he had learned quickly from his proximity to Hollywood.

There is no record of exactly how many people ascended Mt. Washington at 6:00 A.M. on Easter Sunday, but a group photo taken on the lawn shows at least 200, and there is no telling how many were outside the frame. Standing in rows on either side of a floral cross that must have been 10 feet high, they are all—with the exception of the robed Yogananda—white men and women of all ages, with a few children, dressed in their finery. The exact content of Yogananda's sermon is also unknown, but we can surmise that it was similar to those he delivered on subsequent occasions, such as this Easter Message published in *Inner Culture* magazine in April, 1940:

> As Christ resurrected His consciousness from beneath the sepulcher of bodily limitations, so must thou learn to resurrect thy mind from beneath the tomb of material desires. Resurrect thy thoughts by meditation from body confinement to the consciousness of omnipresence.
>
> Resurrect thy divine love from beneath the sod of mundane human attachment. Resurrect thy calmness from beneath the soil of restlessness. Resurrect thy wisdom from beneath the earthliness of ignorance. Resurrect thy love for all from the limited love for family, society and country.
>
> Resurrect thy soul from the imprisonment of body consciousness and unite it with omniscient Spirit through the developed consciousness of Christ.[11]

Every guru who's come to the West—indeed, Hindus in general—has expressed the highest esteem for Jesus. He is regarded as a great holy man at the very least, or as a rare *jagadguru* (world teacher), or even as an *avatar*, an incarnation of God, like Krishna and Rama. Yogananda took the veneration of Christ a step further, producing a massive volume of written and spoken commentary on Jesus and his teachings. And while many gurus have encouraged Christians to take Jesus as their *ishta devata* (preferred form of God), Yogananda named him (he would say Him) as part of his lineage and placed his image on the altars of his temples and centers, along with those of Sri Yukteswar, Lahiri Mahasaya, and Babaji. Not even Krishna held that status during Yogananda's lifetime, except on the altar of the Golden Lotus Temple in Encinitas during its short life (1938 to 1942), because he felt that Americans would react poorly to it (a painting of Krishna was added after Yogananda's death, per his instructions; so was Yogananda's portrait).

His reverence for Jesus invited several accusations: of selling out to attract Christian followers, of "Christianizing" Hinduism, and of handing cultural imperialists an easy way to appropriate Hindu traditions. This was compounded by his use of the term "church" for some of his centers and temples, and by the format of his Sunday services, which are Protestant-like from the rows of pews or chairs to the communal prayer to the collection basket. The more generous assessment is that his embrace of Christ, which was indisputably genuine, not only enabled him to reach larger numbers of Westerners; it also reconfigured for millions the way they understood and related to Jesus. In fact, Yogananda's work gave many disaffected Christians a path to forming a more comfortable relationship with the tradition of their birth. It also gave non-Christians, principally American Jews, a different understanding of the young Hebrew in whose name atrocities had been perpetrated.

But the most important point about Yogananda and Christ is this: part of his stated mission was to revive "Original Christianity," along with the original and authentic teachings of Yoga. He believed that to be his dispensation. In fact, he said on many occasions, Babaji and Christ were astral buddies who cooked up the whole thing. He told his American audiences that the true teachings of both Christ and the Indian rishis had been lost, and his assignment was to resurrect both.

Whatever the Easter service may have done to align the cosmos favorably for Yogananda's campaign, it was, at the very least, a way of affirming that the land on which it was held would be the home of his movement. The property was now consecrated.

It came down to the wire. Additional contributions from students and income from course fees trickled in, but not quite enough. Yogananda believed that God was testing him. "I have to fight for what I accomplish, just like any other person," he once said, correcting the assumption that highly evolved souls get whatever they need effortlessly. "God always comes to my aid in the end, but He makes me work for it." He was as faithful a human being as ever lived, but when it came to getting things done in the world he was faithful to the adage that God helps those who help themselves.

As has happened repeatedly in the annals of spiritual progress, the heroes who stepped up to save the day were female. In this instance, the saviors were two well-heeled women who believed in Yogananda's cause. The first was Miriam A. Clark. Grateful to Yogananda for what she considered a divine healing intervention for her ailing husband, J. Ross Clark, the scion of a wealthy mining family, she offered him $25,000 in cash, interest free. There was one proviso: the money had to be returned in full in three years.

Yogananda was still $5,000 short the day before escrow was to close. He said he prayed nonstop for an hour that felt like a year. Then, on his way to his room, what he called "a miraculous incident" occurred.[12] A window suddenly opened, and a gust of wind hit his face. In that moment, a woman named Julia Trask, whom he'd met only twice, flashed into his mind. He considered it a sign. He looked her up in the phone book and dialed the number. When he explained his predicament, she offered help to the tune of $200. He told her that would leave him $4,800 short. At which point Mrs. Trask remembered that someone to whom she'd lent money had just paid it back unexpectedly. How much? Five thousand dollars. She offered it as a second mortgage, interest free.

The deal closed the next day, and Yogananda's supporters saw to it that some adjacent parcels were also secured, bringing the total holdings to seven and a half acres. The vision he'd had in Kashmir would come true. And, alas, the mortgages would come due.

The property, which came to be known affectionately as the Mother Center, needed a good deal of fixing up at first. While that work was going on, Yogananda and the people he'd gathered around him made plans to spread the word and bring in the funds that organizations—hornets' nests though they may be—require in order to survive. Those efforts included new and revised books, a correspondence course, a Super-Advanced Course, a magazine, and two lecture tours: a West Coast jaunt that summer and a longer, broader one commencing toward the end of the year.

The first tour took him to San Diego, Fresno, Portland, Seattle, Spokane, and San Francisco. During that period, three historic events occurred that can be seen as countervailing forces to the evolutionary Vedic wisdom he promulgated: Hitler's *Mein Kampf* was published in Germany; in Tennessee, the "Scopes Monkey Trial" came down on the side of anti-Darwin fundamentalism; and, on August 8, 40,000 Ku Klux Klansmen paraded in Washington, D.C. In each city he visited, Yogananda maintained his usual hectic schedule of free lectures and paid-for classes. For existing students he offered advanced classes. Some of the new devotees would make significant contributions to his mission. He met two on his return to Seattle in July.

One was Edith Bissett, who was mentioned in the last chapter. Fifty-six at the time, she would move to Mt. Washington in 1932, after her husband's death, and take renunciate vows as Sister Gyanamata. The other was Mildred Hamilton. Not yet 21, Mildred quickly accepted Yogananda as her guru. She later married, had children, and ran the Self-Realization Fellowship's (SRF's) Seattle center for decades. It is said that she was the only woman to whom Yogananda gave the title Yogacharya, which means simply "teacher of Yoga" but is customarily reserved for teachers of distinction. After Yogananda's passing, she went to India and, acting on a statement by her guru that she often quoted—"I don't want people to have Yogananda realization, I want them to have Self-Realization"—she met her second guru, Swami Ramdas. Eventually, she founded a spiritual community called the Cross and the Lotus, and ran it until her passing in 1991.

In what must have been the most grueling segment of his tour, Yogananda gave two classes on two different topics for six straight nights at San Francisco's Scottish Rite Auditorium. The series was titled "Advanced Course on Practical Metaphysics." While in what was then dubbed "The Paris of the West," Yogananda realized that, despite his growing number of students, he had only $200 in the bank. Rashid was so shocked by that news, says Yogananda, that he collapsed to the floor, yelling, "We will go to jail!" To which the ever-faithful swami said God would not have given him the Mt. Washington property only to bankrupt him. He predicted they'd have the money they needed in a week.

Six days later, he said, he left his hotel—the Palace, where the Standard Pose had been photographed—to take a walk. A woman approached him on the street. Her name was Mary Foster, and she had evidently heard him speak. She said she would like to talk with him. In the hotel lobby, she peppered him with questions about his ideas and plans. Then she offered to donate money to his work. Yogananda was hesitant. Mrs. Foster insisted. She wrote a check and inserted it in an envelope. Back in his hotel room, Yogananda opened the envelope, expecting, he said, maybe $100. The check was for $27,000. He saw the hand of God on that check. Today, it should be noted, its purchasing power would exceed $350,000.

With his burden eased by Mrs. Foster's generosity, Spokane, Washington, where he spent the next two weeks, must have seemed as beautiful as Kashmir.

It is hard to imagine a less contemplative lifestyle for a sannyasi. No wonder he told the Lewises that he had become "strangely busy." In addition to almost nightly lectures, he said, "I have to write books, answer myriads of letters and prepare lectures." He could have added: give interviews to the press, meet privately with students, monitor the progress at Mt. Washington, hatch plans for future projects, and deal with money issues.

But he was a vigorous monk. Only 32 at the time, he slept very little and was fueled not by caffeine or egomaniacal ambition but by yogic techniques and a strong sense of divine purpose. "There was a time when I tried to do good things to earn good opinion," he told Dr. Lewis, "but now life has offered me a new proposition. I do good things not goaded by the compelling whip of duty but with the sense of privilege." What did he mean by that? "My only privilege is to please God," he said. He added, in a moving rhythm, "Serve I must, rain or shine, serve I must for that is my joy."[13]

On October 11, he began another series of lectures at Philharmonic Auditorium. One ad for the "Miracles of Yoga" series contained this headline: SWAMI YOGANANDA RETURNS TO HIS BELOVED LOS ANGELES BEFORE GOING EAST. All the items on his plate required money. There was, among other things, the matter of the Mt. Washington debts. In a letter to followers, dated September 14,[14] he solicited donations: "Because I want you to feel that it is your own Center, established for the good and upliftment of America and the world, that is why I feel free and glad to ask your help and good-will." Books for the library and decorative items were also welcome. All were invited to the formal opening.

Knowing he would be on the road a great deal in the foreseeable future to gather new students, nurture old ones, and, not insignificantly, generate income, he once again called for reinforcements. Swami Dhirananda arrived in LA on October 13. In the inaugural issue of *East–West* magazine, published the following month, Yogananda declared of his old friend and colleague, "I am powerless to tell how greatly he has helped me in carrying on my educational work in India and Boston, or of the good which the world has derived from his ideal character and exalted spiritual life." He explained further: "Just as he successfully carried on the work of the Ranchi School during the first two years of my absence from India, so will he likewise take charge of the Los Angeles Headquarters whenever I am of necessity absent from there on lecture tours for the spread of God's message of all-around education and human perfection."[15]

In turn, at the dedication of the Mount Washington Center, Dhirananda said, "Being connected with Swami Yogananda for over fifteen years, I know what he has done to me, and what he can do to others and to the world. If I am of any help to Swami and to the cause which he upholds most sincerely and with the great spirit that he always shows, I am willing to do that. . . . I will be faithful to him and God and to yourselves."[16]

They were a busy duo. There was a magazine to design, edit, and publish. There were other publications to print and distribute, including *The Science of Religion*, the *Psychological Chart*, *Scientific*

Healing Affirmations, the *Yogoda System of Physical, Mental and Spiritual Perfection*, and Dhirananda's own, newly completed book, *Philosophical Insights*, which contained this dedication:

Inscribed to Swami Yogananda Giriji
My College-Friend, Teacher and Guiding Inspiration in Life
With Deep Love and Faith

The project with the most lasting consequences was the Yogoda Correspondence Course. Teachings that had for centuries been transmitted from teacher to student face to face were now typed by a guru's staff and delivered by the United States Postal Service at predictable intervals. The 1920s equivalent of a smartphone app or an online webinar, the mail order course was either a welcome democratization or a dangerous break with tradition, depending on one's point of view.

The initial series consisted of 12 Lessons in a total of 43 pages. It cost $25, and allowances were made for those who could not afford it. The content mirrored the classes Yogananda and Dhirananda taught in person. Students receiving the course were asked to take this pledge: "I declare on my honor not to reveal the following lessons to anyone, unless permitted to do so." The pledge was necessary, the statement said, to "prevent misunderstanding and incorrect teaching," and to maintain proper standards for the propagation of Yogoda's work. Over the decades, the correspondence course would evolve, expand, and undergo changes in content, format, and name. Stenographers took word-for-word notes at the swamis' classes; other material— articles, poems, affirmations, even recipes—were added; and enlarged versions of the course were released. By 1934, after a four-year process, what was called "the Praecepta" totaled 200 Lessons in more than 1,500 pages. During the 1940s, I was told by SRF officials, Yogananda expressed displeasure at certain aspects of the course, which by then (as now) were called the Self-Realization Fellowship Lessons. He ran out of time for making revisions, and after his death disciples he had trained finalized the changes he instructed them to make. A revised version was released in 1956. As of this writing, that set of Lessons is still being distributed, although a major revision is in the works (it was announced at SRF's annual Convocation in August 2017).[17]

Yogananda was well aware that his impersonal delivery system did not go over well with traditionalists in India. No less a yogic innovator than Sri Aurobindo argued that "instructions in Yoga . . . can only be given successfully to a few, to each separately as an intimately personal thing which he must assimilate and make living and true in himself according to his own capacity and nature."[18] Yogananda addressed the issue in the final chapter of his autobiography: "It would indeed be a priceless boon if each student could keep by his side a guru perfected in divine wisdom; but the world is composed of many 'sinners' and few saints. How then may the multitudes be helped by yoga, if not through study in their homes of instructions written by true yogis?"[19] He said many times that after he was gone the teachings would be the guru, and he attempted to make up for the absence of a guru's physical presence—the value of which he knew firsthand, of course—with written pledges, vows, and prerequisites for each new step of teaching. Clearly, he calculated that the rewards of wide dissemination outweighed the risks. And it would be hard for purists to write off the thousands, if not millions, of people who would have remained in the dark about yogic ideas and practices without Yogananda's mail order course, or to ignore the uncountable lives that it changed for the better.

"Come, All Los Angeles, Come," shouted the headline on a newspaper ad. Beneath that, adjacent to the Standard Pose, the copy read: "Be with us to celebrate the cause of Universal Right Education. Swami Yogananda most cordially invites all to the formal opening of Mt. Washington Educational Center on Sunday, Oct. 25, at 2:30 P.M." This was followed by a nontypical understatement: "Very interesting program. You will enjoy it."

With this landmark event looming and a successful tour behind him, Yogananda could not have been blamed if he felt giddy. Then came an odd and somewhat mysterious bump in the road. Two of them in fact, back to back: the dark side of human affairs that renunciates hope to avoid rose up in the form of lawsuits. One was filed in California Superior Court on October 13 by Emma S. Mitchell, who accused Yogananda of fraud in the purchase of her tract of Mt. Washington land. She claimed she made the sale "upon the express condition and consideration that the said property was to be used in the establishment of a certain school . . . for children."[20] The plaintiff now believed that Yogananda, "the defendant," had no such intention. She wanted the court to restore her ownership of the land, and, if that could not be done, to award her the value of the parcel, $13,000. Court records show that the case was dismissed on January 22 of the following year; as is the norm for lawsuits settled out of court, the terms were not revealed.

Nuisance though it may have been, the case did not impede the opening of the center on October 25. Neither did the other, far more curious lawsuit. This one was filed just three days before the opening ceremony by none other than M. Rashid. For his services as "secretary and manager to the defendant," the suit claimed, Rashid had been promised 25 percent of "the net proceeds of all lectures, fees, contributions or other monies received by the defendant."[21] That would be Yogananda, and the sum he owed, Rashid asserted, was $20,750, based on his calculation of revenues from July 1924 to the date of the filing. The situation got dicey when Rashid was granted a writ of attachment on Yogananda's two bank accounts,[22] meaning the funds were essentially frozen and subject to garnishment should the plaintiff prevail in court. The record shows that the case was dismissed on October 26, the day after the Mt. Washington festivities.

Again, the terms of settlement are unknown. Did money change hands? Did Rashid have a change of heart? Also a mystery is exactly what prompted him to take this action, and what may have transpired between him and Yogananda before and after he filed suit. Moving the events from the enigmatic to the bizarre is the fact that Rashid kept on working for Yogananda for another eight or nine months, and a farewell tribute to him appeared in *East–West* when he left for India: "Mr. Rashid has constantly proved his worth and loyalty to the Swami and to

Yogoda, and has rendered the cause much fine intelligent service. The Swami and his staff sincerely regret Mr. Rashid's loss."[23]

The strange legal ticks were Yogananda's first taste of the troubles that can befall a spiritual celebrity in America. He could not have known it at the time, but they were previews of far more distressing litigation to come.

But Mt. Washington was now his. More than 2,000 people showed up for the dedication ceremony. In anticipation of occupying a sylvan hilltop in the American Benares, he waxed poetic. The first stanza of his poem "Life's Dream" reads:

> The summery East
> And the wintry West,
> They say:
> But Mount Washington
> (Named rightly after that pioneer
> Of freedom's great career),
> Thou dost stand, a snowless guardian Himalaya
> Of the Angel Land, in perpetual green regalia.[24]

The verse, published in the inaugural issue of *East–West* and later included in bound collections, commends the landscape and the scenic beauty, and proclaims a future of ecumenical unity:

> Here all other paths shall merge as one.
> Here the love of earthly freedom's paradise, America,
> Shall blend fore'er with love of spiritual freedom's
> paradise, India.

While administrative functions would be housed at the Mother Center, its principal purpose, the official announcement made clear, was educational. Dhirananda's Sunday school classes for children would commence immediately; a variety of adult courses were in the works; and a library, museum, and printing press were being planned (as was a swimming pool). Most notable, especially in light of the Emma Mitchell claim, was the plan to create a Yogoda How-to-Live school to give American youth the "physical, mental and especially spiritual results" seen at Yogananda's schools in India but adapted for America. The school would open "whenever the Divine Power sends His instrument for fulfilling this great spiritual educational need," i.e., when God arranged the financing.[25] The school as such would never materialize. Mt. Washington would instead flourish—surviving various perils through the Great Depression, World War II, and beyond—as a combination administrative headquarters, monastery, and what Yogananda called a "spiritual lighthouse."

The maiden issue of *East–West* weighed in at 34 pages. It cost $.25 an issue, $1.25 for an annual subscription. The centerpiece of the cover was a lotus-shaped drawing with a five-pointed star in the upper center—at the forehead if the logo were a face—and two leaves emanating from the stem, one with "Sat-Sanga" written in it, the other with "Yogoda." Inside, a statement declares the bimonthly's Aim and Purpose: "To inspire, to enlighten and to encourage all to live the Practical Spiritual Life." Dedicated to the benefactor Mary Foster, the magazine contained articles by and about Yogananda, poems by him and others, photos of his projects in India and others of him on his cross-country road trip (e.g., feeding a bear cub in Yellowstone), an essay by Luther Burbank, a poem *about* Luther Burbank, tributes to key people in India, the paean to Dhirananda cited earlier, praise for Yogoda from prominent people, and promotional notices for the organization's products. By all measures, the magazine was off to a good start.[26]

Yogananda would not enjoy the Southern California sunshine that winter. Sometime shortly after November 9, when he hosted the chief of the Yakima tribe, he boarded a train at Union Station. It would be four years before he could celebrate Christmas at Mt. Washington.

CHAPTER 12

ROAD WARRIOR

Yogananda probably logged more hours on trains, station platforms, and waiting rooms in the next four years than his father, the railroad executive, did in his lifetime. Parts of his prolonged itinerary—what he called spiritual campaigning— would be grueling today, let alone when bouncing around on Prohibition-era infrastructure. In mid-November 1925, he disembarked from a 2,000-mile rumble across the southwest and plains into the spanking new beaux arts Union Station in a Chicago run by Al Capone. He spent almost a month in the Windy City, delivering his standard lectures and classes at the Morrison Hotel and addressing various associations.[1] A reported 400 Chicagoans took the Yogoda Course. As in all of his local chapters, female students outnumbered the men, perhaps by as much as two to one. One hopes that one of them welcomed him to Thanksgiving dinner and provided tasty vegetarian fare.

From there, he headed east-northeast along Lake Erie to Rochester, New York, where, if reports are accurate, he spoke to an astonishing 5,000 people in two events on the same day at the Lyceum Theater. Among his Rochester students was George Eastman, whose company made Kodak a household word and cameras a household item. Eastman gave Yogananda two things: another highly respectable name for his endorsement list and the latest model Kodak camera for his pleasure.

He then rolled downstate to New York City for a brief visit, presumably spent meeting with supporters and existing students; then up to Boston for the opening talk at the 14th annual convention of the Hindustan Association of America, reunions with his earliest American devotees, and Christmas with the Lewis family. He probably rang in the new year with his Boston friends as well, but he celebrated his 33rd birthday in Cleveland. He remained in what was then called "The Sixth City" (denoting its relative size) for about a month, then boarded a westbound train for an unanticipated homecoming; among the gifts he received from grateful Clevelanders was a round-trip ticket to Los Angeles.

He was greeted at LA's Union Station on February 11 by ebullient followers bearing garlands and bouquets, and was driven up to Mt. Washington in a car decked out with so many roses it was compared to a New Year's Day parade float. He no doubt had a great deal to discuss with Dhirananda and with staff in charge of various tasks. A few people had come to live and work at Mt. Washington by then. Among the "inner residential workers," as they were called, were Mr. and Mrs. C. P. Scott from Portland, Oregon, and their young daughter. "In the capable hands of Mrs. Scott," the notice proclaimed, "the business details of the work are carefully looked after."[2] Stay tuned for more on the Scotts.

The overall mood was festive. On Saturday evening, the staff put on a show for their Swamiji, and the next morning a far larger congregation than usual showed up for Sunday services and Yogananda's sermon. On Sunday night, he took to the house organ and led the crowd in chants and songs. He must have been delighted and moved by the display of affection. "I never sought crowds as such," he said on many occasions, "but I love crowds of divine souls."

Arranging and managing a multicity lecture is challenging even today, with our ability to connect with anyone anytime from just about anywhere. Imagine what it must have entailed in an era of coin-operated phone booths, long-distance operators, telegrams, and letter writing, especially in the service of a dynamo who needed very little sleep and seemed to be willing to speak anywhere he could, from a fancy ballroom to a humble living room. A list of the clubs at which he spoke would fill up a page with unlikely names—the Hoo Hoo Club, the Quota Club, the Zonta Club, the Gyro Club—along with the usual suspects: Rotary, Kiwanis, Masonic, Lions, and the Men's Club or Women's Club of Wherever. Lining up venues, arranging dates, negotiating finances, placing ads in newspapers, designing and posting flyers and billboards—it all must have required a traveling team, an organized group of locals, and coordination from the Mother Center. For those reasons, M. Rashid deserves credit as an unsung hero of Yogananda's early efforts (he also found time to pen a brief article on Sufism for the second edition of *East–West* magazine[3]).

On tour, the ads for Yogananda's appearances were basically the same as those already described, with the occasional eyebrow raiser. In Pittsburgh, for instance, he was hailed as "A thinker—A Doer—A Teacher—An Author—A Master," and an ad said his message "will appeal to you like the Two Edged Sword of Truth—A THUNDERBOLT FROM GOD." Collectively, his topics suggest an appeal to Western pragmatism, with promises of improvement in various aspects of worldly life—e.g., "The Science of Success and the Art of Getting What You Want" —balanced by an equal, if not larger dose of yogic methodology and Vedic philosophy, e.g., "Highest Technique of Meditation" and "How the Teachings of India's Great Masters Can Help America."

To a skeptical observer, the self-help component might appear to be a compromise or a diminution of the deeper spiritual message that defined his mission. Viewed from another angle, the promise of improved health, enhanced business skills, finding a soul mate, and the like were doorways into the realm of transformational spirituality for those who could not enter it directly. Someone might come to hear him speak, or sign up for his course, for any number of mundane reasons and come away realizing there was more to be had than he or she had bargained for. Yogananda dispensed self-help advice within a larger yogic framework, making it clear that the starting point, and end point, of all self-improvement was union with the Divine.

Regardless of the packaging, the ingredients always contained some Hinduism 101: karma, dharma, reincarnation, samadhi, mantras, chakras; the core principles of Vedanta, the major yogic pathways (*jnana, bhakti, karma*, and *raja*); God as transcendent and formless, and God as immanent with multiple forms. Plus, a Christ who would be more at home in a Himalayan ashram than a church, and a take on the Gospel that would appeal more to Meister Eckhart or Thomas Merton than to the Pope or Aimee Semple McPherson.

The East-West synergy was evident in his manner as well. "He is American in both the terseness of his style and the exuberance of his claims," said Wendell Thomas in *Hinduism Invades America*. "He speaks in words of popular science, and supports his statements by Hindu lore and verses taken from the Bible."[4] His evocation of science was crucial. He was remarkably knowledgeable about the brain and nervous system, interpreting yogic insights in light of what was then known about neurophysiology and anticipating modern discoveries like neural plasticity, which recognizes that the brain can be reconfigured by experience. Most important, he told audiences that belief in the ideas he professed was not necessary; one only had to be curious enough to test his methods in the laboratory of their own consciousness, a classic yogic precept.

By credibly framing his message in rational, empirical terms as opposed to the faith-based language of conventional religion, he was able to appeal to a broad spectrum of Americans. This extended to deep religious dilemmas like the existence or non-existence of God. The only true proof, he maintained, was to be found within, through deep meditation. Accepting the existence of God without that direct experience, he called "the death of wisdom and divine acquaintanceship."

His speeches reflected his growing familiarity with life in America, adding another measure of relatability. "He took great delight in learning American colloquialisms and figures of speech, and using them when appropriate," a disciple who studied his speeches told me in an e-mail exchange. "When he first arrived in Boston, his English was more formally 'Hindu-British,' but later it became more informal." And his natural flair for the dramatic seems to have been augmented by American pizzazz. If later recordings are evidence, his oratorical style mixed soft, personal, intimate tones with such sonorous, grandiloquent flourishes, replete with plentiful "Thees" and "Thous," that one might have thought he was a 19th-century evangelist with a funny accent.

Indeed, for someone who was reticent about public speaking at first, he became quite the performer. In theaters equipped with an organ, such as LA's Philharmonic Auditorium, Rimsky-Korsakov's "Song of India" would precede his entrance. He would recite his own poems and regale audiences with stories from his life and tales of exotic India. When speaking of mind control and the Yogoda exercises, he might invite people to touch his bicep, "which he caused to vibrate with energy in the manner of an electric power machine," as Kamala Silva put it in *The Flawless Mirror*.[5] He might have physicians come onstage to verify that he could stop his breath and heartbeat at will and cause the pulses in each wrist to beat at different counts. On at least one occasion, he asked some beefy security guards to try to dislodge him from his position. They failed, of course. In the coming years, as we'll see, he would be joined by other theatrical personalities, but once again we have to consider the context. Was it only show biz or a way to capture attention so his deep and substantive message would be heard?

In the spring of 1926, Yogananda filled a gap in his speaking schedule in a surprising way: with a trip to Cuba for him and his travel staff. This was 33 years before the revolution led by Fidel Castro, and Cuba was a choice vacation spot for Americans who craved sunshine and something more exotic than, say, Miami Beach. Did Yogananda have a hankering to experience a Latin culture? Was the trip a gift from a grateful student? Had it been planned in advance, or was it a spontaneous decision? None of that is known. His two weeks' stay in Cuba appears to have been a genuine vacation; there is no record of any public presentations. What we do have is a record of his return, by boat, to Key West, Florida, on April 7, and a letter from New York dated April 14 in which Yogananda tells Dr. Lewis he'd returned the day before from Cuba by way of Philadelphia.

THE LIFE OF YOGANANDA

He got back in the swing of things with a series of five lectures over the course of a week at the most prestigious of venues,
Carnegie Hall. His debut in the fabled concert hall was memorable. The scheduled lecture was on "Everlasting Youth," a recurring title for his public talks. It turned into something rather
more fitting for the room in which every musician aspired to
perform. As he later recalled, he'd discussed the idea of having
the audience join him in chanting a devotional song and was
warned that Americans would find such a thing too alien. On
the surface, that would seem to have been a sensible view; the
style of devotional singing mentioned earlier known as kirtan,
in which sacred mantras featuring the various names of God
are sung by the leader and echoed back by the audience in unison, was unheard of America; even 40 years later, when it was
introduced publicly by the Hare Krishna movement, it seemed
bizarre to most. Yogananda disagreed. Because music is a universal language, he argued, the audience could not fail to appreciate
the devotional yearning for God in the chanting.

And so he asked the capacity crowd[6] to join him in song.
He wisely chose not to go with Sanskrit mantras but rather with
his English translation of a bhajan composed by Guru Nanak,
the 15th-century founder of the Sikh faith.[7] The song, which
remains a beloved liturgical feature in organizations propagating Yogananda's work, is called "O God Beautiful" ("Hay Hari
Sundara"). The lyrics:

O God Beautiful; O God Beautiful; At Thy feet, oh, I do bow.
In the forest Thou art green;
In the mountain Thou art high;
In the river Thou art restless;
In the ocean Thou art grave.
O God Beautiful; O God Beautiful! At Thy feet, oh, I do bow!
To the serviceful Thou art service;
To the lover Thou art love;
To the sorrowful Thou art sympathy;
To the yogi Thou art bliss.

It went on for an hour and 25 minutes, round after round of the same verses. The Carnegie congregation must have been astonished. We don't know how many fidgeted, or if any walked out, but the open-minded and spiritually receptive would have discovered unfamiliar feelings of ecstasy and, perhaps, transcendence. "The thousands of voices of the entire audience chanted . . . in a divine atmosphere of joyous praise," Yogananda said about the evening.[8] Sacred music became a standard part of Yogananda's repertoire, and his introduction of kirtan to America has been largely underappreciated. Usually playing a harmonium—an accordion-like keyboard instrument introduced by the British that has become so widely used it is thought of as Indian—he would lead groups in chanting Sanskrit mantras, devotional songs he composed himself, and traditional bhajans he translated into English. In the 1930s, he published a collection of compositions called *Cosmic Chants*. The introduction is a handy guide to the use of music as a medium of worship. "Music is a divine art, to be used not only for pleasure but as a path to God-realization," he wrote. "Vibrations resulting from devotional singing lead to attunement with the Cosmic Vibration or the Word."[9]

In addition to the Carnegie series, Yogananda spoke at all manner of New York venues, from the Authors' League Fellowship to the International New Thought Alliance to the Maha Bodhi Society of America, where Buddha's birth anniversary was celebrated and he shared a platform with other spiritual luminaries. He harvested nearly a thousand new Yogoda students and endorsements from prominent New Yorkers, notably Countess Ilya Tolstoy, the daughter-in-law of Leo Tolstoy, the social reformer and author of *War and Peace*, and a Christian minister named Arthur Porter, who said his week of study with Yogananda gave him more of a genuine education than he'd received in the universities and seminaries he'd attended.

Yogananda shuttled a bit between Philadelphia and New York that May, then headed west to Detroit. His three weeks in the Motor City essentially recapitulated other stops on his tour, with two exceptions. One was an address at the Universal

Islamic Society, as far as I can tell the first time he spoke to a Muslim group. In a proclamation issued on June 20 of that year, the organization thanked their guest speaker and praised his work in breaking down barriers of religion and creed.

The other consequential occurrence in Detroit was the connection he formed with a fellow Bengali, Nirad Ranjan Chowdhury. Chowdhury grew up around yogis and was well-versed in yogic philosophy and practices. A graduate of Calcutta University, he came to the U.S. to study Sanskrit at Berkeley, then transferred to Harvard. While in Cambridge, in 1923, he received Kriya initiation from Yogananda. By 1926 he was working for the Ford Motor Company in Detroit. When Yogananda came to town, Chowdhury went to see him. In a letter dated May 31, 1926, he asks to be made a *brahmachari*, traditionally an initial step toward becoming a swami. He states his desire to work for Yogananda under the standard conditions of renunciate employment: room, board, and basic expenses. To simplify his name for Americans, and to designate his commitment, Chowdhury became Brahmacharee Sri Nerode.[10] Yogananda made him leader of the Detroit Yogoda Center. Theirs would be a fruitful association for more than a decade, but it would not have a happy ending.

In the remaining months of 1926, Yogananda chugged back to Pittsburgh, Cleveland, Detroit, and New York, where Yogoda Sat-Sanga now had an office on the ninth floor of a slim building at a choice address, 509 Fifth Avenue, about halfway between St. Patrick's Cathedral and the grand New York Public Library.[11] He also made a splash in a new city, Cincinnati, Ohio, where his lectures drew historically large crowds. Curiously, his time in that town coincided with an appearance by Annie Besant, the worldwide head of the Theosophy movement and a leader in India's independence struggle. No record exists of the two having met, but it would be surprising if they had not at least tried.

The campaign was interrupted for a monthlong respite in and around LA. The Mother Center had thrived under Dhirananda, who delivered regular sermons (including that year's Easter Sunrise service), conducted classes and Sunday School, offered pastoral counseling to individuals, and oversaw the production of *East–West* (the second issue sold out all 5,000 copies) as well as the correspondence course and other publications (new editions of *Songs of the Soul* and *Science of Religion* were released that year).[12] Yogananda kept an eye on LA developments from a distance. In fact, he kept in touch with all the Yogoda groups. He sent the leaders inspiration, instructions, and advice by mail, as in this letter to Dr. Lewis, who headed the Boston group (he anointed leaders in every city): "You with your co-workers may follow any plan to conduct the weekly meetings in your home, suited to the best needs and wishes of the majority. The final decision of matters concerning Boston Sat-Sanga will rest with you acting in co-operation with my wishes."[13] He requested that Dr. Lewis assure both the quality of the membership and its quantity, through growth of numbers, and he gave instructions for collective readings from his book of affirmations and the *Bhagavad Gita* at their weekly meetings.[14]

He returned to LA on August 18, bearing a supply of mangoes and Amelita Galli-Curci recordings, and he stayed until mid-September. Much of his time was occupied with work, as it generally was, but the record shows that he had some well-earned rest and recreation as well. He went to the Hollywood Bowl; he played tennis; he made mango ice cream; he took a group to Catalina Island for boating and swimming; he stayed with mother and daughter Buchanan—both of whom had taken up residence at the Mother Center—at their homes in Manhattan Beach and Santa Barbara. These passages from Kamala Silva's book give a sense of Yogananda as a vacation companion: "On the way we marketed and later he cooked a meal of East Indian food that was relished by everyone. Friends of ours came by to see us, and Swami delighted their two small children with some games which he taught them to play. Then afterward, we all walked to the beach, where he and one of his guests went in swimming." When the talk turned to Shakespeare, she said, "Swami delighted us with a dramatic portrayal of Anthony's famous oration from 'Julius Caesar.'"[15] If only cameras had been rolling.

But the highlight of his time in LA might very well have been a postcard from India, dated August 11.[16] It read (Yogananda translated from the Bengali):

> Child of my heart, O Yogananda!
>
> Seeing the photos of your school and students, what joy comes in my life I cannot express in words. I am melting in joy to see your yoga students of different cities. Beholding your methods in chant affirmations, healing vibrations, and divine healing prayers, I cannot refrain from thanking you from my heart. Seeing the gate, the winding hilly way upward, and the beautiful scenery spread out beneath the Mount Washington Estates, I yearn to behold it all with my own eyes.
>
> Through the Guru's grace, everything here is going well. Through the grace of God, may you ever be in Bliss.
>
> Your well-wisher, (Signed)
> Sri Yukteswar Giri

Much of America welcomed in the watershed year of 1927 by listening to the annual Rose Bowl football game live, in real time, on the first coast-to-coast radio broadcast ever. The world would shrink some more over the coming year, bit by bit. The first demonstration of television, still more than 20 years away as a consumer product, presaged the future of communications. The first transatlantic phone calls were made. For the first time, autos rolled under the Hudson River through the Holland Tunnel connecting New York and New Jersey. Construction on the George Washington Bridge, which would do the same *above* the river, began. Astonished spectators watched *and heard* Al Jolson sing in the first motion picture with synchronized sound, *The Jazz Singer*. And a bold young aviator named Charles Lindbergh thrilled the world by flying solo from New York to Paris.

It was an astonishing year, and Yogananda was living its animated spirit as he campaigned with the energy of Henry Ford's zippy new Model A. He must have loved the anything-is-possible drive of the country he had come to love. On the previous July 4, the 150th anniversary of America's independence, he had wired some commemorative thoughts from Detroit to LA. The statement was displayed at the Mother Center's main gate and read aloud at the holiday gala, during which the Declaration of Independence was recited and the national anthem sung. It read:

> The longer I stay in America and study her closely, the more I appreciate her true principles and love her people as my own people that are in India. The craving for the Highest Spiritual realization being the common goal of Americans and Hindus interests me most.
>
> Of all the western nations America is the most Spiritual next to India. So I love her. The veil of material civilization and extreme hurry which hides her true character from the superficial observer increase by contrast to more enhance the beauty of her half-hidden golden ideals.
>
> I love and support the hundred per cent Americanism which excludes all superstition, meaningless dogma, untruth and unkindness to brother nations and which is solely and wholly founded on lasting principles of Truth, true patriotism, international inter-racial and inter-religious tolerance and good will to all for which her great men like Lincoln and others lived and died.
>
> My mission is to bring her people closer to one another and bind them by bonds of Truth universal and the Highest Spiritual discipline, so that materially strongest as she is, She may serve also to be the best Spiritual example in the world, and thus avoid the pitfalls into which other powerful nations of history fell through their carelessness and pride.[17]

That budding patriotism must have served him well in the nation's capital, where he kicked off 1927 (he had spent the Christmas holidays with Amelita Galli-Curci and her husband, Homer Samuels, at their home in New York). The two-month Washington campaign began with a lecture on January 9 and was capped on February 22, George Washington's birthday, with a visit to Mt. Vernon, the first President's home and final resting place. He spoke everywhere and anywhere, from Dunbar High School to a Hindu Health Luncheon in his honor to the cavernous Washington Auditorium, where he appeared on 11 consecutive nights. The January 16 session was a Healing Service for a reported 5,000 people. They joined Yogananda in what *The Washington Post* called a "slow, sonorous ritual." The chant ended, said the *Post*, with "several prolonged repetitions of 'I am whole for Thou are with me.'"[18]

Yogananda had conducted Healing Services in other cities, but this one may have been historic in that it yielded perhaps the first description of India's ancient science of sound in a major U.S. newspaper. The *Post* reporter who interviewed Yogananda wrote: "The Swami explained that the power of the healing was drawn by concentration, devotion and faith of affirmation from the Comic [sic][19] Spirit, or God, by himself and transmitted to the audience on the vehicle of vibrating sound, which he declared caused a chemical change in the body cells, and a new ordinance of the cells of the brain, provided, of course, that the recipient of the vibrating waves concentrate properly and was imbued with devotion."

Yogananda encountered the full range of American society in the nation's capital. On the one hand, he was embraced by eminent citizens, was introduced one night by a U.S. Senator, and, to top it off, was welcomed to the White House by President Coolidge on January 24.[20] *The Washington Herald*, under the headline SAGE SEES COOLIDGE, reported that the President greeted Yogananda with "evident pleasure" and agreed with his guest that "it is only spiritual understanding between all nations that can bring lasting peace." The newspaper photo shows Yogananda, looking distinguished in an overcoat and holding a walking stick, posing outside the White House with a representative from the British Embassy; behind them, the President peers at the scene from a window. Earlier, we should add, Yogananda had issued some lifestyle advice for the commander in chief through a *Post* interview: a vegetarian diet, periodic fasting, no ice water, daily fresh-air exercise, twice-daily periods of "introspective silence," and no worrying ("calmly active and actively calm" was his motto). The article actually contained Yogananda's prescribed breakfast, lunch, and dinner menus.[21] There is no record of Coolidge thanking him for the advice.

On the other end of the social spectrum, Yogananda discovered Jim Crow. In each of the two previous years, as many as 50,000 members of a resurgent Ku Klux Klan had marched triumphantly in the nation's capital. Now Yogananda was surprised to learn that only white people were permitted to attend his classes there. He responded by creating a Yogoda Center for African Americans. Viewed side by side, the photos of the two Washington, D.C., Yogoda classes—both packed with well-dressed men and women, one group lily white, the other all black offer a portrait of race in America. Less than a year later, Yogananda himself would be on the receiving end of the nation's ugly racial legacy.

All in all, the D.C. visit was a landmark victory. A large hotel ballroom was needed to house all the students who signed up for Yogoda classes.

The rest of his year included stops in Pittsburgh, Cleveland, Detroit, Buffalo, Cincinnati, Greenwich, Connecticut, Minneapolis, St. Paul, and elsewhere. Two of the people who entered his life in that period beg to be mentioned. One was a 24-year-old seeker named Florina Darling, who heard Yogananda speak in Detroit and went on to study with Sri Nerode. She would become Ma Durga and play a pivotal role at Mt. Washington for decades. Yogananda met the other person of note in Buffalo. His name was Hamid Bey, and Yogananda introduced him to followers as an Egyptian mystic whose esoteric training enabled him to display remarkable powers that Yogananda witnessed. Those feats included reading minds; lying down with a thousand pounds of weight on his chest; mentally controlling his pulse and heart rates; inserting long needles through his throat, cheeks, and tongue without pain or blood; and remaining buried in an air-tight casket for 24 hours. Yogananda would soon share platforms with Hamid Bey, who turned out not to be what he said he was.

His eventful year ended in Michigan, where he also kicked off 1928. That his first public appearance that year (on January 2) should be in a place called Battle Creek, at a gathering called the Race Betterment Conference, is a great irony given the racial subtext of the battles he was about to be dragged into.

CHAPTER 13

TRAVELS, TRIUMPHS, AND TRAVAILS

The headline IRATE HUBBY SOCKS AIDE ON NOSE screamed from the front page of a Buffalo, New York, newspaper in early January 1928, although the incident it described had taken place in Los Angeles nearly two years earlier, in 1926. The substance of the story appeared in papers around the country in variations of the breathless prose used in Buffalo:

> A dark room redolent of the exotic scent of the lotus flower!
>
> Through the swirls of incense, glows the faint spark of a ruby lamp, illuminating the countenance of a Swami, clad in a flaming robe. Seated on his lacquered throne he is murmuring in a musical drome [sic], the sacred mysteries of the Kundalini, that all-powerful power, discovered by Hindu mystics, after centuries of self-mortification, prayer and meditation.[1]
>
> Men and women, who a few moments before stepped from luxurious equipages, outside the temple gates, and who represent the very cream of aristocracy and wealth, dressed in the ceremonial robes of Yoga, are sitting cross-legged on the floor in their bare feet.
>
> They are drinking in every word, every nuance of the Master's voice for he is guiding them, in attaining a power that will assure lasting youth. It is a scene of profound mysticism.

But in a moment it is changed to one in which pan-demonium reigns.

That's when the angry husband barged in and socked the swami "on the holy nose." At least that's what the reporter *said* happened. It was the age of yellow journalism, an invention mastered by the Hearst chain of newspapers. Exaggeration, scandal, sensationalism, and attention-grabbing headlines were its currency, and its purpose was to sell papers in a highly competitive marketplace. Facts were secondary. In this case, a swami had, indeed, received a beating. The victim was Dhirananda, whom the article identified as the "spiritual pinchhitter" for "Swami Yogonanda" [sic], who was teaching in New York at the time. The assailant was the husband of a Yogoda student. The several variations of the report say that the swamis were propagating "strange sex control practices," "weird love theories," "eerie doc-trines of love control," and the like, in literature, classes, and private sessions to (it is implied) naïve, innocent, vulnerable women. The enraged hubby was portrayed as protecting his wife from what various publications depicted as devious pagans with hypnotic powers.

Why the tale reached the newspapers so long after the incident occurred is a story in itself. Based on interviews with SRF officials and archival documents I've been privy to, the con-voluted saga involved clandestine wiretaps, hidden recording devices, stolen letters, and attempted blackmail. The following is a concise summary of what I was able to put together.

A young man named Percy Rogers had discovered Yogananda during one of the latter's early visits to New York. He attained benefit from Yogananda's teachings, and moved cross-country to work for him. He may have become disillusioned and/or been influenced by his father, who was president of the American Theosophical Society at the time. Surprisingly, given Theosophy's links to Eastern spiritual traditions, the society had come out against Yogananda and other Hindu teachers, contending that yogic techniques involving kundalini energy

Thu Jan 5,1893 20:38:00	Timezone: -5:21:00	Ishtakal : 34:11:0
City : Gorakhpur	Daylightsaving : 0	Sunrise : Jan 5,93 06:57:36
State : Uttar Pradesh	Longitude: 79E30'00	Sunset : Jan 5,93 17:19:58
Country : India	Latitude: 26N59'00	Ayanamsha : -22:21:38 Lahiri

Birth Chart

8th h. Pis	9th h. Ari	10th h. Tau	11th h. Gem
Pisces — Ju 23:51 Rev / Ma 13:19 UBh	Aries — Ra 12:41 Ash	Taurus	Gemini
7th h. Aqu — Aquarius	Paramahana Yogananda Thu 01-05-1893 20:38:00 Gorakhpur, Uttar Pradesh India Timezone: -5:21:00 DST: 0 Latitude: 26N59'00 Longitude: 79E30'00 Ayan. -22:21:38 Lahiri		Cancer — 12th h. Can
6th h. Cap — Capricorn			Leo — Mo 03:21 Mag / As 05:55 Mag — 1st h. Leo
Sagittarius — Su 23:13 PSh / Me 00:56 Mul	Scorpio — Ve 24:45 Jye	Libra — Ke 12:41 Swa	Virgo — Sa 20:13 Has
5th h. Sag	4th h. Sco	3rd h. Lib	2nd h. Vir

Navamsha

	Me	Mo As	
Ju Ve			Sa Ra
Ke			
		Su Ma	

Vimshottari

Ke-Me	Thu	04-06-2017
Ve-Ve	Tue	04-03-2018
Ve-Su	Tue	08-03-2021
Ve-Mo	Wed	08-03-2022
Ve-Ma	Wed	04-03-2024
Ve-Ra	Tue	06-03-2025
Ve-Ju	Fri	06-02-2028
Ve-Sa	Sat	02-01-2031
Ve-Me	Mon	04-03-2034
Ve-Ke	Sun	02-01-2037
Su-Su	Sat	04-03-2038
Su-Mo	Thu	07-22-2038
Su-Ma	Thu	01-20-2039
Su-Ra	Sat	03-28-2039
Su-Ju	Sat	04-21-2040

Birth Chart

As	05:55:00	Magha	Mee	2,Ke/E
Su	23:13:17	P.Shad.	Pah	3,Ve/S
Mo	03:21:11	Magha	Mee	2,Ke/S
Ma	13:19:13	U.Bhadra.	Jha	3,Sa/R
Me	00:56:04	Moola	Yay	1,Ke/V
Ju	23:51:26	Revati	Cha	3,Me/I
Ve	24:45:07	Jyeshtha	Yee	3,Me/I
Sa	20:13:28	Hasta	Tuh	4,Mo/I
Ra	12:41:33	Ashwini	Lah	4,Ke/N
Ke	12:41:33	Swati	Ray	2,Ra/N

Birth Chart

	Dignity	SB%	SB#	VB.	AV	Av3	Av5	K7	Func.	In
Su	Grt.Fr.	0.75	1	14	3	Drm.	Old	BK	Benefic	5/5/1
Mo	Neutr.	1.30	3	11	3	Drm.	Infant	GK	Neutral	1/1/9
Ma	Neutr.	0.95	5	10	2	Drm.	Adoles.	PK	Benefic	8/8/4
Me	Frnd.	1.06	3	15	4	Drm.	Infant	DK	Malefic	5/5/1
Ju	Own	1.07	3	14	5	Alr.	Youth.	AmK	Benefic	8/8/4
Ve	Enemy	1.44	3	12	7	Drm.	Infant	AK	Malefic	4/4/12
Sa	Grt.Fr.	1.49	4	15	3	Drm.	Youth.	MK	Malefic	2/2/10
Ra	Neutr.			9	1	Slp.	Adoles.		Benefic	9/9/5
Ke	Neutr.			18		Drm.	Adoles.		Neutral	3/3/11

Yogananda's natal chart prepared by Ayur-Vedic Astrologer Mas Vidal.
Used with the permission of Mas Vidal.

Yogananda's father,
Bhagabati Charan Ghosh.
Courtesy of Self-Realization Fellowship,
Los Angeles, Calif.

Yogananda's mother,
Gyana Prabha Ghosh.
Courtesy of Self-Realization Fellowship,
Los Angeles, Calif.

Yogananda at age 6, the earliest known
photograph of him.
Reprinted with permission of Crystal
Clarity Publishers, Nevada City, California.

Yogananda's birthplace: formerly the Ghosh
family home in Gorakhpur (recent photo).
Ron & Hélène Lindahn copyright©2015

Yogananda's meditation room at 4 Garpar Road, now maintained as a shrine. Ron & Hélène Lindahn copyright©2015

Yogananda's family home, 4 Garpar Road, Calcutta (recent photo).

50 Amherst St., Calcutta, where Yogananda's mother died and where he studied with Mahendra Nath Gupta, aka Master Mahasaya (recent photo).

Bedroom shrine in the ashram of Nagendra Nath Bhaduri,
"The Levitating Saint."

Pitambar Bhattacharya Lane, where Tulsi
Bose lived and where Yogananda created
an ashram in 1909.

Doorway to Lahiri Mahasaya's home,
31/58 Madanura Lane, Benares
(recent photo).

Yogananda with his elder brother,
Ananta, 1914.
Courtesy of Self-Realization Fellowship,
Los Angeles, Calif.

Banyan tree in Serampore, beneath which
Yogananda often sat with Sri Yukteswar
(recent photo).

Panthi Boarding House in Serampore, where Yogananda lodged
circa 1914–1915 (recent photo).

Yogananda with students at his school in Ranchi, circa 1918–1920.
Courtesy of Self-Realization Fellowship, Los Angeles, Calif.

Smriti Mandir in Ranchi, on the site of the storeroom where Yogananda's vision
to go to America occurred in 1920.

Headline in *Washington Post*, February 2, 1912.

Yogananda in Denver, with poster announcing his class series, 1924.
Courtesy of Self-Realization Fellowship, Los Angeles, Calif.

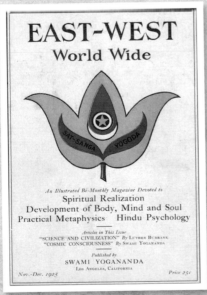

Cover of first issue of *East-West* magazine, November 1925.
Courtesy of Self-Realization Fellowship, Los Angeles, Calif.

Ad for Yogananda's first lecture in Los Angeles, *Los Angeles Times*, 1925.
Courtesy of Self-Realization Fellowship, Los Angeles, Calif.

Yogananda with Yogoda African-American Study Group, Washington, D.C., circa 1927.
Courtesy of Self-Realization Fellowship, Los Angeles, Calif.

Yogananda with James Lynn at Mt. Washington, 1933.
Courtesy of Self-Realization Fellowship, Los Angeles, Calif.

Yogananda at Lake Xochimilco, Mexico, 1929.
Courtesy of Self-Realization Fellowship, Los Angeles, Calif.

Yogananda with Mahatma Gandhi in Wardha, India, 1935.
Courtesy of Self-Realization Fellowship, Los Angeles, Calif.

Yogananda with Ananda Moyi Ma and her husband, Bholanath, circa 1935.
Courtesy of Self-Realization Fellowship, Los Angeles, Calif.

Yogananda with Sri Yukteswar in Calcutta, 1935.
Courtesy of Self-Realization Fellowship, Los Angeles, Calif.

Yogananda at his writing desk in Encinitas, California, 1938.
Courtesy of Self-Realization Fellowship, Los Angeles, Calif.

Yogananda's application for United States citizenship, 1946.

Letter from Yogananda to Donald Walters, later Swami Kriyananda, February 18, 1950. From pp. 348–49 of *The New Path* by Swami Kriyananda,

Reprinted with permission of Crystal Clarity Publishers, Nevada City, California.

Gandhi Memorial at the Self-Realization Fellowship Lake Shrine,
Los Angeles.

Yogananda with California Lieutenant Governor Goodwin Knight
and Mrs. Knight at the dedication
of the Lake Shrine, 1950.

Courtesy of Self-Realization
Fellowship, Los Angeles, Calif.

"The Last Smile," taken shortly before Yogananda passed away, March 7, 1952.

Arthur Say, Reprinted with permission of Crystal Clarity Publishers, Nevada City, California.

भारत
INDIA
1977

25

परमहंस योगानंद 1893-1952
PARAMAHANSA YOGANANDA

Commemorative stamp issued by the Indian government, 1977.
Courtesy of Self-Realization Fellowship, Los Angeles, Calif.

were dangerous. Whatever Rogers's motives were, my sources indicate that he conspired with another resident worker at the Mother Center—the very Mrs. Scott whose business skills had been praised in *East–West* magazine. Written statements from contemporaneous observers, in particular James McLachlan, a former U.S. Congressman who had become Yogananda's student and legal counsel, allege that Mrs. Scott wiretapped phone conversations between Dhirananda and the woman referred to in the sensational newspaper articles and arranged for the woman's husband to listen in. In addition, Mrs. Scott apparently pilfered correspondence between Yogananda and Dhirananda, parts of which were referenced in those same articles. Her motives appear to have been financial.

Whether Dhirananda actually behaved inappropriately with that married woman—or with any other women (allegations were later made)—is not known. According to newspaper reports,[2] Yogananda telegrammed the angry husband from New York, appealing to his "Christian spirit" and urging him to "yield to goodness and God and not to anger" so that Yogoda's good work could continue unimpeded. The husband was evidently pacified; in a letter, he told Yogananda that all was well. Nevertheless, according to the documents I read, Mrs. Scott demanded a large payoff in exchange for not exposing the organization to negative publicity.

James McLachlan, acting on Yogananda's behalf, had Mr. and Mrs. Scott dismissed from Mt. Washington with a $2,000 severance payment. However, Percy Rogers somehow retained possession of the purloined material. In a telegram to Yogananda, he demanded $10,000.[3] Yogananda refused to pay and/or McLachlan let Rogers know that criminal charges could be filed against him. The demand was withdrawn. But, in 1928, just as Yogananda was beginning a major teaching campaign in Miami, Rogers made good on his threat. Perhaps to discredit Yogananda and his work, perhaps for financial gain, or both, he offered what he had to the press, which snapped up the scoop like ice cream on a hot day.

The Los Angeles Examiner, a Hearst paper, launched an investigative series whose reach in syndication extended as far afield as Charleston, South Carolina, where a headline read: WHERE QUEER LOVE CULT LURES MANY WOMEN. The *Examiner* articles were lengthy, detailed, and scurrilous. On January 9, a front-page banner headline read: 'LOVE CONTROL' TAUGHT IN CULT HERE. Readers learned that the LA district attorney's office was looking into the "weird and amazing doctrines of love and sex control" being taught by the Mt. Washington swamis. The DA's main concern was whether underage girls were being seduced into something immoral or illegal. The paper's main concern was to entice readers to part with their $.05. Yogananda's visage beamed from the front page, even though he was a continent away at the time, in Washington, D.C., and hadn't been in LA for half a year. Almost the entirety of pages 2 and 3 were taken up by the continuation of the main story, plus subsidiary articles and three photos: of the main building at Mt. Washington, a full-length Swami Dhirananda in robes, and a smiling, well-dressed woman identified as "Miss A," whose experience was described in the text.

While the report contained a reasonable overview of the purpose and intent of Yogoda, acknowledging the endorsements from prominent people and the benefits claimed by students, the overall tone was cynical and reeked of innuendo. Dhirananda, who was interviewed for the piece, contended that the sexual energy component of the teaching had been misunderstood and that Yogoda's procedures had changed after the pugilistic husband's attack. "I have a secretary sit outside the door when I talk to anyone in this room," he said, and "the door is never closed." Such changes were no doubt made in collaboration with, or at the behest of, Yogananda. In segments of the correspondence quoted in newspapers, he warned Dhirananda to avoid even the appearance of impropriety with women.

The articles allude to the "bizarre and amazing love control theory being taught to many Los Angeles society women and their pretty daughters." Part One of Miss A's tale spotlighted her first impression of Dhirananda. "There isn't a movie actor in Hollywood that has such simply gorgeous eyes," she said, and when he gave her lessons, "he used to search my very soul with those same eyes." Of the approximately 250 people at the first session Miss A attended, only 10 were men, and the women, she reported, "were apparently from homes of refinement, culture and wealth." Still to come, *The Los Angeles Examiner* teased, were details of Miss A's private lessons in Dhirananda's "darkened room," and especially the ninth of those lessons, "Spiritualizing Sex Force," with the "mystic Kundalini sex theory."

It was the Roaring Twenties, when a glimpse of stocking was no longer looked on as something shocking, and heaven knows the era was far more "anything goes" than any that preceded it. But given the theatrical buildup, the follow-up articles seem laughably tame, especially by today's standards. The *Examiner* made much of a dimly lit, incense-filled room in which women sat on the floor swaying and murmuring with Dhirananda. They were, essentially, meditating and chanting, "OM." Miss A revealed that Dhirananda had coached her on the importance of finding a suitable mate. "Don't contaminate the soul craving with sex craving," he told her, "as then you will lose your right discrimination and be misled." Nothing more suggestive than that rather sensible advice was reported, except for the content of some of the classes, such as the use of meditation to "unite sex force and soul force" and "spiritualizing" emotions by drawing them from lower energy centers up to the brain. It is easy to see how these standard yogic concepts might alarm protective fathers and husbands. It didn't help that kundalini was referred to as "serpent energy," eliciting images of Satan in the Garden of Eden.

Dhirananda addressed the controversy in public talks and press interviews, calling the accusations against him an insult to the intelligence of the American people. James McLachlan spoke out in his defense, and Yogananda weighed in from a distance. Writing in *East–West*, he took a swing at yellow journalism without mentioning the LA investigation explicitly: "Certainly the methods of exaggeration and distortion, and the free play of imagination and fictional skill that are employed by some newspapermen in lieu of sober consideration of facts and actual events, can make a harmless rope look like a vicious snake." He wrote of broken homes and ruined reputations and, in a clear reference to himself, lamented that "the fruits of a lifetime of disinterested service to mankind can be reduced to ashes through the soulless efforts of yellow journalism."[4]

In that same long, remarkable essay, he also addressed the larger issue of anti-Hindu and anti-India propaganda. In addition to the scurrilous literature mentioned earlier, a book titled *Mother India* by historian Katherine Mayo had become a huge bestseller in 1927. Condemned by Tagore, Gandhi, and masses of protesting Indians, and called dishonest, distorted, intentionally misleading, and worse by scholars, the book was a relentless broadside against all things Indian. It portrayed the Indian people as irresponsible, untrustworthy, and immoral. "Her representation of India as a land of filth, disease, and above all sexual perversion no doubt infected domestic visions of anyone and anything perceived as hailing from within its borders," wrote Anya P. Foxen of Mayo's book.[5] Yogananda fought back by praising India's civilizational and spiritual gifts to the world. He also gave space in the magazine to others who praised his native land, among them, surprisingly, the silent film star Lillian Gish.[6]

The district attorney's investigation found nothing incriminating against Dhirananda or Yogoda Sat-Sanga. The news was greeted with headlines like HINDU 'LOVE CULT' REPORT ERRONEOUS and INQUIRY IN CULT CASE FRUITLESS. The case was dropped. But damage had been done. Rumors and allegations dogged Yogananda's footsteps all the way to Miami, where he arrived in mid-January for his usual routine of lectures and classes. He was about to have what he called the most severe trial of his life. But before we pick up that story, let's note one passage in *The Los Angeles Examiner* series. It alluded to correspondence between Yogananda and Dhirananda that "reveal a gripping, human interest story of two masters of heavenly harmony hurling discords of reproach at each other and quarreling over the conduct of their heavenly-perfection business, and credit for literary work." The sentence seemed tangential to the gaudy "love cult" content, but it presaged a conflict that would come to a boil the following year.

While Yogananda was, no doubt, keeping abreast of developments in LA, the start of his scheduled two weeks at Miami's Scottish Rite Temple drew healthy crowds. Then, on February 3, the *Miami Daily News* reported that "the love cult exponent" had been told to leave the city. "I'm ordering you out of town to satisfy a horde of protests against your activities," Police Chief Leslie Quigg told Yogananda, "and to save you from a repetition of what happened to you in Los Angeles, when an irate husband handed you one on the nose." Never mind that the nose belonged to Dhirananda (or that a telegram from James McLachlan corrected the mistaken identity at a hearing); the language makes it clear that reports from LA had influenced not only city officials but Miamians who wanted the swami and his entourage gone. About 200 women had been taking Yogananda's classes (there was no mention of men in news reports), and some of their husbands were up in arms. Variations of the Miami articles appeared in newspapers as disparate and dispersed as the *New York Times* and the *Ogden* (Utah) *Standard-Examiner. Time* magazine even took a swipe at opera star Amelita Galli-Curci for endorsing "a man who looks like a plump woman" and had been "ordered by the police to leave Miami."[7]

Yogananda was not inclined to obey the edict. As we've seen, he was not easily cowed. "His life threatened by a delegation of indignant citizens, Swami Yogananda, East Indian love cult leader, was at a hotel tonight determined to stay in Miami 'and fight it out,'" one reporter wrote. He got himself a lawyer, Redmond B. Gautier, who petitioned a federal court for an injunction against "police interference" with Yogananda's activities. He argued that if the police really wanted to protect the swami from an angry mob, as they claimed, they should deal with the people making threats, not the one being threatened. The court rejected his petition; Gautier refiled in state court. Meanwhile, Chief Quigg said that if Yogananda showed up for his next scheduled lecture, he'd have to finish his speech in jail.

As a precautionary measure, a riot squad with tear gas canisters lined up outside the lecture site, the Anglers Club. Yogananda canceled the talk, and moved to an undisclosed location. The series of events was so sensational that Miami newspapers ran major stories almost daily and Yogananda supporters and opponents filled City Hall for the hearings.

To its credit, the *Miami Daily News* gave Yogananda space to write his own response to the charges against him. He seized the opportunity with two columns of emphatic prose, correcting newspaper errors, describing the nature of his mission, outlining his accomplishments, naming some of his eminent supporters, and expressing indignation mixed with irony: "I teach the formation of character and highest moral teaching in self-discipline both to married and unmarried people . . . and in return I get the name of the leader of a 'love cult.' And this in spite of the fact that there is not the slightest foundation for it." He suggests that if he'd wanted to start a love cult it would have been more convenient to go to Kashmir where the women were "just as white and beautiful" as America's.[8]

He was up against a perfect storm of America's worst defects: media sensationalism, religious bigotry, ethnic stereotyping, paternalism, sexual anxiety, and brazen racism. Yogananda was well aware of the racism he and his fellow countrymen had to contend with. "God does not like to be insulted when He wears His dark suits," he once said.

In another twist, it turns out that Miami officials had summoned the British vice consulate to advise them on the matter. In a letter to a superior, dated March 1, one consulate officer says that the Miami city manager and Chief Quigg "recognized the fact that the swami was a British subject and apparently an educated man, but unfortunately he was what is considered in this part of the country a coloured man." Given the South's cultural mores, he noted, "the swami was in great danger of suffering bodily harm from the populace." A British official met with Yogananda privately. "While his manner and conversation were those of a superior person," he reported, "I recognized that his colour, while not negro, was such as might cause high feeling in the community." He advised Yogananda to leave Miami, for his own safety.[9]

We have here another subplot in Yogananda's American narrative. The Empire was keeping an eye on him, and on all its Indian subjects in the United States. They were on the alert for propagandists, fund-raisers, and arms smugglers sympathetic to the independence movement. Yogananda would have known, or at least suspected, this, and the possibility of being deported may have made him more cautious in his speech than he might otherwise have been. What he probably did not know is the extent of the British surveillance. The series of memos from one British official to another suggest that they had detailed knowledge about everything from the people Yogananda associated with to the contents of his letters to his father. A memo from the Los Angeles consulate to an official in New York, dated April 20, 1926, refers to a visit from a couple who had worked for Yogananda. They called him a swindler and accused him of being in cahoots with people who were "stirring up Hindus." They also said that M. Rashid was "a bad character and reputed to be an agent of Gandhi." The informants were Mr. and Mrs. Scott.

Another exchange reveals that a consulate employee scoped out Yogananda's New York lectures: "Swami deals in the usual type of psychological platitudes that emanate from the Hindu apostles of new religions who derive lucrative incomes by imposing upon certain elements of the American public." In the writer's opinion, Yogananda "suffers from seditious tendencies which might break out in violent eruption if circumstances proved favourable." A 1927 letter, which otherwise reeks of British condescension toward Indians, counters that judgment. It seems that before he was allowed to meet President Coolidge, Yogananda had been thoroughly checked out. The Brits found no evidence of seditious activities, and the lecture they attended was deemed "harmless."

Yogananda was finally persuaded to forego his remaining legal options and leave Florida.[10] He made efforts to clear his name, giving statements to newspapers linking the Miami events to the attempted blackmail in LA two years earlier. For the most part, he resumed his customary activities. In mid-March he visited Boston. "O it was so good to be with you all," he wrote the Lewises afterward. "Infinite love and joy was revived—a new life I felt."[11] Indeed, after what he came to call his Miami Crucifixion, the company of loving friends must have felt like a resurrection.

Come spring, and he was rambling once again, to Philadelphia, Buffalo, Pittsburgh, Cincinnati, Detroit, and, on June 10, Washington, D.C., for a significant event. To meet the growing demand for his teachings, Yogananda had again turned to India for reinforcements. Swami Satyananda chose a former Ranchi student named Jotindra. He was one of the two youngsters who had seen Yogananda in the storeroom when he had the vision to come to America. He was also at the dock when the *City of Sparta* carried his guru away. Now, as Brahmachari Jotin, he was introduced by Yogananda as the leader of the Washington center. In 1941, Yogananda would initiate him into the monastic order as Swami Premananda Giri.

Yogananda enjoyed some downtime at the summer homes of affluent devotees, then hopped a train to his ostensible home in Los Angeles. He arrived at Mt. Washington to a hero's welcome on July 15 but stayed only a few weeks, teaching classes, giving talks, and attending to administrative and financial concerns. In early June, a nationwide fund-raising plea was sent out by the Mt. Washington Center Fund Committee. It describes Yogananda's tireless and strenuous efforts to advance his work, and the sacrifice involved in maintaining the Mother Center and paying off the first mortgage. A second mortgage of $25,000 remained on the books, and $5,000 of it was due at the end of June. It was time for the membership to help Swami—who had "bled with difficulties for us"—to settle the onerous debt.

The mortgage burden would not be lifted from his shoulders for another few years. For now, the peripatetic monk hit the road once again. He was in Minneapolis by early August, then Detroit, Cleveland, and Washington, before settling down for a sojourn in Boston, where it had all begun. Eight years earlier, he had landed there anonymous and friendless. Now he was greeted at the State House by Governor Alvan T. Fuller. Whereas once he could barely scrounge up a couple of dozen people to hear him speak, he now filled Symphony Hall. He gave talks at a host of clubs and associations, addressed a throng of enthusiastic Harvard students on the subject of India, and conducted classes at the elegant Copley Plaza Hotel, where he was also an invited guest at a reception for the wife of Herbert Hoover, who was about to be elected President.

He also addressed unseen and uncountable listeners from at least three radio stations (WNAC, WBZ, and WLOE). On one of those broadcasts, he delivered a message to Admiral Richard Byrd, who was leading an expedition to Antarctica. He said, in part: "Greetings from Swami Yogananda of India to you, brave souls, Commander Byrd and your colleagues. As you explore new places, forget not to explore the unexplored mystic territories of your souls. When this adventure of yours is successful and you return, remember there will be nothing more left to explore on earth, so you must start to sail in the boat of Intuition to explore the land of the Infinite." And on January 12 (Vivekananda's birthday, as it happens) he made a triumphant return to the Boston YMCA, the very first place he'd slept in America. He gave a rousing speech on "My Mother India."

Two days later, he lectured at New York's Union Methodist Episcopal Church. To history's benefit, one of the people in attendance that night was the scholar Wendell Thomas, who described the event in *Hinduism Invades America*. The title of the talk was "The Metaphysical Unity of Hinduism and Christianity." Thomas says the church was "comfortably filled," mainly with women. There were a short organ recital, a prayer for unity, the reading of a play, and a series of announcements. Then Yogananda was introduced. Here is the first part of Thomas's account:

> As he rose from his seat in the audience to mount the platform, several persons in the audience rose also, perhaps out of gratitude for some benefit conferred by Yogoda, perhaps in honor of the spirituality of the East,

perhaps in accord with the Indian pupil's respect for his master. The swami is short and plump, with a striking face. His raven hair hung over his shoulders in wavy locks—even longer than is usual among Bengalis—and he wore the vivid orange over his Western attire. His first act was to read one of his own poems, which he called "The Royal Sly Eluder," a record of his personal search for God in ocean, tree and sky, a search which ended in hearing God's voice within the soul, calling out "Hello, playmate, here am I!" The swami's voice was loud and clear, his pronunciation good. He then began his demonstration of the "metaphysical unity of Hinduism and Christianity."[12]

Thomas goes on to describe Yogananda's principal points of discussion: the difference between inference-based and intuition-based interpretations of scripture, the points of unity between Hinduism and Christianity, and the false arguments that demean the Hindu tradition. The author took exception to what he saw as Yogananda's attempt "to explain Christianity in the light of the supposedly deeper knowledge of Hinduism."[13] This has been a common critique of virtually every Hindu who dared interpret the Christ message for Western audiences. Seen another way, however, these are not attempts to Hinduize Christianity so much as an effort to frame *all* religions in the yogic manner of lending primacy to inner experience and universal spiritual principles. Thomas concludes his account of the evening with Yogananda's use of a classic Hindu metaphor about the tendency of humans to search for the Divine in all the wrong places: the musk deer who goes mad trying to find the source of an intoxicating fragrance, not knowing that it emanated from its own navel.

By the spring of 1929, Yogananda had established 13 functioning Yogoda centers in the U.S., with appointed leaders and regular meetings.[14] He had recruited four of his fellow countrymen—Dhirananda, Nerode, Jotin, and one Ranendra Kumar Das in Cincinnati—to help out. He had instigated plans to restructure the organization and relieve its financial difficulties, started a program to train teachers to "spread the Yogoda message," and appealed to students to become official members of Yogoda Sat-Sanga and donate $2 annually. Now came the announcement that new offices had been acquired at 539 South Bowman Ave. in Merion Station, a Philadelphia suburb. All administrative and publishing operations would move there, and so would Yogananda. The operation would be overseen by Harry F. Sieber, a former bank president. Yogananda "expects to reside more or less continuously at Merion, where he plans to finish writing the Yogoda Bible and his universal prayer book, Sacred Demands," the announcement declared.[15] That book of prayers, it should be noted, became the highly popular *Whispers from Eternity.*

"For nine whole years I have incessantly worked for the spiritual good of America," Yogananda wrote in an open letter to Yogodans that May, "but I have found I have been greatly handicapped, due to business and financial responsibilities falling on me." He was, therefore, turning over the business end of Yogoda to Mr. Sieber. By delegating oppressive administrative tasks, he would free himself to write, teach, train, and "keep an unhampered contact with the Divine Father within." The announcement came with a stock offering: 10,000 shares of class A Common Stock and 15,000 shares of class B Common Stock, under terms outlined in some detail. It was a good time for a stock offering. *Everyone* wanted to own stock then, even people who had to borrow money to invest. The Dow Jones Industrial Average had a set a new record in each of the preceding six years. It would all come crashing down that October, but in the spring the Dow was poised to soar above 350 for the very first time. Members of the Philadelphia center subscribed $10,000 to get the ball rolling.

It would seem that Yogananda had every reason to feel both pleased about his progress and confident in the future. Then he had a surprise visit from an old friend, and everything turned upside down once again.

Swami Dhirananda showed up in New York, by all indications unannounced, sometime during the second week of April. Exactly what transpired between him and Yogananda—where they spoke, for how long, and what the content and emotional tone were is not entirely clear. The bottom line is known. Dhirananda wanted out, and he wanted remuneration for his labors over the six and a half years he'd been in America. Yogananda signed a handwritten promissory note, dated April 11, 1928, that read as follows:

> In installments as herein stated, FOR VALUE RECEIVED, I promise to pay to SWAMI GIRIDHIRANANDA, also known as BASU KUMAR BAGCHI, on order, the sum of Eight thousand dollars ($8000.00) on or before January 1, 1936. Payable at the Citizens National Trust & Savings Bank of Los Angeles, No. 457 South Spring Street, Los Angeles, California, in installments of One hundred dollars ($100.00) on the first day of each and every month beginning May 1, 1929 and so continuing each month until the entire principal sum is paid. Should any monthly installment of principal remain unpaid for a period of five (5) months, then, at the option of the holder of this note, the entire principal sum remaining unpaid shall become immediately due and payable.[16]

He signed it twice, once as Swami Yogananda and once as Mukunda Lal Ghosh. The document was duly notarized.

Dhirananda's compensation had been that of a traditional monk: room, board, and essential expenses. Now he insisted on what has come to be called severance pay. Why did he choose to end his working relationship with his close friend and fellow swami? Why did Yogananda sign the note? That's where the speculation comes in. It should be said that a small number of former devotees who discuss these matters on the Internet are convinced that Dhirananda heard that Yogananda was cohabiting with Laurie Pratt, the devotee who would one day edit *Autobiography of a Yogi*, and Dhirananda, having allegedly discovered the rumor to be true, decided to cut all ties.

I have seen no evidence to support that scenario. Dhirananda himself never stated such a thing, at least not publicly, and he had both ample opportunity and ample reason to do so. There are other, more credible, explanations, of course. One is that Dhirananda simply got tired of playing second banana to his charismatic friend and wanted to be his own boss, so to speak. He may not have liked being part of a large organization and preferred something less ambitious. He may have been more interested in building a school than a movement. He may have bristled at the assumption that he was Yogananda's disciple, when he saw himself as a friend and colleague. He may have realized he was not cut out for the monastic life after all. Any combination of those theories is plausible, particularly in light of later developments. After breaking with Yogananda, Dhirananda started teaching on his own. Within a few years, he had disavowed his swamihood, reassumed his original name, earned a Ph.D., become a husband and a father, and embarked on a successful academic career as Dr. Basu Kumar Bagchi.

Dhirananda also seems to have disagreed with some of Yogananda's policies and procedures. Letters from that period show that Yogananda felt Dhirananda did not try hard enough to promote the correspondence course. Indeed, in later years Dhirananda would disparage the course, as well as other practices with commercial overtones. In 1936, he published an article in a Calcutta journal that was as cynical about Indian gurus in the West as any screed by American journalists. "They have adopted the high-powered salesmanship of American business," he wrote, "to boost their course of philosophic and religious teaching to spiritually hungry and nervously sick American men and women, mostly women, using such bait phrases as 'marvelous illumination,' 'instantaneous healing,' 'God-consciousness,' and charging each from 25 to 100 dollars for their courses of lessons." He does not name Yogananda, but he has nothing good to say about generic swamis in the West.[17]

In any event, with the "love cult" headlines and the Miami saga fresh in mind, Yogananda must have been wary of any additional bad publicity. Then again, perhaps he did not need a threat hanging over his head to comply with Dhirananda's demand. In the view of many devotees, his willingness to sign the promissory note was an act of generosity rather than acquiescence to blackmail. In letters written in subsequent years, he says he signed the note because his longtime friend wanted a fresh start and would need money to get by.

Yogananda acted quickly to fill the gap created by Dhirananda's departure. Making a pragmatic decision with immediate benefits and calamitous reverberations in the future, he had Brahmacharee Nerode move from Detroit to Los Angeles. The May–June issue of *East–West* said only that Nerode had been named "residential leader" at Yogoda headquarters and that Dhirananda "has gone away for a period of rest and study"[18]—the swami equivalent, it seems, of an unpopular politician leaving office "to spend more time with his family."

By Yogananda's own account, he was bereft over losing his best friend. Close disciples used terms like "heartbreak," "discouraged," and "distraught" in describing the impact of the incident on their guru, who came to feel so betrayed that, in private correspondence, he sometimes called Dhirananda a Judas. Add to those feelings the exhausting schedule and the ongoing struggle to keep his organization afloat, and it is no wonder that a man who always longed for Himalayan solitude would want to get away. He was able to do so thanks to the family of Oscar Saenger, a famed baritone and voice teacher who had become Yogananda's student and friend. Saenger died shortly after Yogananda's confrontation with Dhirananda (Yogananda conducted the funeral service), and afterward the Saenger family invited him to their home on Lake Chapala in Mexico. It must have seemed like an act of Divine Grace.

"With a heavy heart I am starting for Mexico," he wrote to Dr. Lewis on May 23. He was "cutting loose from everything," he said, to consecrate himself to God.[19] Disciples feared he might never return. With good reason, it seems. Yogananda admitted there were times when he prayed to be relieved of his worldly duties. On one occasion, he said, he beseeched Divine Mother: "Free me. Let me go back to India to serve you there."

CHAPTER 14

REGROUPING
AND REBUILDING

Late in his life, Yogananda reminisced about those times he prayed to be relieved of his missionary burden. "Every time," he said, "Divine Mother takes me by the ear and says, 'Go back.'" So it was after a period of contemplation in Mexico.

He gave some talks south of the border, opened a Yogoda chapter in Mexico City, and met with Mexican president Emilio Cándido Portes Gil. But his most productive time may have been spent at his friends' hacienda on Lake Chapala. In that mile-high setting, about 50 kilometers from Guadalajara, he surely dwelled long and deep in meditation, communing silently with the sacred Source that guided his destiny and soothed and healed his soul.

That Yogananda's psyche might have required soothing strikes some of his disciples as unlikely, or even absurd. Wasn't he a great yogi, and aren't great yogis rooted in the infinite Self, untouched by the discontents that plague the rest of us? So it is said, but yogic adepts are also human beings; their bodies are subject to aging and illness, and their minds and emotions are subject to joys and sorrows and pleasures and pains. In his commentary on Chapter 2, Verse 38 of the *Bhagavad Gita*, Yogananda says of this apparent paradox, "The devotee of divine fortitude remains unchanged like a stainless steel—alike whether under the sunshine of happiness, gain, or victory, or under a corroding vapor from a sea of melancholy, loss, and failure!"¹ Note that he doesn't say an accomplished yogi does not experience life's slings and arrows, only that he *also* remains stationed in the Transcendent, a silent witness to the madness we think of as "reality." We must also remember that Yogananda was still evolving. He was only 36 in 1929. He was not yet the Yogananda who would emerge, after further growth, learning, and profound spiritual experiences, as a middle-aged sage and the scribe who wrote the famous autobiography.

Exactly when he received the divine dictum to get on with his work in America is unknown, but sometime in mid-August he boarded a train to Los Angeles. He was greeted by adoring followers on the 23rd, and on September 1 led an inspired Sunday service at Mt. Washington.

Changes were afoot, personally and organizationally. An item in the November–December issue of *East–West* (publication had been suspended after the May–June edition due to Yogananda's absence) explained the new developments without reference to any of the distressing factors. "The center at Merion Station, Pennsylvania, was found unsuitable for Yogoda purposes," it said. All of the organization's work, including the magazine and the correspondence course, would now be handled at Mt. Washington. "It has long been the wish of Swami Yogananda to supervise the work of the national headquarters at Los Angeles," the article went on, "but due to his constant lecture tours in various parts of America, he could not do so."² Now his plan was to spend as much time as possible in California, writing, meditating, and overseeing the organization.

With LA's warm weather and access to nature, the center's ample space, and his hoped-for release from organizational business, Yogananda could focus on the written word. This would enable him to reach many more people than he could as a speaker. As an added benefit, the organization would be spared the cost of running a business office on the East Coast. Only a few months earlier, prior to his departure for Mexico, having Harry Sieber run things from suburban Philadelphia had been deemed ideal. Perhaps the loss of the trusted Dhirananda forced a reconsideration. Whatever the thought process may have been, it is clear that Yogananda was trying to resolve the central tension in his life between the lure of heavenly silence and his earthly calling, with all its relentless imperatives. Over the years, many of his letters contained poignant passages in which he expressed the hope that one day he would be liberated from his karmic duties and be free like the sadhus who wander the riverbanks and mountain trails of India.

That would never happen, but he would find relief from constant travel—only not right away. He had commitments to keep, devotees in need of guidance, and centers to fortify. And revenue had to be generated. Once again he waved good-bye at Union Station, his luggage filled with garments for less friendly weather and canisters of film from Mexico to show at upcoming events. He spent two days with the Buchanans in Colorado—and it's not every houseguest who does sadhana on snow-covered ground and teaches his hosts' friends to meditate[3]—then shuffled off to Cleveland and Buffalo, followed by a bucolic interlude at the summer homes of student-friends on the East Coast.[4] Onward to Boston, then west to Buffalo, Detroit, St. Paul, and Minneapolis.

On October 29, he was on a train back to Los Angeles when the stock market crashed and panic seized the land. It was the day known to history as Black Tuesday. For the next decade, the Great Depression would weigh heavily on Yogananda, as it would on households across America and around the globe.

During the six years between Yogananda's return from Mexico and his departure for India in 1935, the world economy sank at an unprecedented rate, causing massive deprivation and suffering. In the U.S., unemployment skyrocketed from 3.2 percent in 1929 to 25 percent in 1933. Americans elected Franklin Delano Roosevelt, enacted the social legislation known as the New Deal, and ended Prohibition. Stalin clamped down in the Soviet Union, sending dissenters to the infamous gulag or condemning them to death. Hitler, Mussolini, and Imperial Japan grew increasingly oppressive at home and threatening abroad. In

Britain, an out-of-office Winston Churchill warned accurately of the Fascist menace and, at the same time, railed against every step toward self-rule in India, saying in 1921 that Gandhi "ought to be lain bound hand and foot at the gates of Delhi, and then trampled on by an enormous elephant with the new Viceroy seated on its back."[5] Gandhi marched on, figuratively and literally, initiating a civil disobedience campaign that would eventually break the back of foreign rule.

Yogananda would occasionally comment on world events, sometimes in surprising ways. In the April 1932 *East–West*, for instance, he published a four-page essay titled "How to Burn Out the Roots of Depression by Divine Methods." Leading with compassion for the "well-dressed men and women without money in their pockets or food in their stomachs," he decried society's "tumult of inequalities and injustices" and mocked the calls of business interests for consumers to create demand by purchasing goods on credit. He identified selfishness as the true origin of economic distress, and extolled simple living. His proposed solutions sound almost Marxist, with food, medical care, and education for all. At the same time, while he credits communist Russia for eliminating unemployment, he condemns its "un-Christian, un-spiritual laws of wholesale murder and slaughter." He sang the praises of Mahatma Gandhi frequently in those agitated years, even though doing so might irritate the British, who had the power to get him tossed out of America as an undesirable.[6]

His *East–West* essay then went where political commentators seldom ventured. "How can we by spiritual methods begin a material United States of the World?" he asked. He envisioned meditation-oriented spiritual colonies as the basic units of a "practical Utopia." Other gurus have proffered similar inside-out solutions to social problems, but Yogananda went the extra mile with a detailed, six-paragraph master plan. Groups of 25, married and single, should live frugally and save money for five years, then pool $10,000 each to create a $250,000 trust fund with which to purchase farmland and cottages. He offered guidelines for growing vegetables, raising cows and lambs (for milk and wool, not eating), educating children, and the joint ownership of assets. Communal conformity would be balanced by spiritual freedom so every person was free to develop in his or her own way. Say what you will about the promise of ushering in "universal peace and harmony," the manifesto stands as a remarkable attempt to apply spiritual principles to an intractable economic crisis.

No one with even a rudimentary knowledge of Yogananda would find it surprising that his public statements mixed pragmatism and spiritual idealism. What *is* surprising, at first glance, is the admiration he professed for Hitler and Mussolini in the early 1930s. According to Brother Chidananda, who is now president of SRF, Yogananda's attitude was based on reports he'd received from Hindu friends who had recently visited Germany. The friends were part of the Indian independence movement and were misled, as many others were, by Hitler's promise of peace and prosperity for Germany, as well as the possibility that he might help India in its opposition to British rule.

Yogananda's "Christmas Message to the Nations of the World" (*East–West*, December 1933) praises President Roosevelt for "trying from his Soul" to alleviate the impact of the Depression and calls for freedom for subjugated nations, shared prosperity, and an appeal to brotherhood and generosity.

In that same message, however, he states: "Hitler is to be admired for leaving the League of Nations because peace can never be attained by the victor and vanquished attitude, but only on a basis of equality and brotherhood."[7] He calls on other countries to reduce their own military spending and use the money for humanitarian ends, instead of just thwarting Germany's buildup. He seems to understand the humiliating impact that the Versailles Treaty ending World War I had on the German psyche, and adds, "An insulted, snubbed Germany, if it gets away from the uplifting guidance of Hitler, may join Russia and make her a more powerful enemy of France, and so on."

Two months later, in an interview in which he praised Gandhian nonviolence, he said, in response to a question about individualism and socialism, "A master brain like that of Mussolini does more good than millions of social organizations of group intelligence."[8] Because the ideal conditions—large groups of individuals with great brain power—could not be met at that time, he asserts, we need exceptional people like Mussolini to lead the way. What he calls "Spiritual socialism" will prevail when enough souls have evolved to the requisite level, he says, but until then, true democracy is impossible. Hence, we need "the master mind of a Dictator in order to think right and do right."

Obviously, this is disturbing stuff knowing what we now know. But consider this: Yogananda's example of a wise Dictator—one who can produce "prosperity and international balance"—was Franklin Delano Roosevelt. Call him naïve for using the term *dictator* in that way, and for not initially recognizing the true character of Der Führer and Il Duce, but at that time—less than a year after Hitler was appointed chancellor and eight months before he was elected president of Germany—a lot of smart people did not yet see the writing on the wall. Many did, of course, and others came around in time. According to devotees who were with him in those days, Yogananda expressed profound grief and condemnation—and predicted Hitler's downfall—when Nazi atrocities became evident.

During those "Brother Can You Spare a Dime" days, he struggled mightily to keep his organization afloat. Participation at Mt. Washington declined. Due to Yogananda's long absences, many regulars had come to see Dhirananda as their guru and followed him to his new center. Others were simply too busy trying to make ends meet, or could not afford the gas or carfare. Nationwide, revenue from class fees, book and magazine sales, and donations plummeted. Yogananda's personal expenses had been covered, at least in part, by the 400 rupees his father sent each month, but according to his brother Sananda, who was responsible for sending the bank drafts, the payments ceased in 1930. Unless Sananda misremembered the date, the timing would seem to have been inauspicious.[9]

Physical conditions at Mt. Washington had never been adequately upgraded, and now the operating budget was slashed. But frail furniture and peeling paint were the least of

Yogananda's concerns. In *Trilogy of Divine Love*,[10] a useful book with a close disciple's perspective, Durga Mata (nee Florina Darling) writes that in the early '30s the resident workers at Mt. Washington—15 to 20 of them at various times—received no salaries. Even in 1935, when conditions had improved somewhat, they had to cover their personal expenses, including clothing, with $1 a week.[11] It is said that the situation was sometimes so dire that residents were able to eat only because they grew vegetables on parts of the land.

East–West was published sporadically in 1930 and then shut down completely for more than a year and a half. Remarkably diverse in both subject matter and contributors, the publication contained substantive articles, not only by Yogananda and his teachers but by outside scholars, religious leaders, journalists (e.g., *Los Angeles Times* religion editor James Warnack), and the occasional famous figure, like George Bernard Shaw, Luther Burbank, and the poet Edwin Markham. It was also a revenue source, but capital was obviously required to produce something consumers could buy.

In late 1931 or early 1932, Yogananda mailed a two-page appeal to his national list. "I have bled for this Cause," he wrote, "and staked my freedom for ten years, and given all I had to serve all of you through my Master's great work, and now, in these trying times, the very existence of the work depends upon your cooperation." It was a straightforward solicitation. Expenses at Mt. Washington were $600 to $800 a month, and even small donations could secure the Mother Center and free Yogananda to better serve his constituents through the written word. Donors were promised a monthly lesson "containing the deepest truths."

Accounts by disciples who lived through that period reveal Yogananda as a leader with never-say-die grit who inspired those around him to endure the hardship with positivity and resilience. In *God Alone*, another useful book by a close disciple, Gyanamata reproduces a letter Yogananda wrote in 1933. In it, he says, "Though we have to go through poverty experiences, we must never think ourselves poor and limited. We are rich with

Infinity, unlimited, all the treasures—material and spiritual—which belong to God."[12] He suggests that the very survival of the Mother Center is evidence of God's support, and they should do their part without worrying. He would lighten the mood by, among other things, treating the hard-pressed residents to the occasional Eskimo Pie, the wildly popular bar of chocolate-coated vanilla ice cream. And he rolled up his sleeves to pitch in. According to Daya Mata (originally Faye Wright), in the early 1930s the guru would marshal his disciples onto the ashram grounds in the morning and join them in sweeping, hoeing, planting, and repairing.

At the same time, Yogananda did not deny the difficulties. He often spoke of his trials in starkly dramatic terms, invoking comparisons to the impediments the cosmos placed before Jesus and other religious leaders. He portrayed those challenges as the necessary darkness that reveals the Divine Light, and the requisite evil that allows us to apprehend the Cosmic Good. He rallied his troops like a general up against a formidable foe, and beseeched the Lord for deliverance. As the Depression deepened and his travails intensified, shafts of light broke through. Acts of Grace materialized. His organization not only survived but managed to build a foundation strong enough to support future growth.

Chief among his blessings were the people who gathered around him: the Mother Center staff and the LA volunteers who did the administrative work without which everything would collapse; the network of devotees who kept their local centers going, organized his visits, and contributed their fees and donations; and major supporters who entered Yogananda's realm in the early '30s. Some of them made valuable contributions for a short period of time before leaving the fold, while others became colossally important to their guru and his cause.

One category of significant persons consisted of those who represented Yogananda and his teachings in public. His personal campaigning did not end as quickly as he'd hoped; from 1930 through 1933, his itinerary took him to most major U.S. cities, including New York for a Carnegie Hall sequel and Chicago, where he addressed the Congress of the World Fellowship of Faiths.[13] In his absence, the principal teacher at Mt. Washington was Brahmacharee Nerode, who had stepped into Dhirananda's shoes admirably, combining substantial knowledge, a likeable demeanor, and skillful teaching. A wife and child soon enlarged the Nerode presence on the hill.

The woman who became Mrs. Nerode was Agnes Spencer, a young Coloradan who had moved to Los Angeles to attend UCLA. At one point, money being tight, she took a job at Mt. Washington typing Yogananda's manuscripts. She returned to school in 1928 and subsequently ran into a chum named Gladys Webber, who had also worked at the Mother Center. Gladys arranged a blind double date with two gentlemen from India. One was Brahmacharee Nerode and the other was Dhirananda, who was still in LA. Gladys was legally married to an Indian filmmaker named M. L. Tandon, who had moved back to India without his wife. Later, in 1934, she obtained a divorce and married Dhirananda, who by then had reassumed his original name, Basu Bagchi. The Nerodes married in January 1931 (he was 44, she 24). The term Brahmacharee, with its monastic connotations, was dropped in favor of Sri Nerode.

Because, astonishingly, such mixed marriages were impossible to obtain in California at the time, the couple was legally hitched in New Mexico.[14] On January 23, 1931, Yogananda joined them spiritually on the Mother Center lawn. Newsreel footage of the picturesque ceremony was shown on movie theater screens. In the film, Yogananda says the marriage symbolized the breaking of barriers "between the brown Caucasians of India and the white Caucasians of America." Agnes joined her husband at Mt. Washington, and a year and a half later gave birth to a son, Anil. That happy period would become a rather bitter memory as the decade wore on.

Two colorful characters joined the Yogoda lecture circuit during those years, as Yogananda ratcheted up the showmanship, no doubt in response to economic conditions. At the time, what little money Americans could spare was more likely to be spent on escapist entertainment than edifying philosophy or self-improvement. Hence, the aforementioned Hamid Bey was invited to give mind power demonstrations and lectures under Yogoda's auspices. Most of his appearances were solo, but sometimes the "Miracle Man" was the opening act for Nerode or Yogananda. Dressed in Arabian garb, he stuck long pins through his tongue, stopped his pulse on command, reclined on spikes, had large rocks smashed on his chest, and allowed himself to be buried in a casket for seemingly impossible stretches of time. Some of the ads for "Yogi Hamid Bey, Divine Magnetic Healer and Miracle Man from the Orient" indicate that, while Bey was buried alive, Yogananda would speak on topics such as "Magnetic, Vibratory Healing" and "What Happens 10 Minutes After Death."[15]

Sometime around 1934, Hamid Bey went out on his own. He was accused of publishing material copyrighted by Yogoda Sat-Sanga—which had, for a time, listed him as an honorary vice president—and of teaching Kriya Yoga techniques he said he'd acquired while training in "Egyptian Yoga." In fact, he was about as Egyptian as Cary Grant. He was born Naldino Bombacci in Italy.[16]

Bey was replaced on the circuit by Dr. Roman Ostoja. If the background Ostoja claimed for himself was true, he was a Polish aristocrat who had studied with Indian masters (some accounts say he was born in Cleveland). As "Yogi Ostoja," he gave demonstrations similar to Hamid Bey's, but without the burial. One archival photo shows him bare-chested, lying on a bed of nails with a full-sized man standing on his chest, looking as if he'd just landed a jump. Ostoja was also said to have healing powers. At one point, in fact, he was the resident healer at Mt. Washington, and students were encouraged to take advantage of his services. The affiliation ended in 1938, when it was discovered that Ostoja, who secretly lived large, had run up debts to Yogoda students in several cities.

Why resort to vaudeville-like performances and risk losing credibility or distracting the public from the priceless knowledge of the Himalayan rishis? Why risk the disapproval of Hindu traditionalists? As Anya P. Foxen put it, "Given the general Indian monastic attitudes towards showmanship, and the prevailing notion that siddhis are the byproduct of yogic practice and not its goal, Yogananda's demonstrations of powers on the stage would have been regarded as questionable at best."[17] To the extent that word got back to India about such things, it is safe to assume that Yogananda faced criticism about it, and sources I interviewed in the U.S. and India said that did occur. However, getting people in the door was crucial to Yogananda's mission, and desperate times (i.e., the Great Depression) call for desperate measures. The demonstrations dramatized the ability to control involuntary physical processes through yoga and made people more receptive to the deeper yogic aim of Divine union. By all indications, at no time did Yogananda lose sight of his true message, nor did he ever deprive an audience of hearing it. In this view, he, like other gurus and yoga masters who succeeded in the West, reached out to seekers at their level of receptivity and lifted their gaze.

In any case, Yogananda concluded that phase of his public life by the end of the 1930s, just as he'd previously stopped doing healings because, he said, too many people were interested only in healing their bodies and not in "soul healing." He wanted sincere God-seekers, and, he noted, the path to God was not a circus.

Genuine seekers of high character and deep commitment were the true blessings of Yogananda's life in those years. Their presence not only made possible the longevity of his work; it changed the culture of Mt. Washington. His letters and recorded talks offer moving testimony to his gratitude. He spoke of the dedicated devotees who remained loyal to him and their own spiritual paths like a combination father, brother, friend, and preceptor.

Those dear ones included three women who had met him earlier. Kamala (Mary Isabelle Buchanan) was ordained a lay minister by Yogananda in 1935. She was not active with SRF for a number of years, and then served in a ministerial capacity in the Bay Area from 1949 (when she married for the third time and became Kamala Silva) until she retired in 1974. As mentioned earlier, Edith Bissett moved to Mt. Washington in 1932. As Sister Gyanamata, she became one of Yogananda's most revered disciples and trusted leaders until her death in 1951, four months before Yogananda's own. Equally beloved and relied upon was Florina Darling. A presence at Mt. Washington from 1929 on, she was given the name Ma Durga (later Sri Durga Mata), and served in many capacities, including a long tenure on the board of directors. All three women wrote memoirs that offer valuable insights into life with their guru.[18]

In October 1931, Yogananda conducted a monthlong series of classes in Salt Lake City, Utah. The center of the Mormon universe would not, in those days at least, seem like the best place for a Hindu teacher to garner some of his most eminent disciples, but that's where Yogananda met the Wright family. Descendants of the first generation of Mormons to settle in Utah, five of the Wrights—two sons, two daughters, and the mother—became lifelong devotees. Four of them lived and worked at the Mother Center, and three remained there the rest of their lives. The mother, Rachel Terry Wright, became Shyama Mata; her daughter Virginia became Ananda Mata; Richard kept his name and served as office manager and in other capacities for about a decade (he also accompanied Yogananda to India); and Faye, the older of the two daughters . . . well, an entire book could be written about her, and one is reportedly in progress.

Faye Wright was 17 when she met Yogananda. It is said that his touch on that occasion healed her of a painful and disfiguring blood disorder. Less than two months later, she was living at Mt. Washington. Major decisions made that abruptly often turn out badly, of course, but this one had all the earmarks of destiny, or Grace. She acquired the nickname "Nest Egg" because, Yogananda said, when she arrived he knew that the "nest" of true devotees would grow.[19]

Faye's secretarial skills were put to good use. She took precise stenographic notes at every Yogananda discourse for which she could be present. Her transcripts of lectures and classes—at the Yogoda Course, the Advanced Course, the Super-Advanced

Course, the Super Cosmic Science Course, the Advanced Super Cosmic Science Course—became key resources for the enlarged correspondence course. With the vital help of Richard Wright, the project manager, and two other new residents, Orpha Sahly (later Sraddha Mata) and Louise Royston, the new, seven-step lesson series mentioned earlier, The Praecepta, was completed in 1938.[20] Weighing in at more than 1,500 pages, the Lessons were now more than seven times bigger than all the Yogoda courses combined; they remained the standard until the next major revision, in 1956.[21]

Faye also turned out to be a competent administrator. Ultimately, she grew into a commanding force who would preside over the worldwide operation, as Sri Daya Mata, for an astonishing 55 years (1955–2010). Of most significance for the period under discussion, she may have provided the impetus for Yogananda to create a new monastic community, along the lines of India's ancient swami order.[22] Certainly, she was the first to take renunciate vows. Her sister and others followed. This was a watershed moment in Yogananda's life and work, as Mt. Washington began a gradual transformation from community to monastery. A renunciate order clearly suited both Yogananda's personal predilections and his organizational goals. As a guru, he coveted disciples who were passionately committed to spiritual unfoldment; as the leader of a growing and ambitious organization, he needed dedicated helpers who shared his vision and could focus on the work with as few distractions as possible. The subsequent history of Yogananda's accomplishments was marked by the decision to place vital responsibilities in the hands of monastics[23]—and to empower *female* monastics to an unprecedented degree. Women had always been a driving force in spiritual organizations, but they were mostly behind the scenes, providing food and lodging, arranging venues, hosting salons, contacting journalists and trendsetters, cajoling, imploring, charming, twisting arms, and writing checks or getting their husbands to do so. Yogananda went several steps further in giving authority to skilled, spiritually advanced women, not only by the standards of the 1930s but, in many spiritual institutions, even today.

Ah, but worldly individuals have much to offer as well, and every guru who made a mark in the West has been indebted to resourceful, competent followers who knew how to make things happen and were willing to help. There were many such people in Yogananda's life, like Dr. Lewis, George Eastman, the textile tycoon Alvin Hunsicker, and Warren Vickerman of Philadelphia, to name just a few. One Detroit industrialist who came along during this period stands out in this regard. Oliver Black met Yogananda sometime around 1931, and remained a close devotee while building his company, Peninsular Metal Products, from a literal garage start-up to a multimillion-dollar firm. A few months younger than Yogananda, he became a prominent citizen of the Motor City, and, in time, a teacher of Yogananda's and other yogic methods. Late in his life, Yogananda gave Black the title "Yogacharya." After his retirement, Black wore it proudly as the founder of a spiritual community called Song of the Morning, which still exists.

But there was only one person to whose name Yogananda affixed the word *Saint*. James Lynn was a terrifically wealthy Kansas City resident who had made his fortune in banking, insurance, and other domains. He met his guru in his home town in January 1932. Early on, he said in a 1937 speech, he was sitting with Yogananda when he realized he was unusually still. "I was motionless," he said; "I didn't seem to be breathing." Curious, he looked at Yogananda and "A deep white light appeared, seeming to fill the entire room," and he became part of that divine light.[24]

It was an auspicious beginning for a remarkable guru-disciple relationship and, for Lynn, the launching pad for a radical change of life. He was a classic American seeker, in that he'd realized that enormous success does not bring peace or happiness and had begun the quest to discover what more life had to offer. He had rejected customary religion because it asked him to believe things he could not believe. Yogananda's experience-based yoga was better suited to his pragmatism. It would take a number of years before he was able to move to Southern California and devote himself completely to the spiritual life, but he was at his guru's side as often as he could be while fulfilling his business and family duties at home. From the beginning, he was not only a disciple to Yogananda, but an authentic friend, a beloved brother in many ways, and a benefactor of such magnitude that it is safe to say that the entire mission might have collapsed if James Lynn had been unable to write checks.

Yogananda had been looking for—and praying to Divine Mother for—just such a disciple, someone with a command of material resources and a deep commitment to both his own spiritual advancement and the guru's work. Other wealthy students had apparently made promises they didn't keep.[25] The man he took to calling Saint Lynn was the answer to his prayers. He called him a saint not just because of his extraordinary generosity, but because of his spiritual attainment and his character. In a 1932 letter to him, he wrote: "Nobody in America has drawn such love and appreciation from me as you have by your divine simplicity, self control, and above all your intoxicating, deepening love of God."[26] Yogananda singled out Lynn's "humbleness and his constant oneness with God." He considered him his divine friend, and the love he expressed for him, both in direct correspondence and in letters to other disciples, is profound.

Lynn's first act of kindness was to provide the funds to revive *East–West*. Publication resumed in April 1932, with enough of a budget for monthly, rather than bimonthly, editions.[27] That was just the beginning. Soon he rescued Mt. Washington from the brink by paying off the remaining mortgage. The entire community celebrated the liberation from that heavy millstone by ceremoniously setting the mortgage papers aflame in a bonfire. In keeping with Depression frugality, Yogananda roasted potatoes in the fire. Lynn would continue to make timely contributions and bestow extraordinary gifts for the rest of Yogananda's days—and beyond, as Lynn provided for the organization in his will.[28]

Mount Washington was mortgage free, but not free of finan-cial distress, and the monk/CEO appears to have turned over every stone in hopes of finding cash. The empty rooms at the Mother Center, for instance, were undeployed assets. In a letter to Nerode when the latter was teaching in Texas, he urged him to let people know that "they can live here for $80 per month in a wonderful palatial building and wonderful scenery and healthy mountain top where they are free to meditate or work for the cause as they please." The 80 bucks covered room and board; new tenants were on a three-month probation, and if they stayed three years they became eligible for lifelong membership.

Despite the dire circumstances, Yogananda managed to accomplish a great deal in the first half of the '30s, thanks in large part to his ability to reward supporters with nonmaterial benefits. New local groups were formed, existing ones were solidified with leaders and lay ministers, and a sparkling new temple in downtown Denver was purchased thanks to a gen-erous donor. *Whispers from Eternity*, the collection of his lyrical prayers, sold briskly. He celebrated five straight Christmases at the Mother Center, establishing the tradition of all-day medita-tion that continues to this day.[29] The monastic order was estab-lished. Paint was applied to Mt. Washington for the first time. A "spiritual wishing well" was installed, and a tranquil grove called the Temple of Leaves was created. And in December 1934, what came to be known as the Second Temple was opened in LA, at 711 West 17th Street. Yogananda also made use of the relatively new medium of radio, reaching more people in one broadcast than he might have in a series of local lectures. He was a guest on several programs and had his own Sunday after-noon show for one year each on two different stations (KECA and KNX). The headline on one ad read: "Listen to S. Yogananda in Immortal Self-Illuminating Stories and Spiritual Talks."

Though he worked longer hours than an indentured servant, and also devoted time to his sadhana, Yogananda was described as a jolly guy who enjoyed simple pleasures like cooking up a meal, sharing sweets, playing practical jokes, watching musical and theatrical performances, and organizing auto trips through

America's natural landscape. When it became possible to own a 1930s version of a motor home, he jumped at it. What came to be called "the housecar" was rigged up by mechanics under the supervision of Florina Darling (Durga Mata). Yogananda would pack the housecar with devotees and, sometimes joined by other cars, ride out to the countryside for picnics, hikes, sightseeing, and long meditations in the woods.

Around the start of 1934, when he finally saw his way clear to curtail his "campaign" and devote his energies to the written word, the housecar was turned into a teaching center on wheels. Equipped with a mimeograph machine, a typewriter, and other gear, it was turned over to the Nerodes as a movable home and office. Sri Nerode was now the primary road warrior. While the arrangement proved fruitful for the progress of Yogananda's mission, the living conditions were not easy for a couple with an infant son. This may have been the start of Agnes Nerode's discontent, which would intensify into resentment in the coming years. (A new housecar was subsequently built for Yogananda's use; the house part, complete with shower, toilet, and stove, was constructed by the Pullman Company and mounted onto the chassis of a Dodge truck.)

With all this going on, significant administrative decisions were made. One was a name change. Yogoda Satsanga was replaced by Self-Realization Fellowship, which remains the organization's name in the West today (it is still Yogoda Satsanga in India). What's in a name? In this case, a clear sense of the Western psyche. The new name had an all-American sound, not only because it was shorn of foreign words but because "self-realization" resonates with the Yankee spirit of independence and personal improvement. Yogananda's rationale for the name, Brother Chidananda told me in an e-mail exchange, was that it "perfectly expressed the highest Yogic/Vedantic concept of spirituality: realizing one's individual self (ego) as soul (*atman*); and one's soul as one with the Universal Self ('This *atman* is Brahman')."

On March 29, 1935, Self-Realization Fellowship Church was officially registered as a nonprofit corporation in the state of California, with Yogananda as president, Edith Bisset as vice president, Richard Wright as secretary, and Florina Darling as treasurer. A fifth director, but not an officer, was Karla Schramm, a devotee and a former Hollywood actress who had played the role of Jane in two of the silent Tarzan movies. The word *church* in the new name is significant in that it represents another way of asserting that Yogananda's work was not peripheral to the values of a Christian nation. More important, the organization's status as a religious nonprofit made donations tax deductible and allowed Yogananda to divest himself of all material possessions, and therefore liabilities.

While sitting in deep meditation one day in 1935, Yogananda received a psychic "call" from Sri Yukteswar. The message, he said, was: "Return to India. I have waited for you patiently for fifteen years. Soon I shall swim out of the body and on to the Shining Abode. Yogananda, come!"[30] He took the communication as seriously as he did an actual letter from his father, who was 82 and ailing and wished to see his son. Beckoned by the two beloved elders, he appealed to James Lynn to finance the trip. Lynn came through, plans were made, passage was booked, and farewell banquets were arranged by his students. But the planets were not aligned for smooth sailing.

On Friday, May 3, Basu Kumar Bagchi (Dhirananda) filed suit in Los Angeles Superior Court.[31] He was by then married to Gladys Webber (now Tara Bagchi) and had recently obtained a Ph.D. in electroencephalography from the University of Iowa. Yogananda had made only one of the monthly $100 payments called for in the promissory note he'd signed six years earlier. Dr. Bagchi demanded the remaining $7,900.[32]

Why did Yogananda not make good on the note? One vital factor, and probably the most significant one, was the ongoing financial chokehold of the Depression, then in its sixth devastating year. But it is not unreasonable to conjecture that the severe shortage of funds was compounded by personal pique. Yogananda felt let down and betrayed. It is said that he reached out to mend fences, sending his old friend mangoes either once or every Christmas, depending on the source, only to have them returned unopened. Perhaps that increased his animus. Other reasons were reflected in the cross-complaint he filed on May 12. Yogananda and his legal team contended that Dhirananda, as an ordained member of the Order of Swamis and a disciple at Mt. Washington, had, by tradition, no right to compensation aside from room and board, lodging, incidental expenses, and the cost of clothing. Further, it was alleged that Dhirananda, while in charge of the Mother Center during Yogananda's long absences, had secretly taken from the coffers a total of $16,616.86. This was presumably based on an examination of the books. To that sum was added the $8,000 in the promissory note, which Yogananda claimed to have signed under coercion. Yogananda also rejected Dhirananda's claim to have contributed significantly to *The Science of Religion* and other works. Dhirananda, he said, "had nothing to do with my book nor correspondence course except a few grammatical corrections, which many other clerks and other employees of my institution [also] did."

Bagchi/Dhirananda denied taking unauthorized money and asserted that he had served as Yogananda's partner, not as a traditional disciple. The *LA Times* article describing the claims and counterclaims was headlined: SWAMIS ACCUSE EACH OTHER IN LEGAL BATTLE.

A few weeks later, in a letter to Sri Nerode, Faye Wright said she "can never begin to express to you the sorrow and suffering poor Swamiji [Yogananda] has gone through" over the lawsuit. The harried Yogananda was not only dealing with legal matters but preparing for a journey of indefinite duration and attending to the administrative details at Mt. Washington (Gyanamata/ Bisset was put in charge in his absence, with Durga Mata/ Darling second in command). On May 28, he signed two legal documents. One provided for the assignment of all his personal property to SRF. He gave the new corporation everything he owned, and the articles specified are an almost comical reflection of a life so spartan that its assets could have been disposed of in one trip to a thrift shop: books, magazines, shawls, blankets, typewriters, cooking utensils, icebox, radio, and other humdrum items. The absence of wealth did not make the document any less important. As an attorney familiar with the history told me, "No one could touch the assets now." Yogananda would never again own personal property, or even a bank account.

The second document he signed on May 28 was his last will and testament. It divided any profits that may derive from the sale of his books and other writings equally between the Self-Realization Fellowship in America and Yogoda Satsanga Society in India. The same division would also apply to his ashes should he die "while sojourning in the Empire of India." The executors named were Florina Darling and Edith Bissett.

Three days later, on May 31, Yogananda was deposed in the Dhirananda lawsuit. The hearing would take place in his absence. At midnight on June 9, he set sail from New York to England, the start of a land-and-sea expedition that would, four months later, bring him to Mother India. But any hopes he had of trouble-free sightseeing, unfettered reunions, and the happy bolstering of his movement in his homeland would be compromised by updates from Mt. Washington and bad news from LA Superior Court.

CHAPTER 15

HOMECOMING

For the head of an organization, preparing for a long absence half a world away was no easy task in those pre-Internet days, and Yogananda had the Bagchi/Dhirananda lawsuit to contend with as well. With the help of a dedicated staff, he managed to tie up loose ends, catch a cross-country train and, with a stop in Kansas City to see James Lynn, embark from New York on what turned out to be a 16-month expedition. Joining him on the liner *Europa* were two companions: Richard Wright, who would serve as driver and all-around assistant on the trip, and a Cincinnati matron in her 60s named Ettie Bletsch, who had been living at Mt. Washington and was taking what must have been a dream trip at her own expense. Also on board was a spiffy Ford motor car to get them around on land.[1]

In his autobiography, Yogananda goes into great detail about portions of the journey and glosses over others. Some of the gaps were filled by his letters and by Richard Wright's dispatches to *Inner Culture* magazine, in which he revealed a fine observational eye. On their first stop, Great Britain, Yogananda did some sightseeing, lectured to a large crowd at London's Caxton Hall, and visited the Scotland estate of Sir Harry Lauder, a hugely popular singer of the era. Then the trio crossed the English Channel and motored east to Germany. He was eager to meet the Catholic mystic Therese Neumann in Konnersreuth, a village in the Bavarian hills.

They traversed France, Belgium, and the Netherlands en route. Yogananda lauded the French because they saw no

211

difference "between brown, white, or nubian-dark skins," but he makes no mention of Paris.² Perhaps, to him, the city's charms seemed paltry when compared to a young mystic who had reportedly been healed of blindness and paralysis through prayer, had experienced stigmata (bleeding from the points on the body where Jesus had been wounded on the cross), had ingested nothing more than a daily communion wafer for 12 years, and relived the Passion of Christ in a trance every Friday. Yogananda's eight-page description of his visit to Therese is as colorful and compelling as his tales of Indian sadhus.³

One can't help but wonder what Yogananda's impressions were of Germany. By then, Hitler had declared himself Der Führer (Leader of the Third Reich); the infamous book burnings and the "Night of the Long Knives" had occurred; Dachau and other concentration camps were in operation; anti-Semitism was blatant; and the Nazi military buildup was already massive. What we have, unfortunately, is only this comment, in a summary of the first leg of the trip, dispatched on August 11: "I liked the German awakening—a new Germany."⁴ That sentence can be dissected a thousand ways. Was Yogananda's typically penetrating perception clouded in this instance? Or was he putting a positive spin on Germany's postwar resurgence, hoping its fervent nationalism would take a constructive turn? One perspective worth mentioning is that of Swami Kriyananda, who, as J. Donald Walters, was a monastic disciple in the last years of Yogananda's life. He claimed that his guru saw the writing on the wall and tried to intervene by requesting a meeting with Hitler. Indeed, *Inner Culture* magazine announced that Yogananda intended to meet with both Hitler and Mussolini on his return from India. No such meeting ever occurred, but there is more to the story, and it has to do with past lives.

Yogananda's position on reincarnation was similar to that of virtually every Hindu teacher of note: rebirth is the process by which the soul learns lessons and evolves toward perfection, but spiritual seekers should not spend much time contemplating what their past lives might have been. That said, he sometimes told disciples what he believed their previous identities had been, and he revealed some of his own. One, according to Kriyananda and Durga Mata[5] (as well as disciples I've interviewed), was as Arjuna, the warrior hero whose dialogue with Krishna is depicted in the *Bhagavad Gita*. Another was William the Conqueror, the French-born monarch who ruled England from 1066 to 1087. These claims have sparked numerous theories to explain Yogananda's personality and actions. Be that as it may, one of his reincarnational assertions was that Hitler had been Alexander the Great.[6]

Alexander's fascination with the yogis he encountered in India is well documented by Greek and modern historians.[7] Kriyananda said that Yogananda hoped to revive in Hitler's mind his admiring impressions of the ascetics he'd met as Alexander, and, in so doing, turn the Führer toward the light. That didn't quite work out. But, Kriyananda contended, we have Yogananda to thank for the pivotal turnaround in World War II. In this scenario, Yogananda (and other yogis) "placed the thought in Hitler's mind to invade Russia, thereby dividing his fronts and making it possible for his 'invincible' army to be destroyed."[8] Those unprepared to trust a disciple's remembrances, or the veracity of Yogananda's cognitions, can draw their own conclusions about his understanding of Germany circa 1935.

After Konnersreuth, the Ford climbed the Alps of Austria and Switzerland, whose scenery Yogananda declared "the best in Europe."[9] They wound through Italy, slowed by a broken cylinder head and a costly repair bill, and lingered in Assisi, where Yogananda was moved by the spirit of St. Francis. "As I was visiting his living tomb and put my head on the shrine step," he wrote, "St. Francis appeared to me. Then I saw a tunnel of Eternity in which he disappeared. The entire cellar beneath the church was replete with his vibrations."[10] In Rome, he delivered a lecture, presumably in English, and was captivated by the ruins. He found the sunrise view from the rim of Mt. Vesuvius "especially thrilling," having dreamed of seeing the famous volcano and the Pompeii ruins since childhood.[11]

He offered some political observations as well. "I liked the Italian spirit of unity," he wrote, but he was also upset that Mussolini was on the brink of invading Abyssinia (now Ethiopia) in northeast Africa. A few months later, that invasion having taken place, he wrote to James Lynn that he was "thoroughly disillusioned" by Mussolini, who, he said, "has mighty karma to pay for attacking innocent people without provocation."[12]

From Italy, the travelers headed south and east, moving further back in time at every step. First they crossed the Adriatic Sea to Greece and the roots of Western culture. Yogananda marveled that the Greeks "can almost weave their fancies in alabaster."[13] Then they traversed the Mediterranean to what was known as Palestine, where he expressed sympathy for historic underdogs whose fate in Germany he seemed to not yet fully comprehend: "I liked the awakening of the Jewish people in Palestine, where they are trying to establish a country of their own."[14]

In the Holy Land, he walked in Christ's footsteps. Anyone thinking his expressed reverence for Jesus was merely a ploy to pacify American Christians should read his letters. To James Lynn, he wrote: "His name is alive as before; only the Jesus that was and walked and suffered in the streets of Jerusalem very few people see. He was with me everywhere; and a very special communion I had in Bethlehem . . . He touched me as I entered the ancient menagerie where Mary brought him into the world." As he often did, he transitioned to his natural role as a teacher, letting his disciple know that the true Jerusalem is to be found within.[15]

They crossed the Sinai desert to Egypt. "The sphinx and the pyramids talked to me much about ancient history," he wrote.[16] From there, they sailed on a ship called the *Rajputana*, down the Red Sea, with Arabia and Yemen on the port side and Egypt, Nubia, and Abyssinia to starboard. As the ship turned eastward on the Arabian Sea to India, Yogananda had much to reflect upon, and even more to anticipate. They docked in Bombay (now Mumbai) on August 22 at 2:00 P.M. After 15 long years in the West, he once again inhaled "the blessed air of India."

He would spend a full year in his homeland, longer than anticipated, and his writings during that period reveal the many sides of his personality: the loyal chela, humble before his guru; the man of tender emotions, who loved his family and wept at reunions; the beleaguered executive, putting out fires and raising funds; the teacher, orator, and reaper of souls, delighted to be "amidst people who don't need coaxing to be spiritual"; the inveterate sightseer taking in the scenery from Kashmir to Mysore; the pilgrim soaking up the darshan of holy places and holy people; the evolving soul, anchoring ever more firmly in the Divine; and the frustrated defendant in a lawsuit half a world away, receiving updates, asking questions, and practically shouting instructions.

The biblical adage that a prophet is without honor in his own country clearly does not apply to Indian gurus who succeed in the West. Like Vivekananda before him, Yogananda was greeted like a conquering hero. In Bombay, where he had never been before, he was welcomed at the harbor and garlanded by admirers. Word of his achievements had been spread by a prominent citizen named Dr. V. M. Nawle, who had visited Mt. Washington, and articles about his lecture in London had appeared in Bombay newspapers. Reporters filed into his room at the Taj Mahal Hotel, the largest and perhaps the grandest in the city.[17] But despite the reception and Bombay's lustrous architecture and scenic coastline, he left quickly. "I was impatient," he wrote in his autobiography, "eager to see my beloved guru and other dear ones."[18]

With their trusty Ford loaded into a baggage car, he and his companions boarded what Richard Wright called "an antiquated electric train"[19] and headed east across the subcontinent. The journey to Calcutta would take as long as 38 hours even today, but they disembarked midway in the small city of Wardha, where Mahatma Gandhi was in residence. Yogananda may have been impatient to see his loved ones, but how could he resist meeting a personal, and national, hero?

The *AY* contains nearly 20 pages about the two-day stop-over (August 12–13, 1935), including Yogananda's reflections on Gandhi's life, work, and legacy. "A divine handwriting appears on the granite wall of his life," he wrote, "a warning against the further shedding of blood among brothers."[20] He describes the austere daily routine at Gandhi's ashram, recounts their conversations, and describes the simple meals they shared. He was especially gratified to teach the Yogoda exercises and Kriya Yoga meditation to "Bapu" (as the Mahatma was affectionately called) and his disciples. Gandhi, who had visited Yogananda's school in Ranchi 10 years earlier and said it "deeply impressed my mind," promised to practice the techniques for six years and then tell Yogananda what he thought of them. The leader of a hundred million freedom fighters can be excused if he forgot to send that feedback.

The swami and the Mahatma spoke of many things, from the philosophy of nonviolence to self control to the virtues of avocados. A disciple of Gandhi was present at one conversation, and a portion of his notes was published in a massive Gandhi collection. In reply to Yogananda's question about why there is evil in the world, the Mahatma gave what he called a villager's answer: "If there is good there must also be evil, just as where there is light there is also darkness." But, he added, "It is enough for our spiritual growth to know that God is always with the doer of good." When Yogananda pressed him on why the Almighty permits evil, Gandhi demurred. "I am content with the doing of the task in front of me," he said. "I do not worry about the why and wherefore of things."[21] There is no indication that domestic politics were discussed, but it is unlikely that two proud sons of Mother India could ignore the subject. The British Parliament had just approved the Government of India Act, which, among other things, tried to mollify demands for self-rule by granting a certain amount of autonomy to local governments. It was dismissed as a pacifier by the independence movement and disparaged as a bridge too far by British conservatives. At the time, Gandhi's Congress Party was debating whether to take part in the elections called for by the act (they ended up making significant gains). One can only imagine what the two engaged ascetics had to say about these developments.

Yogananda's welcome at Calcutta's Howrah Station, the site of so many significant arrivals and departures in his youth, was jubilant. His family, friends, and students were proud of his achievements and eager to see the man whom they'd watched grow up, or to see for the first time the uncle, cousin, or famous Bengali they'd only heard about. Hundreds gathered, banging drums and blowing conch shells. The platform was so crowded that passengers had trouble disembarking. Heading the reception were baby brother Bishnu, now 32 and a renowned teacher of physical culture and Hatha Yoga, and Maharaja Shrish Chandra Nundy, the son of Yogananda's patron, the Maharaja of Kasimbazar, who had passed away in 1929. Yogananda and his American friends were ushered through the multitude, weighed down by garlands draped around their necks. A procession of cars and motorbikes rolled slowly to Garpar Road.

The home in which he'd grown to manhood was taller now; another story had been added, and rooms now surrounded his meditation chamber. The entranceway and the interior were decked out as if for a wedding. Music blared, and flower petals and rice were tossed on Yogananda as he entered. He was engulfed by effusive relatives and friends, some of whom had come from afar. Many kneeled and touched his feet, even, contrary to custom, relatives who were older than he, like his sister Roma; they had come to see him as their guru. Yogananda touched the feet of one person: his father. Mr. Ghosh, 82, had recently recovered from a serious illness, but his condition did not prevent him from throwing his arms around his son. "My aged parent embraced me as one returning from the dead," Yogananda recalled in the *AY*.[22] His brother Sananda put it this way in *Mejda*: "They embraced one another as though their reunion were a gift from God."[23]

Another chronicler, Sananda's son Hare Krishna Ghosh, who was 15 at the time, recalled another moving moment from that day. In 1920, shortly before he left for America, Yogananda blessed his nephew in his mother's womb and assured his parents, whose first child had lived less than a year, that they would have a healthy boy. As insurance, he gave them a bangle of gold, silver, and copper to place on the baby's arm. Hare Krishna was still wearing it when he was introduced to his uncle that day in 1935. Yogananda removed the bangle and said, "This boy does not require this anymore. He is quite safe." Hare Krishna also reported that Yogananda initiated him and other relatives into Kriya Yoga.[24]

Yogananda's reunion with his spiritual father was as heartwarming as the one with his biological father. Telepathic messages from halfway around the world may seem fanciful, but to him they were as real as telegrams. He was no doubt relieved, therefore, that Sri Yukteswar, then 80, was alive and well. On his arrival in Bombay, a letter from the guru had awaited him, expressing his pleasure in knowing they would soon reunite. The meeting took place in Serampore a few days after Yogananda arrived in Calcutta. Master and disciple embraced, but not before a more traditional greeting. As Richard Wright observed it, "Yoganandaji dropped to his knees, and with bowed head offered his soul's gratitude and greeting; touching with his hand the guru's feet, and then, in humble obeisance, his own forehead."[25]

He could not stay long on that occasion; another reunion awaited, in Ranchi. With Wright and some friends and family members, he made the 400-kilometer journey by road. After a long, adventurous delay caused by two flat tires, they arrived at Brahmacharya Vidyalaya at 3 A.M. To their surprise, they were greeted by shouting students. Yogananda was moved to tears by the reception, and by the sight of those who had kept the school going in his absence, especially his childhood friend Swami Satyanananda, the former Manomohan Mazumdar.[26]

But all was not well. The Maharaja's death had deprived the school of its major funding, and because he had passed with outstanding debts, his estate was frozen in glacial court proceedings. On top of that, the British government had curtailed its financial aid because some of the faculty were Gandhi supporters. The new Maharaja was helpless to assist financially, but he offered to sell the property to Yogananda on very good terms. With his precious school's very existence in question, Yogananda slipped into CEO mode. "I had not spent years in America without learning some of its practical wisdom, its undaunted spirit before obstacles," he wrote in the *AY.*[27]

In a series of frenzied actions, he mobilized the needed funds from a variety of sources: his father, prominent Calcuttans, and American devotees. One of the key items on his India agenda from the start had been to build a temple in Calcutta. Toward that end, he'd mounted a fund-raising campaign through mailings and notices in his magazine. James Lynn pledged a sum at the same time he agreed to pay for the trip itself. But attempts to find a suitable location for the temple had bogged down. Now, instead, the money would be used to secure Ranchi's future. By October, the deal was sealed. To honor his paramguru, he added a name to Ranchi's institutions: "Shyama Charan Lahiri Mission." At the same time, Yogoda Satsanga Society was incorporated as a nonprofit under the direction of Self-Realization Fellowship in the United States, and the future of Yogananda's beloved school was guaranteed. In letters to Mr. Lynn, his gratitude was unrestrained, as it would be for the rest of his life.

Yogananda's schedule was as intense in India as it was in the U.S., if not more so. "Hundreds visiting me, clamoring for lessons," he wrote to Lynn. "I am busy from morning till one o'clock at night. I am bound hand and foot with the love of people, initiations, songs, and meditations."[28] His teenage nephew Hare Krishna, who was drawn to his uncle's side and called him Guruji, said in his memoir, "We had a permanent stage constructed by the side of our house, so there Guruji used to give lectures every day to the many devotees. . . . Whenever I used to go to school, I would see him in the morning, surrounded by devotees and Guruji answering so many questions. And when I came back from school at 4:00 in the afternoon, I used to see the same thing. Always, Guruji sitting in the middle and surrounded by devotees."[29]

He found the spiritually hungry Indian audiences invigorating after 15 years of American skepticism. At times, thousands showed up at his talks, some of which featured demonstrations by brother Bishnu and his physical culture students. In the coming months, Yogananda would lecture and teach not just in Bengal and Bihar (where Ranchi is located), but in Bombay, Mysore, Madras (now Chennai), Bangalore, and other cities. His speech at Serampore College must have been especially gratifying: "Mad Monk," the indifferent underachiever, returns to his alma mater as a celebrated spiritual leader.

Some of the press coverage was effusive in praise of his speaking skills. "For over two and a half hours, the Swamiji held the audience spellbound by his oration," wrote the *Sunday Times* of Madras. "It was a consummate address. . . . He is certainly the master orator who can sway mass meetings at will." It is not surprising that he was tempted to stay in India. But he knew he would not. And always he voiced that familiar ambivalence: thrilled that he was reaching so many souls, and wishing he could join the sadhus who wander free.

His reception in India was not all mangoes and lotus petals. Newspaper attacks were leveled at him—and, more broadly, at all the gurus in the West—by Dr. Sudhindra Bose, an Indian-born political scientist who had been teaching at the University of Iowa for more than 20 years. In earlier times, Dr. Bose had called Yogananda one of India's "most effective cultural missionaries" and compared him to the revered Vivekananda. Now he turned against him, calling himself gullible for his previous support. In one article, headlined "Swami Business in America," he criticized as "tripe" some of the Yogoda teachings, and he mocked the correspondence course. Decrying teachers he considered "charlatans," he threw around terms like "humbugging the American public" and the "vulgarization of Hinduism."[30] Needless to say, Yogananda objected strongly to the critique, arguing that he was, of necessity, "using business methods in religion," not making a business of religion—as evidenced by the fact that no one was profiting financially from his work.[31] He would reiterate that point many times over the years.

Dr. Bose also referred specifically to the legal battle between Yogananda and Basu Kumar Bagchi—who, as mentioned earlier, had also denounced what he considered predatory gurus in a leading Indian journal.[32] Bose did not reveal that Bagchi was his friend and colleague at the University of Iowa, a fact that infuriated Yogananda almost as much as the vilification itself. In his frequent letters to LA, he exhorted SRF's lawyers to sue Bose for libel, slander, malicious intent, or defamation—or at least threaten such action so the scholar would back off.

To my knowledge, no legal action was ever taken—perhaps because the lawyers felt it would have little chance of succeeding—but Yogananda fought back in the court of public opinion with articles of his own, and at least one by Richard Wright. In the end, he came to see the attacks in a positive light. Bad as it was, the publicity made his presence and his work better known in his homeland.

Sudhindra Bose was a public relations nightmare, but what truly hurt Yogananda's heart and occupied his mind was the Bagchi lawsuit. The trial began on August 21, 1935, the day before Yogananda's ship docked in Bombay (given the time difference, it might have been the *same* day). The absent defendant was represented in court by his attorney, Willedd Andrews. Briefs were filed, evidence was introduced, and testimony was given. Headlines such as SWAMI ASSAILS SWAMI IN LITIGATION OVER NOTE appeared in LA papers. In court, attorney Andrews called on a professor named Edwin J. Dingle to explain the traditional behavior of a chela to a guru. Dingle called "unthinkable" the notion of a disciple receiving financial compensation. Bagchi countered that he was never Yogananda's disciple, and in fact had been made a swami under "ridiculous and farcical" circumstances.

In the end, the judge, Henry M. Willis, bought Bagchi's argument. He also rejected Yogananda's other counterclaims, such as the alleged theft of $16,616.86, for insufficient evidence. The clincher was the promissory note; Judge Willis determined it was not signed under "threats, duress, menace or coercion."

On October 16, he ruled that the plaintiff was to be paid the full $7,900 plus interest compounded at 7 percent annually.

To say that the legal proceedings put a damper on Yogananda's first few celebratory months in India would be like saying an iceberg spoiled a party on the *Titanic*. But he was a fighter, and he would not quit in the face of what he regarded as unfair attacks and false criticism. He fought, he said, for the sake of his students. His close disciple and eventual successor, Daya Mata (nee Faye Wright), said that when supporters got angry about negative comments about their guru, he would call upon them to moderate their reactions and avoid counterattacks: "Never try to appear tall by chopping off the heads of others." Countless students of Yogananda's have reaped the rewards of that advice, but it must be said that, in private correspondence at least, he was not always above lashing out.

In letters from India,[33] he called Bagchi/Dhirananda Judas and Satan, a forger, a betrayer, and a deserter. At times, he urged his attorneys to fight fire with fire by filing charges of forgery; by exposing aspects of Bagchi's past—e.g., the irate husband's punch in the nose; by convincing the immigration department to deport him as an undesirable; and by making it known that the filmmaker M. L. Tandon had sued Bagchi for alienation of his wife's affection.[34] If any of those suggestions were carried out, the effort clearly was in vain. After the verdict, various courses of action—e.g., appeal, move for retrial—were contemplated. In the end, it was decided to negotiate a settlement. Once again, it was James Lynn to the rescue. Bagchi settled for $4,000. It is said that his lawyers pocketed all or most of it.

Two things need to be added before we close the door on the Dhirananda episode. First, Yogananda would always say it was deeply painful to lose the friend he'd loved. Dhirananda may not have considered himself a disciple, but Yogananda clearly saw himself as his teacher, and he claimed to have lavished attention on Dhirananda's spiritual progress. The arrival of a new and exalted disciple, James Lynn, was the spiritual equivalent of finding an ideal mate after a crushing breakup. Yogananda said many times that Lynn was not only an indispensable benefactor but the illumined disciple he'd dreamed of finding.

Second, he said that Sri Yukteswar had warned him about Dhirananda and had predicted trouble when Yogananda brought him to America. In fact, Yogananda said he'd had such premonitions himself. Why, then, did he pull Dhirananda close rather than keep him at arm's length? The answer for many disciples is that Yogananda felt it was his duty, based on karma from their previous incarnation, to set Dhirananda on the right path. He believed Dhirananda had been his son when he, Yogananda, was William the Conqueror. Specifically, according to Swami Kriyananda, Robert Curthose, the oldest of William's three sons, had rebelled against his father in the 11th century and, as Dhirananda in the 20th, wreaked havoc for Yogananda.[35] Depending on one's perspective, of course, the story can be taken as gospel, or as plausible but unprovable, or as simply absurd. To Yogananda, it may have been as real as his memories of Garpar Road.

Less than two weeks after Judge Willis's ruling, Yogananda was in South India as the guest of the princely ruler of Mysore State, one of the largest semi-independent principalities in India. The monthlong idyll, as he calls it in his autobiography,[36] encompassed his usual combination of lectures, classes, initiations, sightseeing, temple excursions, and intimate encounters with saints. He was also such a faithful correspondent that his writing hand must have needed extra Yogoda workouts. His descriptions of India's South, a region with "definite and yet indefinable charm," will awaken sensory memories for those who have spent time there, although modern visitors to bustling Bangalore and hyperactive Hyderabad will find his depictions quaint.[37] One highlight was his visit to the Tiruvannamalai ashram of Ramana Maharshi, perhaps the most revered saint in India at the time. His account of their meeting is short and sweet. But a disciple of Ramana's, Sri Munagala Venkataramiah, was on hand to take notes, and his transcription can be found in his book, *Talks with Sri Ramana Maharshi.*

The author's first impression of Yogananda was, "He looks big, but gentle and well-groomed." He recounts the questions Richard Wright and Yogananda asked and Ramana's pithy, sometimes enigmatic, answers. The account ends with this exchange:

Swami Yogananda: Why should there be suffering?

Sri Ramana Maharshi: Who suffers? What is suffering?

The reply was not meant to be flippant, and it should not be taken as indifference to suffering. Ramana was essentially asking, Who or what is the sufferer? It was a variation of his trademark self-enquiry method, in which devotees ask themselves, repeatedly, "Who am I?" The process leads beyond the intellect, beyond concepts, and beyond words, to the ever-abiding, eternal Self. The only suitable answer, really, is the one Yogananda gave: silence. Or, as the witness to the conversation put it, "No answer." The vignette concluded this way: "Finally the Yogi rose up, prayed for Sri Bhagavan's blessings for his own work and expressed great regret for his hasty return. He looked very sincere and devoted and even emotional."[38]

As was his wont, Yogananda met a number of other sadhus and holy personages in India, and he devoted considerable space to those encounters in the *AY.* One that warranted an entire chapter was his meeting with Ananda Moyi Ma, the adored female equivalent of Ramana Maharshi.[39] He translated her name as "Joy-Permeated Mother" or "Blissful Mother," and described her presence accordingly. She never took him up on his invitation to come to America, but she did visit the Ranchi school, and the students were unlikely ever to forget it. Ramana Maharshi passed in 1950, and Ananda Moyi Ma in 1982, but they are better known in the West now than they were in their lifetimes, thanks in large part to Yogananda's portraits of them.[40]

He also made sure to carve out time for one precious thing he was deprived of in America: his family. Some of his siblings were middle-aged now, and the younger ones he'd known only as kids. In some cases, he was meeting their spouses and children for the first time. One of them, his nephew Hare Krishna, depicts the uncle in him: "He loved children and mixed with all the people alike. He was an early riser. When every morning he used to see us, the children, at home sleeping late, he used to roll small pieces of paper and put those in our ears and noses to make us rise early. He used to say, 'Get up! Get up children! You are sleeping so late in the morning. See the sun is above the sky, so get up quick!'"[41]

His prime concern, of course, was his father. In a poignant moment in a talk he gave on New Year's Day, 1950, he says that, while in Calcutta, he offered to hire a maid for his widowed parent. The old man turned him down. "Service to me ended with your mother," he said. Tears came to the son's eyes. "I bow down to you," he said. "You are a great man." That aspect of his father's life was finished, Yogananda told the audience that day. "He had found some other love, in the love of Divine Mother."[42] When it was time to return to America, Yogananda said good-bye to his father for what turned out to be the last time.

In Serampore that December (1935), Yogananda once more basked in his guru's holy presence. One morning, when the two of them were alone, he exposed a vulnerability that anyone who ever craved a father's or a mentor's unqualified affection will relate to. "I know you love me," he told his aging guru, "but my mortal ears ache to hear you say so." Sri Yukteswar told him that, in his householder years, he'd wanted a son. He found that son in Yogananda. "I love you always," he told him.[43]

"I felt a weight lift from my heart, dissolved forever at his words," said Yogananda. He says that he had often feared that he had not fully won Sri Yukteswar's approval. The admission of insecurity, coming from an evolved yogi who is assumed to be implacably self-contained, is one of the reasons *Autobiography of a Yogi* is cherished by so many readers. According to devotees and scholars I interviewed here and in India, Sri Yukteswar did wonder if Yogananda hadn't become too Westernized in America and had perhaps made too many compromises. If that is so, and there is no way of knowing for sure, his concerns were surely assuaged, as the relationship was clearly as loving as ever.

That Christmas, Yogananda said, he received a precious gift. As he movingly recalls in Chapter 42 of the *AY*, Sri Yukteswar bestowed upon him the honorific by which he has been known ever since: Paramahansa.[44] *Parama* means highest (think paramount), and *hansa* means swan—a symbol of discernment, thanks to the bird's ability to remove only the milk from a mixture of milk and water. Like "Maharaj" and "Maharshi," the title of Paramahansa is given—sometimes by gurus, sometimes by devotees, sometimes by communities—to spiritual masters regarded as exceptional.[45] Yogananda joked that his American followers would have trouble pronouncing the word.

Guru and disciple also had business to attend to. Like a man who knows the end is near, Sri Yukteswar was putting his affairs in order. He told Yogananda his wishes for the governance of his ashrams, the absorption of his organization (Sadhu Saba) into Yogoda Satsanga, and the disposition of his personal estate. Yogananda admitted that he subconsciously denied the obvious implication that Sri Yukteswar knew his time was running out. He also chose to ignore the guru's tacit disapproval when he said he wanted to attend the *kumbh mela* in Allahabad.

For millennia these massive religious festivals have been held every three years in one of four sacred locations. Millions of Hindus—and a growing number of tourists and curiosity seekers—descend on those sites at the appointed times, and the most auspicious time is every 12 years in Allahabad. Bathing at the confluence of the Ganges and Jumna rivers during a kumbh mela is to Hindu pilgrims what a hajj to Mecca is to Muslims. Sadhus leave their caves and forest dwellings and trek to the site (about 120 kilometers from Varanasi); every prominent guru in India hosts a contingent and offers discourses and initiations; and ordinary pilgrims from every corner of the country save their rupees and find a way to get there, packed like sardines in trains, trucks, and buses, sometimes clinging for dear life to the roof and sides of a vehicle or walking enormous distances. Most camp in tents of various quality or sleep in the open on the ground. As a spectacle, the festivals are unsurpassed—the spiritual equivalent of the Olympics, the Academy Awards, and a papal inauguration rolled into one and multiplied by a hundred. So it is no wonder that Yogananda would want to seize the opportunity, knowing it might be the only kumbh he'd ever attend.

He arrived in Allahabad on January 23, 1936, with Richard Wright, brothers Bishnu and Sananda, and cousin Prabhas.[46] They stayed at the home of Prabhas's brother and spent days and evenings on the vast, flat plain of the mela grounds. Yogananda's colorful description (Chapter 42 of the *AY*) has whetted the appetite of many a reader over the decades, and few who managed to get to a kumbh mela have been disappointed. Predictably, he highlights the remarkable yogis he saw and conversed with, and the feeling triggered by those encounters is poignant. They made him yearn once again for the life of the footloose sadhu wandering by the Ganges. But that was not his dharma, and he knew it.

As we've seen, he voiced that longing many times. But the voice was especially powerful in letters from India, where he also describes profound spiritual experiences. They stand as remarkable personal accounts of a yogi's evolving internal landscape. Some excerpts:

> Every thought, every action—even desire—has become a temple of God. The great silent God is playing hide-and-seek with me. . . . God's joy is ever new and ever newly entertaining.

> I can hear carping criticism with as much equal joy as praise. I am in the praising and the criticizing voice; I am both voices. They are unutterable without me.

> How wonderful to love everything, not in a passing way but with deep concentration until love opens a portal into the Love which is everything.

> Last night I was in *samadhi*. My pulse, my heart, stopped; my body was dead and my life force like a comet sprang through the spinal tunnel and head into the blue heavens.

> All matter became my dead body, and within it I saw the Light of all life.

I find I am settled in Bliss. I am awake in Bliss, ever watching the body and mind when they are awake or asleep or dreaming.[47]

On their way back to Calcutta, Yogananda and his troupe made several stops: in Agra to gaze once again at the Taj Mahal; in Brindaban, where he interviewed 90-year-old Swami Keshabananda about Lahiri Mahasaya[48]; in Delhi, for a poignant visit with eldest sister Roma and her husband, Satish[49]; in Meerut, where his late brother Ananta had lived; in Bareilly and Gorakhpur, where he had spent much of his childhood; and in Benares, where Lahiri Mahasaya had lived and where his own life had taken a momentous turn. He arrived in Serampore in late February or early March, eager to see his guru again. Alas, Sri Yukteswar was at his residence in Puri.

On March 8, while at his father's house in Calcutta, Yogananda learned that one of his *gurubais* (brother disciples) had received a telegram saying, "Come to Puri ashram at once." Alarmed, he prayed for his guru's life and started to leave for the train station. A voice came to him saying he should not go to Puri that night. In compliance with what he considered a divine missive, he waited until the next day and took the overnight train with Sananda and Richard Wright. On the way, he says, Sri Yukteswar appeared to him in a vision and let him know he had left his body. The news was verified at the ashram on the morning of March 10, where they found the lifeless "Lion of Bengal" seated erect in lotus posture, as is customary, surrounded by grieving disciples. Yogananda wept. He told Sananda he would never forgive himself for failing to see his master alive one last time.

He was more forgiving in retrospect. He felt it was God's intent that he not have to endure the experience of watching Sri Yukteswar pass, and he noted that when other loved ones died, "God has compassionately arranged that I be distant from the scene."[50] Of course, cynics and psychoanalysts might call it avoidance, not divine compassion, but so much about

Yogananda's life was uncanny, mysterious, and miraculous that debating his interpretation would seem useless, if not rude.

He conducted the funeral services and saw to it that the proper rituals were performed. Sri Yukteswar's body was entombed, in lotus position, in the ashram garden in accord with Hindu custom (the bodies of eminent renunciates are seldom cremated).[51] Years later, on Yogananda's instructions, Sananda supervised the building of a temple on the site.

Yogananda was candid about his protracted grief, using terms like "black brooding" and "tormented spirit" to describe it. Then, three months after his master's death, the darkness was dispelled with another miraculous event. On June 19, the bodily form of Sri Yukteswar came to him. The visitation occurred in his hotel room in Bombay a week after he saw a vision of Lord Krishna from a window in that same room. The conversation, if that's the right term, takes up 20 pages of the *AY*.[52] It consists of a Sri Yukteswar discourse on various philosophical subjects and, most remarkably, a kind of heavenly Baedeker—a vivid, meticulously detailed guide to astral planes, celestial realms, subtle and causal bodies, and the experience of a soul released from its human enclosure. The dialogue was included in his memoir at Sri Yukteswar's behest, Yogananda said, and he acknowledged that many will find it confounding. Some of the readers I interviewed were indeed confounded, calling the account a fiction, a dream, a delusion, an attempt to deceive. But for a large number of readers (probably a larger number), it is among the book's most memorable chapters—illuminating, inspiring, and, in some instances, life changing.[53]

For Yogananda personally, the two-hour event was salutary: "Gone was the sorrow of parting," he wrote, "The pity and grief for his death, long a robber of my peace, now fled in stark shame." It was replaced, he says, by a fountain of bliss.[54]

Yogananda's departure from India was rescheduled a few times. Once so he could again imbibe the beauty of Kashmir; once because there was too much work to be done; and once, at the last minute, because the ship on which they'd booked passage did not have room for the Ford. During the last delay, he returned to Calcutta for unspecified reasons, and on August 14 he filed his last will and testament; he bequeathed his personal accounts at American Express and the Imperial Bank of India to the Yogoda Satsanga Society of India. On August 22, a year to the day since his arrival, he boarded the liner *Naldera* and sailed from Bombay to England.

He spent more than a month in the U.K., occupied with his usual work, along with some sightseeing in London and the English countryside. His London speeches were so well attended that he had to give back-to-back talks, one in a packed Caxton Hall and, an hour and a half later, in another crowded auditorium for those turned away from the first. In light of Yogananda's anxiety 16 years earlier about his command of English, he must have been delighted by the reviewer who wrote, "I have heard few equals of the Swami as an orator."[55] The article also lauded Yogananda's sense of humor; he apparently brought down the house with an imitation of a distracted woman trying to meditate.

In mid-October, it was time to cross the Atlantic. He felt pulled by both Mother India and the America that had adopted him. He had duties in both countries, and he wished they were closer together on the surface of earth. Aboard the *Bremen*, a German liner, his soul was filled with love and loss; his mind was full of plans and obligations; and his body . . . well, his body was full. Indians have a saying, "The guest is God," and they really mean it. "Less than a year of Indian hospitality, and I had gained fifty pounds!" he said.[56]

On October 23, the ship entered New York Harbor. The raised torch of the Statue of Liberty, he said, "brought to our throats joyous emotional gulps."[57] Despite making travel plans on several occasions, Yogananda would never see his homeland again. He would, however, die with the love of India on his lips.

CHAPTER 16

HEIGHTS
AND DEPTHS

The good ship *Bremen* docked on October 23, but Yogananda could not step immediately onto the streets of lower Manhattan. He was detained on Ellis Island, as was noted on a document called "Record of Aliens Held for Special Inquiry." Was he detained because the Dhirananda settlement had not yet been paid (Satisfaction of Judgment was filed on October 30)? Because of his association with Gandhi and support of Indian independence? Both possibilities have been contemplated over the years, but the actual reason for his brief detention was probably far more mundane. Replies to my queries from the U.S. Citizenship and Immigration Services indicate that he was questioned either because he traveled under two names (Swami Yogananda and Mukunda Lal Ghosh) or, the more likely scenario, because his reentry permit had expired. He had renewed it on February 11 when he decided to stay longer in India, but the extension was for only six months; hence it would have expired in August. In any event, things got straightened out, and he reentered America on October 27 at 11:40 A.M. One of the first things he did was enjoy two mangoes from the first harvest of a tree he'd planted at Mt. Washington; they had been air-mailed cross-country to welcome him home.

In his autobiography, Yogananda says that the sturdy Ford, which had traversed thousands of miles in Europe and India, "now took in its stride the transcontinental trip to California."[1] He leaves out that he was not in the car—at least not all the way. He arrived by train at Kansas City's Wabash Station on November 10 for a grand reunion with James Lynn. Another, larger reunion awaited him at the Salt Lake City station, where he arrived on the 16th after brief stops in St. Louis and Denver. A contingent from Mt. Washington had come to meet him. They may have been surprised to find their guru changed. Not only was his body puffed up from Indian cooking, but something had shifted in his soul. That change may not have been visible to the others, but it would manifest in his decisions and actions in the time ahead.

On the way back to Los Angeles, they stopped to view what time and nature had sculpted at Zion National Park and other wonders of the American Southwest. Then, in the California desert town of Barstow, only a couple of hours from home, Yogananda and Durga Mata hopped a train headed 400 miles in an entirely different direction. His destination was San Francisco, where his devotee and former editor, Laurie Pratt, had moved with her daughter after filing for divorce in Atlanta. Yogananda planned to do a lot of writing in this next phase of his life, and he aimed to convince Pratt to move to LA and help him. He succeeded. Laurie Pratt—later Sister Tara, then Tara Mata—would play a major role in the prolific 16 years remaining in her guru's life. They arrived at the Mother Center in plenty of time to organize a festive and heartwarming Christmas.

Conditions in the larger world were more ominous than festive. In the time Yogananda was away, the woeful march of global hostilities accelerated. Hitler's Germany signed a pact with Mussolini's Italy. The two powers began to support the Fascists in the recently erupted Spanish Civil War, and Germany also formed an alliance with Japan. In the Soviet Union, Stalin began his Great Purge, which would claim 8 to 10 million lives in the next two years. On the other side of the world divide, England's King Edward abdicated to marry a divorced American,[2] and President Roosevelt was reelected in a landslide. While FDR's New Deal had helped large numbers of desperate people survive, unemployment was at 17 percent and nearly 40 percent of American families were living below the poverty line. As a spiritual leader, Yogananda was deeply troubled by world events; as the head of an organization, his goals were handicapped by the persistent economic gloom.

But on Thanksgiving, he and his followers had much to be grateful for, and at Christmastime their days were merry and bright. Not long after Yogananda's joyful welcome in LA, James Lynn and Durga took him on a drive, on false pretenses, to the seaside town of Encinitas, north of San Diego. The sisters Wright and their brother Richard surreptitiously drove down ahead of them. A grand surprise had been arranged. Lynn had purchased for his guru a four-and-a-half-acre property on a spectacular clifftop overlooking the Pacific Ocean and a long stretch of coastline.

In fact, Yogananda had selected the property himself. He would, on occasion, set aside time to search the Southern California coast for a suitable retreat site where devotees could go deep in meditation on weekends and holidays, where he could take silence and write, and where James Lynn, the obvious benefactor of such a place, could eventually retire. Opportunities had come and gone, but one property remained on Yogananda's mind. He first saw it in the summer of 1934. "It would be an ideal retreat," he wrote, "a combination of sea and mountains, trees, beach, and complete seclusion." He wrote to Durga from India, urging her to take Mr. Lynn to see the land. "Try your utmost," he said.[3]

She did not have to try too hard. Lynn made the purchase in March 1936. Contractors were given the task of building at least part of a functioning hermitage before Yogananda returned. When his disciples surprised him that autumn day, enough had been completed for him and Lynn to occupy the quarters designed for each of them, and for the rest of the party to share the apartment above a three-car garage. They could even sit in the two meditation caves built into the side of the cliff, reachable by steps, from which only ocean and sky could be seen.

Yogananda was thrilled. He said that he'd had, since child-hood, recurring visions of three buildings. One day, when he was an acolyte in Sri Yukteswar's ashram, he was daydreaming about those buildings when the master snapped him out of it. "In your mental background you were creating three institutions," the master told him. "One was a sylvan retreat on a plain, another on a hilltop, still another by the ocean."[4] They turned out to be, respectively, the school in Ranchi, the Mother Center, and now the Encinitas Hermitage. In the remaining years of his life, he would enjoy countless hours of seclusion and prolific writing—including most of his autobiography—in that serene setting.

Dedicated students along with ministers at Self-Realization Fellowship centers around the country—among them, the Lew-ises, Brahmachari Jotin, Ranendra Kumar Das, Roman Ostoja, Sri Nerode, and of course James Lynn—descended on Mt. Washing-ton to celebrate the holy days and the guru's return. The all-day pre-Christmas meditation was no doubt deeper and more pow-erful than it had been in the absence of Yogananda's wattage the year before. The Christmas Day feast probably seemed tastier and more bountiful. It was certainly more exotic, as were the gifts under the decorated tree; Yogananda and his travel com-panions had hauled and shipped enough foreign merchandise and foodstuffs to open an import shop. One of his pleasures was the seasonal ritual of playing Santa and giving out handpicked gifts. As he did so, Durga Mata recalled, he touched his finger to the forehead of each close disciple and blessed them, saying, "Kali is writing her name in flames on your foreheads."[5]

The day after Christmas, he and a contingent drove the hun-dred miles from LA to see the new ashram, on which additional construction had been completed. Variously called the Yogoda Dream Hermitage, the Hermitage by the Sea, and simply the Encinitas Hermitage, it would soon be expanded and further beautified. When Yogananda took up residence there, he initi-ated a pet project: a four-story, large-windowed Temple of All Religions with an observation tower and a meeting hall over-looking the sea.

The joy and optimism carried into the new year. A Yogoda Convocation was held in early January at Mt. Washington. It featured musical entertainment, "delectable and novel Hindu delicacies," and, of course, speeches. SRF leaders gave brief, ebullient talks celebrating the institution's achievements and praising Yogananda to the skies. Notable for reasons we'll soon discover were the words of Sri Nerode, who at that point was running the SRF center in Miami: "Since I met Swamiji many years ago, little by little I have tried to gather light from his great flame." Yogananda's concluding lecture was titled "Strange Spiritual Experiences and the Resurrection of My Master," in which he told the story of Sri Yukteswar's post-death appearance in Bombay.

As 1937 left the starting gate, there were 19 SRF centers in the U.S., with trained "Conducting Teachers" at the helm in most, and centers in England and India as well. The so-called "Second Temple" in LA was also up and running. Located in a modest residential area about seven miles south of the Mother Center, the small structure at 711 West 17th Street looks in photos like it would fit better in Moorish Spain than in India, with its ornate door and window designs and minaret-like towers on either end.[6] The person in charge at the time was another empowered female disciple, Seva Devi, formerly Jean Chamberlin. Like the Wright family, she had met Yogananda in 1931 in Salt Lake City.[7] Sri Nerode would soon be given responsibility for that center.

The optimism was, of necessity, not without constraints. You didn't have to be Henry Ford or J. P. Morgan to know that demand for products and services had taken a nosedive and the chances of recovery any time soon were as slim as the bodies of the destitute on soup kitchen lines. For the vast majority of Americans, spiritual and self-improvement products were now unaffordable luxuries, much like automobiles and radios and nonessential apparel. Hence money was tight at Mt. Washington, and while James Lynn and, to a lesser extent, other SRF supporters were munificent, they too had limits.

One response to the financial pressure can be seen in the back pages of *Inner Culture*, where SRF items were advertised for sale: Yogananda's books[8]; sheet music for devotional songs; photographs of Yogananda; Self-Realization pins and lapel buttons; books by Ranendra Kumar Das and Brahmachari Jotin (probably more like pamphlets, judging by the low cost); Ora-Mint Alfalfa Tea; Nutritive Nuggets ("the best qualities of meat without its harmful effects"); India Nut Steak (another meat substitute); Mount Washington Prunes (honey-dipped); India Incense; magazine subscriptions; and, most important, the correspondence course.

There were also full-page notices, with a mail-in coupon, for something called the Horn of Plenty Bank. The bank itself was little more than an envelope in which to stash coins or bills on a regular basis. But the package also included metaphysical principles combining essential Vedanta and the prosperity mind-set of New Thought. The purpose, the ad told readers, was to help you "demonstrate in your life the abundance and success which are yours by Divine right." Part of the package was a booklet titled *The Law of Demonstration.* It taught that meditation, prayer, and affirmations could be used to cultivate habits of mind for the fulfillment of material desires. On the theory of "Give and it shall be given unto you," followers were encouraged to send a portion of their savings to the Mother Center "to help carry on the holy work of spreading God's message to suffering humanity."[9]

It is reasonable to assume that Yogananda was not entirely comfortable with what could be seen as commercialism. At his opening talk at the Convocation, he noted that financial struggle was typical for spiritual teachers who start movements, and acknowledged that he'd been forced to think of ways to bring in money to maintain and expand the organization. When SRF was finally on sound financial footing, he said, he would stop charging for classes. He never quite saw that day; some classes would always entail a fee, although he offered hundreds of free talks and classes in his Southern California temples during his remaining years.

But he did see, immediately, the fulfillment of one important desire. He could, at long last, cease his peripatetic ways and stay put, commune with God, and broaden the reach of his work by training future leaders and writing. He now had two peaceful, comfortable locales in which to do that. With the exception of a trip to San Francisco, Yellowstone, and Salt Lake City in 1938 and one to the East Coast in the fall of 1941, he spent the next six years in Southern California (a planned vacation to Mexico in 1940 was canceled because the government advised that it would be unsafe). The itinerant spiritual teacher settled more deeply into his dual roles as satguru—a preceptor who guides the spiritual progress of close disciples—and jagadguru—a world teacher who expounds perennial wisdom to the masses.

He now had more peace and quiet, but his was an intensely active seclusion. He worked on books, first completing *Cosmic Chants*, a collection of original and adapted devotional songs; he penned articles for the then monthly magazine[10] on subjects ranging from his yogic interpretation of Omar Khayyam's *Rubaiyat* to commentaries on the increasingly dire world situation; he conducted services and led classes in Encinitas and LA; he supervised landscaping and construction in Encinitas; he gave talks at various institutions; he created new Lessons for advanced students; he met with devotees for private instruction and spiritual guidance; and he oversaw, through perpetual correspondence, the progress of his centers in India and the U.S. He was a very busy hermit. But he always advocated biting off more than you can chew, and then chewing it.

In this new phase of his life, Yogananda was an ongoing presence to disciples and workers. As a result, we have descriptions of him as a guru, an executive, a boss, and a unique personality.[11] The memoirs of devoted disciples, typically lavish in praise of their guru, are indispensable witnesses, but they are no more complete than a loving child's eulogy to a parent. Bearing that in mind, the portrait that takes shape is of an exceptional human being, similar in early middle age to the teenager who came of age in Calcutta. He was a serious man with a serious and singular mission, a determined, disciplined, demanding dynamo who slept only three or four hours a night (he was reportedly a good napper) and kept his disciples hopping, and yawning. He was also fun loving, playful, mischievous, and childlike, with an easy, infectious laugh, a practical joker who liked silly gags, such as (according to Swami Kriyananda) "Your teeth are like the stars. They come out at night." He found joy in simple pleasures, got excited by gadgets and toys, and delighted in beauty both man-made and natural. The New York spiritual teacher Hilda Charlton told of a time Yogananda became highly animated by something he'd seen. She thought it might have been some ecstatic vision. It was a garbage disposal, and he was eager to show it to her.

Yogananda told disciples not to waste time with diversions like radio and movies, but to use their spare time to turn inward and commune silently with God. Still, he took pleasure in innocent diversions. He enjoyed mechanical toys, for instance, like the French singing bird he delighted in receiving as a present one Christmas late in his life. He listened to the radio, read popular comic strips like *Blondie* and *Bringing Up Father*, and enjoyed the cinema. "Master went to the movies to get away from the telephone or interviews," Durga Mata recalled in her book. "He liked westerns, horror, or fighting pictures." He would play practical jokes on devotees during the films, "poking this or that one with his cane, and then pretending innocence," and surreptitiously putting wadded-up pieces of tissue in their hair.[12] The movies may have been entertainment, but they also gave Yogananda a metaphor he used repeatedly: life as we experience it is the cinema of God. We get caught up in the human spectacle like theatergoers are gripped by the comedies and tragedies on the screen, and we mistakenly think the images and illusions constitute the whole of reality. Don't be troubled by any of it, he urged his students. Take your attention back to the projection booth and see the pure beam of infinite, eternal light, from which all the transient dramas arise.

In a culture where religious leaders were often somber and grave, it must have been refreshing, if not revelatory, to find one who could, on the one hand, raise the rafters like a Hindu Southern Baptist who preached in stentorian tones and beseeched God in antique "Thee"s and "Thou"s, and also guffaw over Charlie

Chaplin, pour water on the heads of disciples below his window, and turn a love song like "Ah, Sweet Mystery of Life" into a devotional chant.[13] Yogananda never stopped enjoying picnics and auto trips, whether spontaneous or planned. He would take off with a few disciples and maybe camp on a cliff near the ocean or in a wooded grove, him in the housecar's foldout bed and his companions on the ground in sleeping bags. He gazed at stars through a telescope. And while he saw nature's grandeur as both a gift from God and a doorway into the Divine, he also liked watching Fourth of July fireworks and flying kites.

He swam in the pool built mainly for that purpose at Encinitas, and in the ocean below the hermitage, even in the winter when the Pacific can be so cold that few today venture in without wet suits. He also delighted in games, and sometimes challenged people to a race or a tennis match. Roy Eugene Davis, who became a disciple in 1949, wrote about the time he happened by the Ping-Pong table at Mt. Washington just as Yogananda was passing by with the Wright sisters. "He motioned for me to pick up a paddle," says Davis. They volleyed gently for a bit, and then, with a gleam in his eye, Yogananda whacked the ball past his opponent "with a fast, forceful stroke of his paddle." Then he asked the women, rhetorically, "And *who* used to be the best table-tennis player around here?"[14]

He also remained as much of a foodie as he had been in India. He could comfortably go long periods of time without eating, it seems, but when he ate he dug in with gusto. According to Durga Mata, he typically consumed only one cooked meal a day—Indian-style, with his fingers, except around guests—and would nibble from the Mother Center refrigerator. He loved to cook, and as a chef was a perfectionist. Hosting feasts was a favorite pastime. In his repertoire were meat and egg substitutes, and he loved it when guests could not tell them apart from the real thing.[15] Clearly possessed of a sweet tooth, he adored mangoes and lychee nuts, enjoyed American ice cream, and was especially passionate about traditional Indian "sweetmeats," sometimes spending hours cooking up varieties like halwa. He eventually lost most of the 50 pounds he had gained on his travels, but he fought the belly bulge in subsequent years.

Other traits assigned to him include: psychic powers and healing abilities; sentimentality (his letters contain effusive expressions of praise and affection); profound loyalty; generosity (he loved to give things away, and was said to bargain down prices only to tip the salesperson more than he'd saved); energetic, even fiery; sometimes quick moving, sometimes languorous, always inwardly calm; possessed of penetrating insight into what made people tick; stalwart and persistent; positive, confident, enthusiastic; charming, magnetic, charismatic. About that last quality, he clearly commanded attention and retained the natural leadership qualities he'd displayed as Mukunda. "Wherever he went, people deferred to him," Kriyananda wrote.

He was also one tough guru. He expected—demanded—a great deal from the people around him, and he did not pull punches when they failed to measure up. Being stern and uncompromising with disciples was consistent with Sri Yukteswar's example—and standard operating procedure for a great many gurus who smoothed the rough edges of egos with psychological sandpaper. He voiced Sri Yukteswar's admonition "Learn to behave," and he made the point emphatically in feedback ranging from gentle sarcasm and good-natured coaxing to rip-roaring rebuke. With the possible exception of Saint Lynn, it seems that none of the close disciples was spared, and those who survived and flourished under that exacting tutelage were uniform in their gratitude. "I admit there were times when I went to my room and shed tears," said Daya Mata (Faye Wright) of being scolded in front of others. "But I didn't let him know it, because I knew he was right. Every time Guruji disciplined me . . . I never could find fault with his judgment. I always knew he was right: I must correct *myself*."[16]

Another early disciple, Mrinalini Mata, who served as president of SRF from 2011 to 2017,[17] concurred with her predecessor: "The relationship we had with Gurudeva was of the closest divine friendship that you could imagine in this world," she once said. She added, "To those who were receptive, to those of us who asked for his guidance in overcoming the delusive ego, he was relentless—and we wanted him to be."[18]

Perceptive gurus, and clearly Yogananda was one of them, work on recalcitrant egos according to the disciple's needs and personal traits. In some cases, instead of a reprimand, the sandpaper might take the form of disregard or withdrawal of attention. That seems to have been the case with Gyanamata (Edith Bissett), and she understood. "No matter what you refused or withheld from me," she wrote to Yogananda, "I never thought you were in the wrong. I always knew that any pang I might feel came from the shadow thrown on my life by desire—wanting something for myself." She sensed that her age may have had something to do with how the guru treated her. A woman of considerable dignity, she was 24 years his senior. She asked him for a favor: "That you will not spare me on account of my age if I ever merit reproof," because, she added, "I have come to you for Self-realization, not self-pleasing."[19]

Yogananda explained his own severity in much the same way he came to understand Sri Yukteswar's. Directly or indirectly, he let disciples know that he did what he did to make them as strong as he was. The true disciple's job is to serve, to do the guru's bidding, to emulate the master and tune in to his consciousness. It is a life of surrender, trust, and unconditional acceptance. Gyanamata sums it up in the guru's own words with an anecdote about a time when Yogananda was prepping followers for a wedding he was about to perform. A woman complained that he gave her a red rose when she wanted a pink one. He said, "What *I* give, *you* take."[20]

Clearly, the traditional guru-disciple model works only when a skilled, ethical, and highly conscious guru attracts stable disciples with whom he or she is well matched. A poorly matched guru and chela can be as dysfunctional as the marital equivalent. True disciples see humble surrender to the master's will as essential to their spiritual development. To others, it amounts to subservience, oppression, or dependency. As Yogananda observed of those around Sri Yukteswar, many are called to discipleship, because the perceived spiritual benefits are enticing, but few are chosen, because the life is too demanding for most. Over time, seekers generally gravitate to more appropriate orbits around the atomic nucleus of the guru. Yogananda seemed to have acknowledged as much, telling Gyanamata, for instance, that "you and a very few others have fully lived up to my expected standard of highest spiritual life."[21] Hence, disciples are few and students are many.

Which brings us to Sri Nerode and his wife, the former Agnes Spencer. Judging from public statements and letters between Yogananda and Sri Nerode, the two Bengalis clearly held one another in high regard throughout most of their association, with the occasional disagreement over matters of money or marketing. Most of Sri Nerode's correspondence reflected a disciple's deference to and respect for the guru. In one example, from December, 1936, he calls Yogananda "Gurudeva" and signs off "yours in eternal discipleship." The following year, in a speech at Mt. Washington, he said, "Our relation has been a relation of master and disciple."[22] In later years, however, Sri Nerode indicated that he saw himself more as an employee, colleague, and friend than as a disciple in the classical sense, and Agnes suggests she was Yogananda's student and a worker for his cause, but her commitment was not on the level of others at the Mother Center.

As noted earlier, the Nerodes lived and worked at Mt. Washington for the better part of three years, then traversed the country in the SRF housecar. From Sacramento to Shreveport, Duluth to Dallas, their years on the road were no doubt grueling, and the conditions for raising a small child less than ideal. It was also the height of the Great Depression, and their letters are marked by an ongoing struggle to generate enough revenue from Sri Nerode's courses to pay the bills. It was probably a relief, especially for Agnes, when they seemed to have found a home in Miami. According to their son, Anil Nerode, who grew up to be a mathematician and professor at Cornell University, his parents had planned to establish an SRF temple in Miami.

Yogananda had other ideas. He called them back to LA to run the 17th Street temple.

As a young wife and mother, Agnes probably did not relish living ashram-style again. In those early years, Mt. Washington was one part idyllic refuge and one part hornet's nest. Spiritual communities are by no means immune to the afflictions of other human groupings—backbiting, maneuvering for influence, competition for perks and the favor of authority figures—and they can even be breeding grounds for such dynamics. While the Mother Center was exemplary in many ways, Yogananda was sometimes compelled to admonish inhabitants to behave better and to work out their differences without the need for his intervention.

The Nerodes returned to LA in April 1937. After what appears to have been a cheerful beginning, things went gradually downhill. Exchanges between the couple and Yogananda grew testy, mainly over finances, accommodations, and friction between the Nerodes and some of the other residents. At one point, Nerode's weekly remittance was reduced (as were those of other ashram residents, according to SRF archivists) and the family was moved from their rooms on the second floor, below Yogananda's quarters, to a smaller, darker space on the bottom level. Agnes did not like this. In her notes she seems to strain to show the expected politeness and respect while also making her demands plain. Yogananda's replies were firm. The Depression raged on, Mt. Washington could not meet expenses, and the Second Temple, which he'd hoped would be self-sustaining, was instead costing money. Out of necessity, he said, the Nerode's original quarters had to be given to rent-paying residents. He indicated that other devotees were making similar sacrifices.

The tension came to a head, and the Nerodes were ousted in the fall of 1939. The official notice of termination cites multiple reasons for the dismissal.[23] In October, Sri Nerode filed suit in Los Angeles Superior Court under his original name, Nirad Ranjan Chowdhury. Like his predecessor, Dhirananda, he claimed to have been Yogananda's partner, based on an oral agreement. Now he moved to dissolve the supposed partnership and obtain his share, which he claimed to be $500,000 (more than $8 million today).

The case dragged out for more than a year, through legal wrangling, delays, depositions, and testimony—and, at intervals, heated press coverage. In December 1940, the inevitable verdict came down. Judge Ingall W. Bull found no legal basis for a partnership agreement, even if the concept of partner had any real meaning in a nonprofit corporation. More to the point, in 1929, in the aftermath of the Dhirananda debacle, Sri Nerode had signed a document stating that what was then called Yogoda Sat-Sanga Society "will be in no way responsible for paying me a salary" and "I am giving my services of my own accord without any remuneration or compensation other than provided me by the local centre." He further agreed never to claim a salary or any portion of the income derived from Yogananda's books and other products. Case dismissed.[24]

The Nerode saga as a whole was not as neat as the courtroom verdict, however, and its ancillary fallout persists to this day in private debates and social media exchanges. Nerode's original complaint included accusations that Yogananda's "personal way of living and conduct" was "repugnant and prejudicial to the interest and objects of the partnership." He put forth a colorful list of allegations, which included: that Yogananda taught that he was God; that he claimed God spoke through him alone; that he tried to break up the Nerodes' marriage; that he lived well and dined lavishly while his followers subsisted on meager rations; and even that he had encouraged followers to practice polygamy. Predictably, the press pounced on the lurid allegations about Yogananda and women. Articles citing court records shouted that the guru surrounded himself with young girls who went in and out of his room at all hours of the night. Yogananda categorically denied the accusations, of course, and other Mt. Washington residents offered to testify in his defense. Like the astronomical $500,000 demand, the inclusion of the sensational claims could be seen as an attempt to induce a favorable out-of-court settlement.[25] To SRF officials, the appropriate term is extortion. In fact, Yogananda claimed in writing that, prior to filing the lawsuit, Nerode had demanded $20,000 under threat of going public with damaging information. Which is probably why local headlines roared that Yogananda called Nerode a "dirty chiseler."[26] Yogananda's counsel, a prominent lawyer named A. Brigham Rose, moved to have the more lurid charges stricken on the grounds that they were not pertinent to issues of partnership and money. The judge granted the request, labeling the allegations not only irrelevant but "slanderous and libelous." Nerode's lawyer redrafted the suit, and the new filing was eventually ruled upon as described above.

The tales of sexual impropriety disappeared from the courtroom, but not from the Nerode family archives or from online discussion groups, where a small but passionate group of Yogananda followers and ex-followers debate such issues. This book does not have the space to adjudicate the claims and counterclaims adequately, or to fairly present the documentation that has been marshaled to support both positions. I have examined all of it and have communicated with individuals who have devoted considerable time to accumulating Yogananda-related materials. Had I found verifiable evidence that Yogananda had sexual affairs or exploited female disciples, I would not have hesitated to report it. But I did not. I found hearsay, inference, speculation, and a handful of statements from a few people who were in Yogananda's orbit at the time but whose objectivity would have to be considered questionable.

Regarding the allegations that Yogananda ran Mt. Washington as some kind of harem, SRF leaders then and now have pointed out that men and older women also lived on the third floor, where the guru's quarters were located, and they too went in and out of his rooms at odd hours. Because he slept so little, they note, people often worked deep into the night (a common phenomenon around gurus). It is also argued that illicit activity involving a number of people would be impossible to keep secret in the fishbowl of an ashram, and no one who lived there, other than the Nerodes, ever made such charges. Some explicitly refuted the claims, and one, Faye Wright/Daya Mata, did so under oath many years later.[27]

Clandestine affairs are a different matter, of course, and no objective observer could definitively rule them out of *anyone's* life. Surely, for most of his students and admirers, the idea of Yogananda participating in such a thing is inconceivable and entirely out of character—a perfectly defensible position given the abundance of firsthand descriptions of him as a man of moral probity. Also understandable, given the history of scandalized gurus and spiritual leaders, are those who find it hard to accept that even an accomplished yogi with an arsenal of methods for redirecting sexual energy (and who said he found God more tempting than temptation) could remain celibate when surrounded by adoring women. But those are subjective viewpoints. The salient fact is this: no woman ever claimed to have had sexual relations with Yogananda—not even in posthumous letters, diaries, or memoirs.

One young aspiring actress who resided for a short period at Mt. Washington in the late '30s claimed in a letter to Sri Nerode that Yogananda had attempted repeatedly and unsuccessfully to seduce her.[28] SRF maintains that the letter was part of Mr. and Mrs. Nerode's alleged blackmail scheme. In their view, the couple persuaded the girl to concoct the story and predate the letter to a time before the lawsuit, by promising a large sum from the money they hoped to acquire in a settlement. That contention was supported by a written statement from Yogananda's former chauffeur, who said he was an intimate friend of the girl and had been offered $10,000 by the Nerodes to testify falsely about Yogananda's character. (A document signed by another SRF employee described a similar bribery attempt.) Predictably, rebuttals and counter-rebuttals have been made by both sides, and an irrefutable verdict would be impossible to render. The fact remains that, to my knowledge, none of the accusations of improper behavior by Yogananda rises to a reasonable standard of evidence.

Another allegation surfaced long after Yogananda's death: that he had fathered a child.[29] In 2001, a now-defunct alternative newspaper called *New Times LA* created a stir with an article about an Oregon miner named Ben Erskine, then 68, who believed he was Yogananda's son. His late mother, a professional photographer named Adelaide Erskine, had been a Yogananda devotee. The youngest of Adelaide's five children, Ben was the only dark-skinned one, and her husband evidently knew he was not the boy's father. It should be stated emphatically that Adelaide never told Ben who his actual father was.[30] Two DNA tests showed that Yogananda and Ben were not related, but the sampling procedures were called into question and a third test was done. This time SRF hired a former San Diego prosecutor, G. Michael Still (of the law firm Liedle Getty & Wilson), to oversee an independent test. The lab work was performed by two different companies, one in Missouri and one in Louisiana.[31] Each concluded separately that no biological connection existed between Yogananda and Erskine.[32]

To repeat, my research did not uncover any credible evidence that Yogananda ever broke his vow of celibacy. Add to that his positive impact on millions of lives and the reverence with which he was held by the great majority of people who knew him, and it would seem that he deserves the benefit of the doubt, at the very least.[33]

Before we leave this delicate subject, we must ask why it is that people get so exercised about the purported sex lives of spiritual leaders. One reason is that we tend to place them on pedestals so high that many of them would rather not climb on board. The veneration not only sets up followers for disappointment when the gurus turn out to be human, as they all are; it also invites backlash, as some people love to topple pedestals as much as others love building them. Portraying gurus as godlike also denies them the credit they deserve for growing, learning, maturing, and evolving as human beings. Yogananda said that a saint was a sinner who didn't give up. We can't possibly know what inner struggles he may have kept to himself on his way to the sanctified status that was eventually bestowed upon him. But if we did know, would the spiritual principles he articulated so well be any less true? Would his Kriya Yoga be any less effective? He asked people to examine his ideas with rigor, and to practice his methods with diligence; he did not ask to be turned into an object of worship. He said, many times in many ways, "I am not the guru. God is the guru. I am God's servant." He also said, "After my passing, the SRF teachings will be the guru."[34]

In the larger picture of Yogananda's life and legacy, the Nerode upheaval was a bump in the road—a noisy and bruising one to be sure, but, as he once wrote to Dr. and Mrs. Lewis, "A life without trouble and vicissitudes is tasteless, insipid. Troubles come, let them come, they will be your stepping stones for your upward climb."[35] He had been remarkably productive in the three years before the Nerode lawsuit, and he continued apace during and after it.

In general, the nature of his work shifted after his trip to India. Perhaps the change was catalyzed by his return to his roots, or by his guru's passing, or by his new, more exalted title of Paramahansa.[36] Clearly, the time had come to delegate certain tasks and to focus on posterity. Quality of disciples rather than quantity of students became his priority. The culture around him at Mt. Washington and Encinitas became more monastic, and the residents were more committed.

Most of his lectures now were at his home bases on Thursday nights and Sunday mornings, and hence more like sermons to the flock than orations to strangers. Many of the talks were dutifully transcribed by Faye Wright and others, ultimately to be collected in anthologies such as *The Divine Romance* and *Man's Eternal Quest*. In his public talks, the occult demonstrations of the past were gone. He was philosophical and instructional, but also spoke about world conditions—the ongoing economic depression and persistent despair, the buildup to war, and the need to cultivate inner peace as a prerequisite for the outer kind. He kept up with the news and made his perspective known.

In fact, shortly after the Nazis invaded Poland and Britain and France declared war on Germany (September 3, 1939), he wrote to British Prime Minister Neville Chamberlain with a win-win proposition: Britain should grant India complete self-government; in return, Indians would give their wholehearted support to the war effort. The suggestion was, of course, decisively ignored. Needless to say, Yogananda could not stop Pearl Harbor or the devastation that followed. But he never stopped speaking out, and the urgency that drove his labors was partly fueled by the tenuous condition of humanity. He felt that the teachings he represented were what the world needed, and he pushed himself accordingly, perhaps to the detriment of his health.

Other notable developments occurred in the years following his return from India. In 1938–39, to cite an especially meaningful example, his brother Bishnu came to America. With the help of Yogananda's imprimatur and James Lynn's financial aid, Bishnu and his principal student (and future son-in-law), Buddha Bose, demonstrated and taught muscle control, as well as Hatha Yoga techniques, in various locations.[37] The brothers' reunion must have been especially poignant because, in 1937, their older sister Roma had passed away at age 50. Bishnu was the last member of his immediate family whom Yogananda ever saw.

Of most enduring import were his literary and organizational activities during this period. In addition to the transcribed sermons, the magazine articles, and the many poems and songs, he progressed with his commentary on the life and teachings of Jesus. The work would eventually be edited and organized by disciples and published posthumously in two volumes (more than 1,500 pages) as *The Second Coming of Christ: The Resurrection of the Christ Within You.*[38] Along the way, articles by that title were featured in issues of *East–West/Inner Culture.* Of most significance, he also made progress on the personal reflections that became *Autobiography of a Yogi.*

He also clearly felt a strong need to solidify what he'd achieved and to secure the future of his work. His literary output was part of that effort, and so was nurturing the spiritual development of his eventual heirs, strengthening existing centers and establishing new ones, producing guidelines for utopian "brotherhood colonies," and initiating the building of permanent structures. One such project came to fruition in October 1939, but he never got to see it. Yogoda Satsanga Society of India opened a serene, handsomely landscaped ashram overlooking the Ganges in Dakshineswar, just down the road from the

Kali temple where young Mukunda had spent so much time in divine communion.[39]

The architectural center of his attention was Encinitas, where he did his most productive writing, in a quiet corner of his study with a spectacular view.[40] He took a hands-on approach to the property's expansion, beautification, and development, the heart and soul of which was the Golden Lotus Temple of All Religions. With its gold, lotus-shaped crowns serving as a beacon to automobiles on Highway 101, the temple opened formally on Sunday, January 2, 1938. As many as 3,000 people reportedly showed up, necessitating two services instead of the scheduled one. Yogananda described the experience of being in the sanctuary, with its statues of Jesus, Krishna, Babaji, Lahiri Mahasaya, and Sri Yukteswar,[41] and its large window facing west, as "a commingling of the soul with the vastness of the sky and ocean as one offers his devotion to God on the altar of the horizon."

For the next four years, he held forth on more Sundays in Encinitas than he did in LA. And then, on July 21, 1942, with American troops fighting in the Pacific, with Japanese-Americans herded into relocation camps, and with German soldiers occupying much of Europe, Yogananda's beloved temple started to slide down the cliff toward the sea.

CHAPTER 17

THE YOGI
IN WINTER

The last 10 years of Yogananda's life—spanning World War II, Indian independence, the postwar recovery, and the beginning of the Cold War—were, in most essential ways, a continuation of the previous five, only more so. Increasingly inward and withdrawn, he was nevertheless inordinately productive, not only by sannyasi measures but even by the standards of prolific writers and heads of spiritual organizations. Those two roles reinforced one another; the durability of his hard-won achievements depended on a solid, financially secure organization manned by dedicated, competent, spiritually advanced disciples who had in their arsenal an archive of written materials to extol the wisdom of the rishis, generation after generation. He also knew that both his practical aims and his spiritual aspirations were best served by time spent in silent communion with the Divine.

His was a thoroughly engaged seclusion with forays into public life balanced by long dives within. During and after the war, he addressed world affairs in his writing, in his public talks, and in gatherings of devotees. Sometimes he spoke about specific issues, such as postwar U.S. policy toward China or the bitter partition of his homeland into India and Pakistan. At other times he issued broad appeals to world peace, the brotherhood of man, and the unity of nations and religions, in the spirit of

THE LIFE OF YOGANANDA

the Sanskrit maxim *Vasudhaiva Kutumbakam* (the world is one family). He compared war to a disease caused by the release of toxins in the body: "When there is too much selfishness in the international system, that poison breaks out in the world as the disease of war." And war will always be with us, he lamented, "until perchance we all become so spiritual that by the evolution of our individual natures we will make war unnecessary."[1]

In the first issue of *Inner Culture* after Pearl Harbor, Yogananda urged readers to buy Defense Bonds to help safeguard "Motherland America." He spoke of the strength of "our united soul-force" and urged everyone to seek first the Kingdom because "God and ideal living are the best bomb-shelters." That message was consistent throughout the carnage and the grief. In his first New Year's message after the Allied victory (January 1946), he implored followers to help war-ravaged Europe and India not only materially but with prayer and meditation, and by sharing copies of *Autobiography of a Yogi*—an odd suggestion because the book would not be published until December of that year. Faster timing must have been anticipated.

Yogananda told Americans that victory was certain because their country was not waging an aggressive war and had accrued plentiful good karma. After the war, he asserted that the benevolent karma would enable America to prevail against any future aggressor (one wonders what he would have said about Vietnam). He linked his own karma to his adopted country more officially when, in 1946, he took advantage of a change in immigration laws and applied for citizenship. He had argued on behalf of eligibility for Indians when the old policy was being debated, stating in a letter to the editor in the *New York Times* (February 18, 1944) that "America and India can make valuable contributions to each other's well-being." His application was approved in 1949 and he became a naturalized U.S. citizen.[2]

During the war years, Yogananda's heart must have ached for Mother India, as its people suffered horribly. More than 2.5 million Indian soldiers and 14 million laborers were mobilized by the British, who also drained the country's resources—iron ore, textiles, coal, timber, medical supplies, and foodstuffs—for its own wartime use, creating severe economic distress and massive food shortages. Approximately 3 million Bengalis died in the famine of 1943. On top of everything, the Japanese bombed Calcutta, which was a major British transportation hub. Prime Minister Winston Churchill, a heroic figure in the annals of World War II, revealed his dark side in response to India's woes: "I hate Indians," he said. "They are a beastly people with a beastly religion."[3] The famine was India's own fault, Churchill said, because its people breed like rabbits. Amid reports of all the horrors came news of personal loss that surely broke Yogananda's heart. His beloved father, the beneficent soul of the Ghosh family, passed away in 1942 at 89. Four years later, his sister Nalini died at 51. And that same year, during four gruesome days of Hindu-Muslim violence in Bengal, his brother Sananda was wounded by a bullet and his nephew, Sananda's son Shyamsunder, was killed.[4]

Whatever joy world affairs brought in those years came from the Allied victory over Fascism and, at long last, India's independence. Yogananda had correctly predicted that the war would mark the end of European colonialism in Asia and Africa—indeed, he said that freedom for the oppressed colonies was the war's karmic purpose—and he was overjoyed when the Gandhian ideal was vindicated on Independence Day, August 15, 1947. A proud patriot, he penned an article for *East-West* titled "India Free at Last—What Joy."[5] He took a train to San Francisco in November 1949 to meet India's first prime minister, Jawaharlal Nehru, at a special reception, and two months later, when the new Constitution took effect and the Indian republic was officially birthed, he said, "Those who have not suffered political fetters cannot imagine my feelings tonight." He spoke of freedom as "the birthright of the soul" and, as always, turned to God: "He has created the dark and the yellow and the white. Let no man be proud of his skin, but of God's light shining in the multicolored lamps of flesh."

That the only true peace and the only true freedom are found in Divine communion was, of course, Yogananda's core message, and in those perilous times, when even victory in war and freedom from foreign rule were contaminated by dreadful sorrow, it was especially potent. He was distressed by the massacres that erupted when, in the aftermath of independence, Pakistan split off from India, taking not only a large portion of the nation's northwest but the eastern half of Bengal.[6] Further clouding the joy of Indian freedom was Gandhi's assassination in January 1948.[7] Yogananda conducted a memorial service for the Mahatma and paid homage with several pages in *East–West* (March–April 1948) and on SRF's radio broadcast, "The Voice of Self-Realization." "Statues may be erected in his honor," he said at the memorial service, "but we must erect in one corner of our heart a statue to nonviolence if Gandhi is to be rightly remembered."[8]

India was never far from his mind, and in the last years of his life he made plans to go there several times, once booking passage on the *Queen Mary*. He never made it.

Like most visionary founders, Yogananda had an exceptional ability to inspire others. He could arouse their passion and sense of purpose regarding the merits and significance of their enterprise. He knew he needed people who were good at managing, administering, marketing, budgeting, and other organizational tasks, although his hands were tied by the limited talent pool available to spiritual leaders who can't pay well or reach too far beyond the ranks of loyal disciples. He was a hands-on and detail-oriented leader—often to a degree that might be called micromanaging if it were done by someone less empathetic—but he also relied on those he trusted to carry out his wishes. That trust seemed to depend less on the person's skills than on his or her attunement with the guru's mind. Among those he empowered to run the day-to-day operations at Mt. Washington were, at different times, Richard Wright; a businessman named Faraon Moss; Ranendra Kumar Das; and the key female monastics, Sister Gyanamata, Durga Mata, and Faye Wright. Increasingly, he vested authority in monastics, whom he felt were best equipped to internalize his teachings and focus on the work without distraction.[9]

Judging from the accounts of those who worked closely with him, Yogananda's management style was decidedly top down; the guru-disciple dynamic doesn't lend itself to a horizontal sharing of authority. But it was also what might today be called "people centered" or "humanistic." Daya Mata once enumerated some of the guidelines he gave to leaders for working well with others. They included: "Work with their virtues, and with the best that they have within them," "Expect nothing, but be grateful for all they do and all they give," and "Don't expect them all to be saints. Be glad if you find among them one saint in a hundred." As we've seen, he could also be demanding, painstaking, and perfectionistic—not necessarily a bad thing, he noted, since God was also a perfectionist. "No use doing anything unless you do it right," he is said to have remarked. "And if you aren't willing to do it right, let me know so that I can have an opportunity to have it done right by someone else."[10]

As a leader, he exhorted his charges to overcome fear and negative thinking, and instead to summon confidence, boldness, and steadfast persistence. He appeared to be conscious of how important it was that he, the guru and leader, model those attributes, and he did so seemingly without artifice. Also, perhaps because he understood the pitfalls of human interaction in tight-knit communities, he considered interpersonal harmony essential. He reminded disciples that a hive without the honey of God is meaningless, and at one point threatened to leave if they quarreled.

The Karma Yoga concept of treating work as a spiritual practice was another of his ideals. He extolled the *Bhagavad Gita*'s directive to perform one's duty impeccably and yet be unattached to the fruits of one's actions, as he modeled when nature (in the form of soil erosion) uprooted the Golden Lotus Temple at Encinitas and dragged it like a child's toy down toward the Pacific Ocean (unsalvageable, the structure was dismantled).[11] The catastrophe was hard to bear, he admitted, but he regarded it as a test, and he saw in it the hand of God. He had come to see the ups and downs of worldly existence as *lila*, the divine play of the Infinite One.

From a business perspective, Yogananda grew increasingly attentive to securing long-term structural and financial stability for SRF and especially for YSS as India struggled through the uncertain infancy of its nationhood. At a special board meeting in December 1942, it was determined that SRF would send its Indian sister $100 per month or half the month's net income, whichever was larger. Later, in 1949, a trust fund was established for YSS, secured by blue-chip stock presumably supplied by James Lynn. SRF's officer corps and board were periodically reconfigured and its corporate bylaws redefined. Notably, the percentage of women in leadership positions was always unusually high (more than half the board by the end of the 1940s).

Lynn was the closest of the close disciples. Yogananda's letters and the recollections of devotees portray an extraordinary relationship that, at different times, resembled a deep friendship between peers, a father-son or brother-brother devotion, or a traditional guru-disciple dynamic. Lynn was the chosen successor. That decision, an obvious one given his combination of business expertise, spiritual advancement, and devotion, was made official as early as 1942, at that same special board meeting. It was announced publicly on August 25, 1951, at the last SRF Convocation in Yogananda's lifetime, at which time Lynn took sannyasi vows and received the name Rajarsi Janakananda.[12] As disciples learned after Yogananda's passing, the new president was not to be the new guru. The *parampara*, or succession of gurus, would stop with Yogananda; he would forever after be the master to whom devotees pledged their loyalty and from whom guidance would be obtained.

To prepare for the inevitable post-Yogananda era, he focused on guiding the leadership to deeper spiritual states and grounding them in his essential teachings. He did this in his sermons, articles, and public talks, in intimate gatherings and private meetings, in his voluminous correspondence, and in countless informal interactions with ashram inhabitants as they went about their business, ate their meals, celebrated special occasions, and enjoyed pleasurable moments together. When he withdrew to focus on his writing, Faye Wright said, he told her,

"My work is over, and now yours begins." When she came to him with decisions to be made and problems to be solved, as she had for nearly two decades, he would tell her to deal with them herself. Over time, she grew from an uncertain young woman into a capable administrator, and then into Daya Mata, who succeeded Rajarsi in 1955.

Yogananda never stopped worrying about the organization's future. He fretted over large financial issues and also small details, such as what he considered the unwise sale of a papaya greenhouse in Encinitas that he'd hoped would generate income for SRF.[13] He never stopped asking Lynn and other disciples of means to step up and assure the organization's long-term financial health. By all accounts Lynn was as munificent as he could possibly be while also taking care of his family, especially his wife, Frieda, who suffered for decades from debilitating physical and mental illnesses. He wrote check after check, and Yogananda's gratitude was effusive.[14] But the concerns he longed to wipe from his slate remained largely unerased into the final months of his life.

When the Encinitas temple was destroyed, Yogananda told his followers that it happened because God knew he might otherwise settle for only one temple instead of building more. More came, some almost immediately and others over time. In fact, at least two were already in the works when he made that remark.

Three years earlier, Dr. and Mrs. Lewis had purchased for SRF a choice plot of land with a couple of houses on it. Its convenient location, on Sunset Boulevard, less than three miles east of Hollywood's world-famous Grauman's Chinese Theater (Sid Grauman was a devotee), was ideal for regular services and other congregational activities. With America's entry into the war and available funds needed for repairs on Mt. Washington, money to develop the property was scarce. But one day Yogananda was asked by a lawyer if he had any use for a church. A client had purchased an estate with an unwanted chapel on the land. SRF obtained it at a bargain price and moved it to Hollywood. Disciples and volunteers were mobilized, funds were raised from all over the country, and Yogananda became a combination of architect, interior designer, contractor, and construction foreman while continuing with his more customary duties.

As was described in *Inner Culture*, the end results included "a gold and stained-glass pergola, a wishing well, a set of quaint stone seats under an elm tree, many beautiful shrubs and flowers, and a large pool, surrounded by plants and stone deer, which reflects the gleaming gold-leafed stained-glass windows of the church."[15] The church was Gothic, trimmed in blue, white, and gold (said to be Yogananda's favorite colors), with gold-leaf spires and a charming interior with a pipe organ and niches for symbols of the world's religions. Yogananda's well-known perfectionism extended to the environment, as visitors to any of SRF's and YSS's immaculately landscaped properties can attest.

The Self-Realization Church of All Religions, colloquially known as the Hollywood Temple, opened on August 30, 1942, little more than a month after the Encinitas catastrophe. It was a gala affair, packed with devotees, students, curious citizens, and eminent guests and speakers. Yogananda dedicated the church to "the ideal of human brotherhood and the definite realization of God as the One Father of all mankind."[16] With him personally conducting services there every other Sunday, the center thrived, and on April 18, 1951, he hosted another gala celebration on the site. It was attended by a thousand people, including cast members of the film *Stars in My Crown*, a western starring Joel McCrea as a heroic preacher. Under the guru's direction, a squadron of monks had added a sizable building next to the chapel. Called the India Center, it contained an auditorium, living quarters for the monastics in charge of the center, a meditation garden, and, most notably, a vegetarian restaurant.[17] Called SRF Cafe, it became a popular eating place for health-minded Angelinos who fancied a Luncheon Plate of, say, Almond Loaf with two vegetables and either a dinner salad or soup ($1.35), or perhaps a simple curry on rice ($.95). Hungrier patrons could feast on the Curry Dinner ($2.10), which consisted of several dishes and an American-style or Indian dessert. The menu was plentiful, with omelets, salads, mock chicken dishes, and other items, including Yogananda's own creation, a mushroom burger served on a toasted garlic bun, with a green salad, for $.60. The restaurant closed in 1969—oddly enough, just when LA hippies were turning vegetarian—and a meeting hall and bookstore took its place. The center and temple thrive to this day.

Another Church of All Religions opened in September 1943, close to downtown San Diego and bucolic Balboa Park. At the inauguration, Yogananda asked for God's blessing, and added this cautionary request: "[W]hen we discuss theology and philosophy, may we not get sidetracked by the pitfalls of intellectual egotism and blind emotion, but travel straight to the highway of Self-Realization and truth which leads to Thee."[18] The temple, still in operation, was where Dr. Lewis presided for many years after he and Mildred moved west from New England, and where, in 1945, a 14-year-old named Merna Brown met Yogananda. The following year, she entered the Encinitas ashram.[19] As a young renunciate, she served her guru faithfully, and continued to do so after his death, eventually becoming vice president and then succeeding Daya Mata as president in 2011 (by then her name was Mrinalini Mata). She held the position until her death in 2017.

Two other Churches of All Religions were established in Yogananda's master builder phase—in Long Beach, California, and Phoenix, Arizona—and new centers opened in other locations. He also obtained an isolated property in Twentynine Palms, a tiny desert town about 140 miles from LA. There, he would spend long stretches of time writing and meditating. But the crowning glory of his unrivaled karma for sacred real estate was the acreage SRF acquired in 1949 at the western end of the long and winding Sunset Boulevard, about half a mile from the ocean. Once a silent movie set, the land was shaped by the surrounding hills into a natural amphitheater. When a real estate magnate acquired it and began to level the ground, it filled with water from underground springs. The 10-acre site was now considered useless for development, but it appealed to a studio executive who moved his houseboat there and added a mill house and a Dutch-style windmill. The subsequent owner planned to build a resort hotel on the property, but, as SRF tells the story, he one night dreamed that it housed a "Church of All Religions." He looked up the phrase in the LA phone directory, saw the Hollywood Temple listed, and, presumably mind-blown, wrote to Yogananda with an offer to sell. The ever-reliable Saint Lynn secured the purchase and added adjacent land for future expansion.

Yogananda envisioned an open-air Church of All Religions—a temple without walls. Once again, the sturdy monastics and other volunteers got to work, with Yogananda supervising from the houseboat. The festive opening ceremony was held on August 20, 1950, in conjunction with the first official SRF Convocation at Mt. Washington.[20] With about 1,500 in attendance, Yogananda inaugurated what came to be called the Lake Shrine in typically ornate prose: "I dedicate this church of all religions . . . unto all the soul temples of Christians, Moslems, Buddhists, Hebrews and Hindus, wherein the Cosmic Heart is throbbing equally always, and unto all the multicolored lamps of various true teachings, in which shines the same white flame of God, and unto all churches, mosques, viharas, tabernacles and temples of the world."

The jewel in this particular crown was, and remains, the Gandhi World Peace Memorial. Through the efforts of Dr. Nawle, the Bombay publisher who did advance work for Yogananda in 1935, SRF managed to obtain the only portion of the Mahatma's ashes to leave India. The brass-and-silver vessel containing the remains was ceremoniously interred in a Chinese sarcophagus said to be a thousand years old. The outdoor memorial, adorned by white towers topped with the golden lotuses salvaged from the Encinitas temple, remains a site of homage for those who hold Gandhi dear, especially visiting Indians. And the Lake Shrine as a whole remains one of LA's most pastoral landmarks, an oasis where people come to stroll around the tranquil water—home to swans and turtles and carp—enveloped by lush greenery, flower beds, a waterfall, and shrines to every religion. The mill house is now a gift shop and the windmill a picturesque chapel where services were held, with Sunday crowds overflowing onto folding chairs outside, until a sparkling hilltop temple was opened in 1995.[21] A retreat center and monk's quarters were also added.

The impact of Yogananda's literary legacy has been surpassed by very few spiritual figures in history. He produced it through countless hours writing in longhand on blank pages and editing typed manuscripts; through late nights and early mornings and long afternoons dictating to disciples who recorded his words in shorthand or typed as he spoke; through discussions with Laurie Pratt about rewrites and editorial choices; and through transcribed lectures, sermons, and informal talks.

With some notable exceptions, such as a Muslim League banquet in 1950 or his keynote address at a June 1945 conference in conjunction with the signing of the United Nations Charter in San Francisco, Yogananda's late-life public speaking was limited to Southern California. "The Master seldom made even the slightest preparation for his lectures," Daya Mata wrote in the Preface to *Man's Eternal Quest*; "if he prepared anything at all, it might consist of a factual note or two, hastily jotted down. Very often, while riding in the car on the way to the temple, he would casually ask one of us: 'What is my subject today?'"[22] He evidently began his sermons by asking, "How is everybody?" to which the customary group response was, "Awake and ready." In his later years, newfangled recording devices preserved his voice the way film preserved his image. The recordings offer invaluable documentation of his speaking style, vocal quirks, and personality, revealing a commanding figure who at times exuded an endearing humility and deep affection for his disciples, and at other times rose up and roared theatrically— on the one hand a warm, jocular, sometimes sentimental raconteur, and on the other hand a thunderous preacher with an old-fashioned vocabulary.[23] At all times, he was a teacher who bridged East and West, abstract philosophy and pragmatic application, science and religion.

Also to be counted in his literary output during those fecund years are upgrades he prepared for the SRF correspondence course, aka the Lessons. Between 1949 and 1951, he carved out time to make revisions in the Praecepta, which had been in use since the mid-'30s. The extensive changes he envisioned were not completed during his lifetime, but his directives were incorporated in a new version released in 1956. Those Lessons have been mailed to SRF students ever since. A thorough revamping of the course is slated for release in 2018; it will incorporate additional material that Yogananda dictated during that prolific period as well as guidelines he issued to his editorial staff. We might also include his contribution to the popularity of Hatha Yoga over the decades. In the 1940s and into the '50s, he set aside space in just about every issue of SRF's magazine for instructions, with photographs, of the yoga asanas (postures) that have become the very image of modern yoga.[24]

As was noted earlier, two of the projects to which he was most devoted were published posthumously, each in two volumes. One was his *Bhagavad Gita* translation and commentary titled *God Talks with Arjuna*. The other was *The Second Coming of Christ*, whose core message he summarized this way: "The Christ Consciousness of Jesus, free from theological crucifixion, can be brought back a second time into the souls of men."[25] The composition of that book was aided by the vision he claimed to have had in Encinitas while writing commentary on the New Testament. He reached out in prayer for Christ's guidance in interpreting the message he believed had been misrepresented since it was delivered in the Holy Land two millennia earlier. Soon thereafter, the room "filled with an opal-blue light," out of which emerged the form of young Jesus. More wonders followed, and then Christ "uttered beautiful words, so personal in their nature that I keep them in my heart."[26]

A different kind of mystery surrounds his *Gita*. Letters indicate that Yogananda finished dictating a draft of it in 1950 and expected to publish it quickly. Prepublication ads for the *Gita* appeared in *Self-Realization* magazine. For whatever reason, the book was not published at that time. Instead, it was serialized in the magazine over the course of many years, and the complete two-volume, 1,173-page book version finally appeared in 1995.

But his crowning achievement, and the most enduring monument to his earthly expedition, was *Autobiography of a Yogi*. As initially conceived, the book was not really an autobiography as such. The original title was *Yogi Christs of India*, later modified to *My Experiences with Yogi-Christs of India and Other Saints*. By some accounting, Yogananda started work on it as early as 1931. He nursed it over the next five or six years, then picked up the pace. Most of the work was accomplished in Encinitas, at a writing desk with a commanding view of the Pacific. Stenographers and typists were mobilized to convert his handwritten and spoken words into manuscript form for Laurie Pratt to work with. At one point, personal memoir blended with the Yogi-Christ element, creating the final, unusual hybrid. Readers have been surprised by how much of the autobiography is about people other than the author, and about events at which the author was not present. Also included was information he gathered in India about Lahiri Mahasaya's life; his paramguru received a chapter of his own plus other reverent passages.[27]

Yogananda and his team worked intensely on the book. He spent most evenings and random intervals on it. The parts he dictated were read back to him for fine-tuning, and the typed versions were given piecemeal to Laurie Pratt. Yogananda wanted his editors and transcribers to not only be skilled, but so tuned in to him that they could discern the meaning behind his torrent of words and ideas. Pratt evidently had that attunement. She was well-versed in Indian philosophy and other esoteric studies and also had the requisite skills. She may also have been more stubbornly independent than other close disciples; I was told by former SRF monastics that she dared to disagree with her guru over editing issues she felt strongly about (that may be apocryphal, of course). When the *AY* was finally published, her "long editorial labors" were acknowledged in the book, and Yogananda inscribed her personal copy with this: "God and the Gurus ever bless you for your valiant & loving part in bringing this book out."

The road to publication was fraught. In 1944, Pratt moved to New York to find a publisher and usher the book through publication. Housed in an unheated cold-water flat—located, it seems, in Queens—she met with rejection after rejection. The esoteric subject matter and the abundance of miracles and miracle workers were no doubt a deterrent; so might have been elements of the book's structure and style. Yogananda and Pratt continued to edit the old-fashioned way, by mailing pages back and forth across the country. Meanwhile, the war that had killed 50 to 80 million people came to a merciful end, but only by announcing, with the biggest of bangs, the dawn of the Atomic Age. The unspeakable destruction of nuclear weapons purportedly spurred Yogananda to even more urgent productivity. (One wonders how he reacted when he heard that J. Robert Oppenheimer, the physicist in charge of the bomb's development, evoked the *Bhagavad Gita* as the first nuclear mushroom cloud rose above the New Mexico desert.)

The publishing company that finally stepped up to the plate was Philosophical Library, which was then only five years old and has since published 22 Nobel Prize winners. The contract, only three legal pages long—practically Tweet-size by today's standards—was signed on August 12, 1946. The terms called for an initial printing of 7,000 copies. Royalties were set at 10 percent of the retail price, $3.50. There was no advance. On the contrary, Yogananda was required to purchase, in two installments, 3,000 copies at $2.10 each for resale to individuals. The contract was signed in Yogananda's name by "Laurie V. Pratt (attorney-in-fact)."

Autobiography of a Yogi was published December 1, 1946, just in time for Christmas giving.[28] And a wondrous gift it was for the denizens of Mt. Washington, Encinitas, and other SRF strongholds. Yogananda was thrilled when the first shipment arrived, and he again proclaimed his gratitude in a telegram to Laurie Pratt in New York: "Cannot express what happiness you brought us when four boxes of 160 books arrived. Self-Realization will march on thru ages thru this divine book and your efforts deathlessly embedded in it. Ceaseless love and blessings from me and all."[29]

In many respects, the timing could not have been better. Americans once again had money to spend, optimism was in the air, and spiritual quests that had been suspended for the Depression and the war were resumed. Additional soil had been tilled by other authors, notably philosopher Aldous Huxley and novelist Christopher Isherwood, whose books and articles on Vedanta had penetrated intellectual circles. But few realistic observers would have predicted that the book would still be going strong seven decades hence. Well, maybe Yogananda did. He prophesied that when he was gone the book would change millions of lives.

Reviews were more plentiful and more favorable than one might have predicted. The *Louisville Times*[30] said it "gives the reader an amazing insight into Hindus' lives and their mystic country." The *New York Times* called it "a rare account of the Indian cult from within, by one who practices it."[31] While the book is one yogi's story, noted *The San Jose Mercury-News*, it is "necessarily the essence of the very old combination of religion and science through which its devotees heal and also achieve oneness with the Infinite Spirit of God."[32] A Charleston, South Carolina, reviewer noted that India's pending independence made the *AY* especially timely, "since it endeavors to raise one of the many dark curtains that have enshrouded the deep mysteries of that ancient country too long."[33]

Similar opinions were proffered in popular magazines and scholarly journals ("There has been nothing before, written in English or in any other European language, like this presentation of Yoga," declared Columbia University Press),[34] as well as dozens of newspapers in cities large and small. While it was acknowledged that Yogananda's accounts of the miraculous would "exceed the credulity of many," and while some objected to his treating Jesus like one of many masters instead of the unique Son of God, he was commended for his humor, his frankness, his "disarming zest," his sincerity, and his clarity in explaining the precepts of Indian philosophy.

Time magazine begged to differ. In a review titled "Here Comes the Yogiman," the writer remarked that the autobiography "is not likely to give the uninitiated much insight into India's ancient teachings." He added, snidely, "It does show exceedingly well how an alien culture may change when transplanted by a businesslike nurseryman from the tough soil of religious asceticism into hothouses of financial wealth and spiritual despair." The other major weekly, *Newsweek*, was friendlier: "Writing for a Western world that seldom understands and often scoffs at the yogi search for union with the Cosmic Spirit, Yogananda, an authentic Hindu yogi, has tried to explain by telling the story of his life. 'Autobiography of a Yogi' is more than an apology for yoga and its techniques of meditation; it is a fascinating and clearly annotated study of a religious way of life, ingenuously described in the lush style of the Orient."[35]

That lush style, it must be said, has made many literary types—writers, editors, English professors—cringe. The vocabulary is overly ornate, they say, soaked throughout by stilted, florid, fancy-pants words. Too many "lo"s and "behold"s and "perforce"s and other antiquities, they complain. Too many superfluous adjectives and adverbs—and odd ones, like "ejaculatory" and "smilingly." Too much dialogue that sounds more like a formal letter or a Shakespearean soliloquy than modern human speech ("Sir, whither are we bound this morning?"). And some have complained that its structure is sketchy, with carefully observed detail here and cavernous gaps there, as four or five years in the subject's life are written off in one breezy sentence.

In Yogananda's defense, it is very likely that British schools in the India of his youth taught an opulent Victorian English, and Bengali literature is said to have been, as a rule, flowery. Yogananda was a veritable horticulturist of flowery prose, and his style has charmed a far greater number of readers than it has annoyed. In fact, some of the book's departures from the standard memoir form have always been part of its appeal.

Then there are the miracles. A graduate journalism student (hired by this author) counted 132 miraculous occurrences of one kind or another, and calculated that they take up 44 percent of the book. For some readers, the astounding tales are the most memorable portions of the *AY* and its main attraction; for them, the wondrous stories are eye-openers that changed the way they saw the world. Others consider them to be either fables or magic tricks, and they wish Yogananda had stuck to his philosophical discourses and endearing personal stories.[36] Yet many of those same skeptics recommend the book anyway, and commend its author for attempting to explain the miraculous in rational terms. As for Yogananda's motives for devoting so much space to what we regard as miracles, perhaps he told us himself by including this biblical epigraph on the *Autobiography* title page: "Except ye see signs and wonders, ye will not believe" (John 4:48).

The almost reluctant affection some people have for the book helps explain its astonishing success. Pick it apart if you must, as many have, but there is no denying its endearing charms. Take exception to its quirks, but recognize that those very quirks are part of its allure. Disregard what you don't like, but consider what you are left with: a compelling tale of a unique life; a rare glimpse of exotic India at a certain period of time; portraits of bona fide holy persons; illuminating insights from ancient sages rendered in modern terms; a practical, nonsectarian tutorial in spiritual development; and concepts that make you think, perhaps more deeply and more out of the box than you had before. It is, therefore, no wonder that the book won endorsements from prominent people, like the scholar W. Y. Evans-Wentz, who wrote the Preface, and the celebrated German novelist and Nobel laureate Thomas Mann.

The autobiography broke no sales records upon its release,[37] but it dramatically increased public awareness of Yogananda and his work, triggering a surge in center attendance and correspondence course enrollment. When the book was published, there were thirteen SRF centers in the U.S., plus several in India and one each in London, Mexico City, and the Gold Coast (now Ghana) in West Africa. Five years later, there were still more in India, twenty-four in America (and some existing ones had been expanded); six in Mexico; five in West Africa; four in Holland;

three each in Canada, France, England, and Czechoslovakia; two in Germany, South Africa, and the Philippines; and one each in British Guiana, Cuba, Hawaii (it was not yet a state), Finland, Norway, Sweden, Scotland, and even the Faroe Islands, a Danish archipelago in the North Atlantic. As that list suggests, the gradual distribution of the English-language edition (including in India) and the licensing of translation rights gave Yogananda a truly international reach for the first time. His autobiography was accomplishing, he said, "what I meagerly did while traveling and lecturing to thousands."

He also said, in the November–December 1948 issue of *Self-Realization* (as it was now called), "Renunciates, in a steady stream, are joining our Headquarters Colony and our Encinitas Colony—and there is a long waiting line." Readers wanted the benefits of yoga that the book so vividly described, and some of them wanted the whole samosa. The monastic order grew as a number of hungry seekers dropped their current obligations and headed to Southern California. There would be attrition along the way (as was noted earlier, the monastic life is only for the rare few), but many of the renunciates who signed on in the late '40s and early '50s became SRF mainstays and vital contributors to the organization's work (among them were Brothers Anandamoy, Bimalananda, and Mokshananda and the female monastics Mukti Mata, Meera Mata, Uma Mata, and Vijoya Mata). Also among them were three young men who went on to represent Yogananda's teachings outside of the SRF structure.[38]

Norman Paulsen arrived at Mt. Washington in 1947 at age 18. Four years later, he returned to his native Santa Barbara and eventually began teaching, drawing from Kriya Yoga and other systems. He passed away in 2006, but the Sunburst community he started in the late 1960s lives on in the hills north of Santa Barbara.

Another teenager, mentioned earlier, Roy Eugene Davis, saw an ad for *Autobiography of a Yogi* in a fitness magazine while recuperating from an illness on his family's farm in Ohio. He bought the book, read it, signed up for the Lessons, and eventually quit his job selling magazines door to door and hitchhiked from

Florida to the West Coast. He met Yogananda at Mt. Washington the evening of December 23, 1949. The next day, he joined the all-day meditation. Eventually, Davis, who never took final monastic vows, married, had two children, and established the Center for Spiritual Awareness in rural Georgia. He has taught and trained ministers worldwide, always as a disciple of Yogananda, and continues to do so as of this writing, at age 86.[39]

The third disciple who went on to a long career as a spiritual leader was, like Davis, introduced to the guru through the *AY*. J. Donald Walters was a 22-year-old New Yorker when he read the book in 1948, and almost immediately boarded a bus to LA. He moved into the ashram and was soon given exceptional responsibilities for his age. After Yogananda's death, he took vows as Swami Kriyananda and continued to serve SRF in different roles, including board member and vice president. In 1962, he fell out of favor and was expelled. Eventually, he started teaching on his own. Inspired by Yogananda's unfulfilled vision of world-brotherhood colonies, he founded Ananda Village in the foothills of the California Sierras in 1969. He passed away in 2013, but the community continues to flourish, along with its sister colonies in America, Europe, and India.[40]

The vast majority who were drawn to Yogananda's work through the autobiography, of course, were not monastically inclined. One of the more interesting and worldly disciples to get close to Yogananda at that time was Herb Jeffries, a multiracial, multiethnic actor and singer who was dark enough to play an African American in films. The "Bronze Buckaroo," as he was called, used to swim with Yogananda at the Lake Shrine and occasionally dine with him. In the documentary *Awake: The Life of Yogananda*, he tells an amusing story that illustrates Yogananda's worldly savvy. Jeffries told his guru he'd grown tired of the "thou shalt nots" of religion and wanted to know what he, as a disciple, "canst do." Yogananda ran through the basics—smoking, alcohol, and sexual promiscuity. Jeffries admitted he did them all. To his surprise, Yogananda said he could continue. Then he added a caveat: "But I will not promise you that if you continue to study these teachings, that the desire to do these things will not fall away from you."[41]

The autobiography was updated and expanded in 1951. "I have long wished to revise the book," Yogananda had written to the publisher, "to remove some grammatical errors, to correct some minor misstatements of facts, and to add some material in answer to questions which readers have asked me since the first publication of the book." A new final chapter, titled "The Years 1940–1951," brought the story forward in time and added new philosophical detail. Also added was an homage to India, by then a democratic republic, along with a lengthy footnote that proudly recounts the nation's historic glories.

In October 1953, almost 20 months after Yogananda's death, SRF reacquired the rights to the book for $1,500. Periodically updated, edited, and embellished with new photographs, captions, and footnotes, it has sold at least 4 million English-language copies and has been translated into nearly 50 languages. Critics, Swami Kriyananda chief among them, have taken exception to some of the changes made to Yogananda's original; SRF insists that most of the modifications were made in accordance with the author's explicit instructions, given before his death, while others were minor alterations to keep up with changing times and new discoveries.[42]

Regardless of which edition readers acquired over the years, the ad slogan used today would have applied: "The book that changed the lives of millions." That was especially true as the staid '50s gave way to the tumultuous '60s, when a large segment of baby boomers embraced Eastern spirituality as passionately as they opposed the Vietnam War. In counterculture circles, the autobiography, with the now-familiar ochre-colored background to the deep-eyed visage of Yogananda in the Standard Pose, was by far the most beloved, borrowed, gifted, and ripped-off spiritual text. If you were lucky enough to know George Harrison, you might have received one from the stack he kept on hand to give away when people needed "regrooving," because, he said, "If I hadn't read that, I probably wouldn't have a life—really."[43]

The *AY* has been going strong ever since. Sales rose when the movie *Awake* was released and when word got out that copies had been given away at Steve Jobs's memorial service when the Apple founder died in 2011. Now, more than seven decades after its publication, it can be found everywhere from small-town school libraries to hipster health food stores and, of course, amid the fancy outfits and accessories in the shops of yoga studios that owe their existence, at least in part, to the book and its author.

CHAPTER 18

LIBERATION AND LEGACY

In his final years, Yogananda's spirit soared while the body it inhabited declined. Those who were close to him said he frequently slipped into sustained spiritual ecstasy, and his own writings indicate that he entered the permanent state of the Divine union extolled in yogic texts. So inwardly absorbed would he become that his awed disciples worried he might never come out; he instructed them to chant "OM" softly in his right ear should they become alarmed. The apex occurred in June 1948 at the Mother Center. What came to be called the Great Samadhi spanned almost 12 hours, from late one evening until 10 o'clock the following morning, during which time, Daya Mata later reported, "a few of us disciples were privileged to glimpse something of this unique experience through his ecstatic description of the cosmic revelation as it unfolded."[1] The high point of the drama was a prolonged dialogue between Yogananda and Divine Mother. He "conversed like a child" it was said, even voicing grievances disciples didn't know he'd harbored, and Divine Mother replied through him.

Soon afterward, Yogananda said, "I shall always be in this state of *nirbikalpa samadhi*, but no one will be able to tell." The term samadhi generally applies to the experience of unified consciousness, and yogic texts describe several forms of it. Translations of *nirbikalpa* (more typically spelled *nirvikalpa*) and its companion *sabikalpa* or *savikalpa* samadhi vary.[2] Suffice it to say that the "always" in Yogananda's remark is the key word; permanence is a hallmark of a definitive state of liberated awareness, in which the realized soul remains in unbroken union with the Infinite. The "no one will be able to tell" is a corrective to the erroneous assumption that enlightened beings can be identified by the rest of us based on their appearance, speech, or actions. In Yogananda's case, disciples said he was visibly more beatific and more removed after the Great Samadhi, but outwardly he was still the Yogananda who wrote feverishly, ate meals, joked around, scolded, made decisions, delivered discourses, answered questions, signed legal documents, and fretted over money and the future of his work—all while, based on his own reports, his indwelling spirit remained untouched and unshakably at one with the Eternal.

"I killed Yogananda a long time ago," he said in the period that followed. "It is the Father who speaks through me." In case anyone misunderstood, he added: "But it's not right to say I am God because the wave can't exist without the ocean but the ocean can exist without the wave." In that classic metaphor, the individual entity called Yogananda—and, by extension, each of us—is the wave, and God, or Brahman, is the timeless, boundless ocean of Being. The state of Self-realization he describes is accompanied by the nonattachment lauded by the sages. "I am living only for Him," Yogananda said. "I am interested only in His work. To the last breath I shall work for Him, I shall worry about His work; but not for myself, not for me at all."

The September 1948 issue of *Self-Realization* contained a Special Notice advising students that Yogananda was now "observing a stricter seclusion than he has done in the past." Letters addressed to him would not be answered as promptly as before. "Because of his constant immersion in God," the notice explained, "it is not always possible for his secretaries to intrude on his attention."[3] He spent the abundance of his time in the desert, working day and night on his books, assisted by a team of note takers and editors.

In his hardworking seclusion, his body began to lose its characteristic vigor. His inner bliss and freedom may have been sublime, but, as he acknowledged, he still had to deal with the constraints of a body and the karmic demands of material existence. Everyone does, of course, even Ramakrishna and Ramana Maharshi and other revered saints whose flesh was racked with disease at the end. As the calendar shifted into the 1950s, an unnamed condition weakened Yogananda's legs. According to Roy Eugene Davis, he found amusement in his need to be moved about in a wheelchair for some time. He was not able to appear in person at Mt. Washington's 1950 Christmas celebration, nor at his annual birthday party the following January 5. He addressed the attendees via loudspeaker from his upstairs quarters. Christmas 1951 and his birthday in 1952 were his last such celebrations and, fittingly, they were especially moving occasions. He was weakening, and he knew it. To the chagrin of disciples within earshot, he would occasionally state, matter-of-factly, that his remaining days on the planet were numbered.

What ailed Yogananda? The official explanation is that his body suffered the consequences of taking on the karma of disciples—what was called after his death "a metaphysically induced illness."[4] The phenomenon of saints and sages absorbing the karma of others for healing purposes has a venerable pedigree in mystical traditions. Yogananda wrote about it, and spoke about it in recorded talks, and he indicated in the *AY* that masters employ specific techniques on behalf of disciples who need their intervention. The discipline, however, is known to weaken the practitioner's body. For Yogananda's disciples, that transfer of energy from the afflicted to the healer is a sufficient diagnosis for the ailments he endured in his final years.

Of course, even a "metaphysically induced illness" would manifest in a diagnosable and namable form. A doctor I spoke to suggested that Yogananda could have had diabetes, undiagnosed or unrevealed. It is an understandable hypothesis, given his sweet tooth, his tendency to gain weight, and the exceptionally high rate of diabetes in the Indian population.[5] The cause of death on his official death certificate was "acute coronary occlusion"; that is, a heart attack. "Coronary arteriosclerosis" is named as an antecedent cause. Surprisingly, "rheumatic heart disease" is entered in the box for "conditions contributing to the death but not related to the disease or condition causing death." Its onset, according to the certificate, was 10 years earlier. It is, of course, impossible to ascertain the accuracy of that information, but the "informant" named on the form is Orpha Sahly, aka Sraddha Mata, who had been a nurse prior to moving to Mt. Washington in 1934.

Whatever may have been going on in his body, Yogananda asserted many times in those years that the bliss of his unitive awareness was uninterrupted. The *Bhagavad Gita* declares that this paradigmatic state is marked by "equanimity in pleasure and pain, in gain and loss, in victory and defeat."[6] The pain might be bodily, the loss might be of health, the defeat might be to the ability to keep breathing, but the equanimity is of the soul. Clearly, Yogananda was fully prepared to go gently into his good night.

Los Angeles awakened on March 7, 1952, to flooded streets and road closures, the result of an exceptionally heavy rainstorm the night before. It was still rainy and windy that morning, and temperatures were not expected to rise above 55 degrees Fahrenheit. In the news, battles raged in Korea, as they did every day; pundits speculated about who would be nominated to run in the upcoming presidential election; the Soviet Union announced its biggest military budget since World War II; and President Harry S. Truman called for an $8 billion foreign aid program to counter Russia's threat to the "survival of civilization."

Yogananda had come to Los Angeles from his desert retreat a few days earlier because newly independent India's ambassador to the U.S., Binay Ranjan Sen, was in town. On the morning of March 4, he gave the ambassador and other Indian dignitaries a tour of Mt. Washington. Then they were taken to the Hollywood Temple for a tour of that facility and a festive lunch. A visit to the Lake Shrine capped the day. He was no doubt delighted when the consul general said that, while diplomats may come and go, he,

Yogananda, was "a true ambassador of India." He spent March 5 quietly at Mt. Washington, and that evening shared a meal of Indian food—a more elaborate feast than usual—with disciples. Those present came to call it the Last Supper. Early the following morning, March 6, he joined Ambassador Sen, Mrs. Sen, and other prominent Indians for breakfast at the Ambassador Hotel. Disciples who ferried him there said he had difficulty walking but refused a wheelchair. That afternoon, he made what would be his last visit to the Lake Shrine. He circled the lake, surveyed the damage from recent rains, and took to the chapel organ for a round of heartfelt devotional songs. Back at the Mother Center, a crate from Florida awaited him. It was filled with green coconuts, a favorite Indian delicacy. He ate the meat and drank the juice with relish. "I am just fulfilling these last little desires," he said. That night, Daya Mata later revealed, he said to her, "Do you realize that it is just a matter of hours and I will be gone from this earth?"[7]

A banquet for the ambassador was scheduled for the evening of March 7 at the Biltmore Hotel. Yogananda was to be the featured speaker. He spent most of that day quietly in his Mt. Washington quarters. At around 4 P.M. he took the elevator down and spoke with some disciples. Then he and a small entourage drove to the hotel he'd checked into when he first arrived in LA, 27 years, two months, and five days earlier. The rain had given way to mist. The traffic into downtown was heavy.

Shortly after 5 o'clock, the party settled into the two-room suite reserved for Yogananda's pre-banquet use, and for the night should he choose to stay over. He was unusually quiet—"interiorized," as Daya Mata put it—and said at one point, "Do not disturb my thoughts." As he waited to be summoned to the banquet, he sat in an easy chair with close disciples seated before him on the floor. After a period of meditation, he gazed into the loving face of each person, one at a time. Daya Mata says she knew it was his farewell *darshan*—the term used for being in the energetic presence of a holy person. He joined the 250 other guests in the Biltmore's Music Room. In the last photograph ever taken of him, shot at the banquet, the eyes belong to someone who knows things most of us do not, and what he knows is sublime. The photo is known as *The Last Smile*.

Yogananda's final moments seem almost too theatrical, too much like a Hollywood script or apocryphal myth-making, but the details are well documented. It is said that he had prophesied on more than one occasion that he would not die in bed, but speaking of God and India. That he did. His was the last speech scheduled before Ambassador Sen's address, and whatever may have been going on in his body did not affect his mind or his vocal power. He was apparently in top oratorical form. He concluded by reciting selected lines from one of his own poems, a stirring tribute to his homeland by a proud native son, titled "My India." One can imagine the heartfelt emotion and the stirring delivery:

> Mortal fires may raze all her homes and golden paddy fields;
> Yet to sleep on her ashes and dream immortality,
> O India, I will be there!

> God made the earth, and man made confining countries
> And their fancy-frozen boundaries. Where Ganges, woods, Himalayan
> caves, and men dream God—I am hallowed; my body touched that sod.[8]

They were his last words. According to witnesses, his gaze went up to the *kutastha chakra*—the point between the eyebrows where attention was directed in his meditation techniques—and he collapsed to the floor. An ambulance was summoned. Disciples ran to his side and chanted "OM" in his right ear, as they were instructed to do when he was lost in ecstasy. This time there was no coming out. The official time of his *mahasamadhi*—the term given to a master's final release from the chains of physicality—was 9:30 P.M., March 7, 1952. The date is commemorated every year by devotees in at least 175 countries.

The funeral service was held on March 11 at Mt. Washington. The main hall was packed with flowers and mourners. The monks wore white; the nuns wore yellow saris. Rajarsi Janakananda, nee James Lynn, presided. He, Ambassador Sen, and others delivered eulogies. A musician-devotee named Korla Pandit[9] performed a half-hour organ recital. Yogananda's body lay in an open casket, and seven white roses were ceremoniously placed on his chest.[10] Newspapers described the two-hour service, fittingly, as "half-Indian, half-Christian." Dr. Lewis read from the Bible; Swami Premananda recited Vedic verses and quoted Gandhi.

Disciples wanted Yogananda to be buried at Mt. Washington or the Lake Shrine. Because of difficulties involved in fulfilling the legal requirements for burial facilities, he was interred instead in a mausoleum at Forest Lawn Memorial Park in Glendale. It was supposed to be a temporary resting place. His remains are still there.[11]

One of the most intriguing and talked-about components of *Autobiography of a Yogi* is the black-bordered page with the heading:

PARAMAHANSA YOGANANDA
A YOGI IN DEATH AS IN LIFE

Its famous claim reads, in part: "Weeks after his departure his unchanged face shone with the divine luster of incorruptibility." The proclamation includes two paragraphs from a notarized statement by Harry T. Rowe, the mortuary director at Forest Lawn Memorial Park, containing phrases such as "absence of any visual signs of decay," "no physical disintegration," "no indication of mold," and "no odor of decay." Twenty days after his death, it states, Yogananda's appearance had not changed. "This state of perfect preservation of a body is, so far as we know from mortuary annals, an unparalleled one."[12]

Naturally, this has been presented as evidence of Yogananda's advanced spiritual state and a testament to the value of his yoga. The story even appeared in *Time* magazine. However, the claim has not been free of dissenting voices. Skeptics have pointed out that the rest of Rowe's letter contains a couple of salient facts, namely that Yogananda's nose had begun to show signs of desiccation (drying) and that his body had been embalmed. A 20-day absence of decay in an embalmed body kept under heavy glass is not unusual, some embalmers have testified.

Sixty-six years after Yogananda's passing, the issue is still being argued online. To this writer, it seems a useless and futile debate. Would absolute proof of an uncorrupted corpse burnish Yogananda's legacy significantly? Would his enduring influence be any less if his body turned out to have deteriorated like other bodies? Based on my conversations with devotees, students, and casual fans, the answers are overwhelmingly "no" and "no." His legacy is assured by virtue of his powerhouse presence in the years he lived, the depth and breadth of his written and spoken words, and the practical value of the yogic techniques he introduced to the West. That those methods continue to transform lives surely matters more than the postmortem condition of a body he seemed rather eager to discard. In fact, Yogananda's presence among today's spiritual seekers is so vital, so palpable, that it is easy to forget that he drew his last breath eight months before Dwight D. Eisenhower was elected President of his adopted country.

The principal reason for that ongoing influence is the astonishing durability of his seminal autobiography, which has rightly been dubbed one of the most important spiritual books of the 20th century. But credit also goes to the disciples, three generations on at this point, who have made it their mission to preserve and promote Yogananda's work. "He had implanted his consciousness in those he trained; and they made the commitment to devote their lives and ambitions solely to carrying on the spiritual legacy that he put in place," Brother Chidananda, who is now SRF's president, once told an interviewer. Yogananda selected "vowed and committed" monastics for the task, because, Chidananda said, "you have to have a solid core of non-negotiable principles, and that is what he built into his monastic order."[13]

Among other things, the leadership has, over the decades, produced new collections of their guru's speeches and articles, updated existing books and created new ones from his writings, published memoirs by people who knew him, digitized and released recordings of his talks, served existing members and enrolled new ones, and introduced Yogananda's work to new areas of the globe. As of this writing, there are SRF/YSS members in 178 countries, with about 800 centers, temples, and retreat facilities spread about every continent. In addition, Kriyananda's Ananda Sangha has more than 70 active groups in the U.S., 40 in Europe, and others in India and other parts of the world. Roy Eugene Davis's Center for Spiritual Awareness also has an international presence.

The preservation and expansion of Yogananda's teachings have not been without conflict and controversy. Like most spiritual organizations after the death of their founders, his has survived disgruntlement, amicable partings of the ways, angry departures, periods of stagnation, criticism from within and without, and at least one costly lawsuit (the one with Ananda Sangha dragged on for 12 years). Arguments have raged over changes SRF made in the years following Yogananda's death—tweaks to the *AY*, changing "Paramhansa" to "Paramahansa," adjustments in the eligibility standards for Kriya initiation, and the addition of Krishna's image to the altar,[14] to name just a few. The monastic order whose diligent labor is credited with safeguarding the integrity of Yogananda's teaching has also been criticized for being authoritarian, failing to adapt to changing times, not appreciating the challenges of householder life, and other ostensible shortcomings, from lack of transparency to terminal tedium. Too protective to some, not protective enough to others; too Westernized for some, too Hindu for others. In short, variations of the kinds of divisions that beset most spiritual organizations over time. Anyone who can name a sizable institution that has not sustained such critiques has simply not done enough research. In fact, most guru lineages struggle after the passing of their charismatic founders, and some quietly fade away. The organizations teaching in Yogananda's name have flourished to a remarkable degree.

However one assesses it, Yogananda's impact on the religious and spiritual history of the West—and, increasingly, India—is unique and unassailable. For that he will always be remembered and celebrated. Just as the Transcendentalists and Swami Vivekananda paved the way for him, he paved the way for a procession of swamis, gurus, maharishis, and yoga masters who came, saw, and conquered in the 1960s and '70s, as well as the legion of teachers, both Eastern and Western, who flourish in today's yoga-friendly world. He predicted that one day millions would seek spiritual enlightenment, and that yoga would be taught in schools. Both have come to be, thanks in large part to his efforts. History is likely to record that the export of India's interior sciences to the West was as significant spiritually as the export of Western science has been to the East's material progress. No single person contributed more to that East-to-West current than Paramahansa Yogananda.

In a talk to his disciples on his 56th birthday, Yogananda pointed out that few people quote the lines that follow Rudyard Kipling's famous assertion that East is East and West is West, and never the twain shall meet.[15] Those lines read:

> But there is neither East nor West, Border, nor Breed, nor Birth,
> When two strong men stand face to face, tho' they come from the ends of the earth!

Yogananda was a strong man from the East who crossed the earth to stand face to face with the mighty West, saying *"Namaste"* with hands joined at his chest. But he was of neither East nor West. He represented the universal Spirit that knows no border, breed, or birth. Through the strength of his character and his skillful transmission of perennial wisdom, he showed the way for millions to transcend those and other barriers to the liberation of the soul.

He would happily give Mother India the last word. On the 25th anniversary of his death, the Indian government issued a commemorative stamp with his likeness (the Standard Pose). The announcement read, in part: "Though the major part of his life was spent outside India, still he takes his place among our great saints. His work continues to grow and shine ever more brightly, drawing people everywhere on the path of the pilgrimage of the Spirit."

ENDNOTES

Introduction

1 "If You Would Know the Guru," an Informal Talk by Sri Mrinalini Mata, audio CD available from Self-Realization Fellowship. Excerpted in *Self-Realization* magazine, Spring 2003, pp. 42–43.

Chapter 1

1 Sri Aurobindo was a distant cousin of Yogananda's.

2 David Frawley (Vamadeva Shastri), *Astrology of the Seers* (Twin Lakes, WI: Lotus Press, 2000).

3 Cited in the documentary *Awake: The Life of Yogananda*, a film by Paola di Florio and Lisa Leeman.

4 The seminal memoir *Autobiography of a Yogi* by Paramahansa Yogananda was originally published in 1946 by Philosophical Library. Self-Realization Fellowship has owned the rights since 1953 and has published several updated editions.

5 Paramahansa Yogananda, *Autobiography*, 2013 edition, 4.

6 Mahasaya is a Sanskrit honorific. Yogananda translated it as "large-minded." Alternatives include "magnanimous one."

7 Exactly how limited is impossible to know. Such methods have, for millennia, been handed down inconspicuously from guru to disciple in countless sequestered ashrams throughout India.

8 Paramahansa Yogananda, *Autobiography of a Yogi* (Self-Realization Fellowship, 2013), 8. For a complete description of Kriya Yoga, see Chapter 26, "The Science of Kriya Yoga."

9 Sananda Lal Ghosh, *Mejda: The Family and Early Life of Paramahansa Yogananda* (Los Angeles: Self-Realization Fellowship, 1980), 52.

10 Ghosh, *Mejda*, 23.

11 Paramahansa Yogananda, *Autobiography*, 2013 edition, 8.

12 Paramahansa Yogananda, *Autobiography*, 2013 edition, 9.

13 The illustrious reformers include Siddhartha Gautama, historically known as the Buddha; Mahavira, who founded Jainism in the 6th century B.C.E.; Guru Nanak, who did the same for Sikhism about 500 years ago; and Shankara, the 8th-century C.E. exponent of Advaita Vedanta and founder of

the monastic order to which virtually every swami since then—including Yogananda—has traced his lineage.

14 Ghosh, *Mejda*, 29.

15 Ghosh, *Mejda*, 42.

16 Ghosh, *Mejda*, 31.

17 *Bhagavan,* from the Sanskrit root *bhaj,* meaning to honor or adore, is one of many terms for the personal form of God in Hinduism.

18 Iswara, sometimes spelled *Ishwara* or *Isvara,* is one of many Sanskrit words for the personal aspect of Divinity.

19 Paramahansa Yogananda, *Autobiography*, 2013 edition, 10.

Chapter 2

1 It is now the second largest city in Pakistan, located 24 kilometers from the tense border with India.

2 Yogananda tells the previous two stories in Chapter 1 of *Autobiography of a Yogi.*

3 The last two stories are told by Sananda Ghosh in *Mejda.*

4 Amherst Street is now Raja Rammohan Roy Sarani (*sarani* means path or road). Ram Mohan Roy was an important 19th-century Bengali intellectual and social reformer whose modern interpretations of Hindu philosophy were highly influential among Western thinkers such as Ralph Waldo Emerson, as well as in India.

5 Ghosh, *Mejda*, 50.

6 Paramahansa Yogananda, *Autobiography*, 2013 edition, 14.

7 Paramahansa Yogananda, *Autobiography*, 2013 edition, 14.

8 The entire poem can be found as "My Mother's Eyes," in *Songs of the Soul*, Self-Realization Fellowship, 1983, 102.

9 He died in 1942, at the age of 89.

10 Paramahansa Yogananda, *Autobiography*, 2013 edition, 14.

11 Paramahansa Yogananda, *Autobiography*, 2013 edition, 19.

12 Mark Twain, *Following the Equator: A Journey Around the World* (Hartford, CT: The American Publishing Company), 480.

13 Paramahansa Yogananda, *Autobiography*, 2013 edition, 239.

14 Paramahansa Yogananda, *Autobiography*, 2013 edition, 24. It is said that, upon his death, Swami Pranabananda's body (as per his own instructions) was placed in a trunk, locked with chains, and submerged overnight in the Ganges. The next morning, the trunk was empty.

15 The story is recounted in Chapter 7 of *Mejda*, page 82.

16 Paramahansa Yogananda, *Autobiography*, 2013 edition, 17.

17 The amulet story is described in Chapter 2 of *Autobiography of a Yogi*. It vanishes in Chapter 10.

18 Swami Vivekananda, *The Complete Works of Swami Vivekananda*, Vol. 1 (Calcutta: Advaita Ashrama), 1915.

19 Bengal was subsequently reuinited, but split again during the Pakistan-India partition; East Bengal was absorbed into East Pakistan and then, in 1971, became Bangladesh.

Chapter 3

1 The headquarters of Yogananda's organization in India, Yogoda Satsanga Society, is a short stroll downriver from the Kali temple. It was built on a site chosen by Yogananda himself and was completed during his lifetime, but he never got to see it.

2 The Rig Veda maxim Ekam sat vipraha bahudha vadanti, usually translated "Truth is One, and the wise call it by many names," became the motto of Swami Vivekananda's Vedanta Society.

3 4 Garpar Road is now the home of Sananda Ghosh's grandson and Yogananda's grandnephew Somnath Ghosh; he and his wife, Sarita, maintain sections of the building for devotees of their famous relative to pay homage.

4 Vivekananda's birthplace is now called the Ramakrishna Mission Swami Vivekananda's Ancestral House and Cultural Centre. The Tagore estate is now the Rabindra Bharati Museum. The Ray home was converted to the Athenaeum Institution School.

5 Though it was off most Indians' radar at the time, 1906 also saw Mahatma Gandhi's first campaign of civil disobedience in South Africa, a training ground for the leadership he would one day assert in his homeland.

6 The term *bhajan* is typically used for devotional songs performed by one singer, or by more than one in unison. *Kirtan* usually refers to a group performance characterized by call-and-response between singers and audience.

7 Swami Rama Tirtha taught "practical Vedanta" in America between 1902 and 1904.

8 One of the prizes that day was an air gun (the other was an inkwell), which Mukunda intentionally rendered useless after accidentally shooting a sparrow.

9 The institute Bishnu Ghosh established in 1923 is a few blocks from Garpar Road. Called Ghosh's College of Physical Education & Ghosh's Yoga College, it was run after the founder's death by his son Biswanath and is now maintained by his granddaughter, Muktamala Mitra.

10 Later renamed Ladies Park.

11 Ghosh, *Mejda*, 91.

12 Swami Satyananda Giri, *A Collection of Biographies of 4 Kriya Yoga Gurus* (Battle Creek, MI: Yoga Niketan, 2004). In addition to Yogananda, the book covers Lahiri Mahasaya, Hansaswami Kebalananda, and Sri Yukteswar.

13 Swami Satyananda Giri, *A Collection of Biographies*, 156. It is interesting to
    note in this context that A. C. Bhaktivedanta Swami Prabhupada, who
    brought the Hare Krishna movement to the West, was born and raised
    on Harrison Road. His birth name was Abhay Charan; he was three years
    younger than Yogananda and attended the same college.

14 Paramahansa Yogananda, *Autobiography*, 2013 edition, 25.

Chapter 4

1 Mas Vidal, *Sun, Moon, and Earth* (Twin Lakes, WI: Lotus Press, 2016),
   173. Vidal, an American yoga instructor, claims that Lahiri Mahasaya
   included some asanas as part of his disciples' sadhana, and that one of
   those disciples, Yogananda's father, "carried on his Guru's influence by
   recommending practical healing formulas and simple uses of asana and
   pranayama for various health issues." Also, a couple of traditional asanas
   are incorporated in the Kriya Yoga techniques.

2 A traditional feature of Hindu ritual involving the offering of flames usually lit
   by ghee-soaked wicks or camphor.

3 Some tantric practices have been categorized as "left-handed," consisting of
   convention-defying rituals regarded as degenerate by society. In the "right-
   handed" category are practices that adhere to ethical standards and societal
   norms.

4 Paramahansa Yogananda, *Autobiography*, 2013 edition, 73.

5 The complete talk can be heard on the CD *To Make Heaven on Earth*, Self-
   Realization Fellowship, 2004.

6 What was once a field is now part of the urban sprawl, and where Sadhana
   Mandir once stood is a center belonging to Yogananda's Yogoda Sat-Sanga
   Society of India. The Bose home still exists. On the blue exterior wall is an
   inscription, framed in white, that reads, "Tulsi Narayan Bose, boy hood
   friend of Paramhansa Yogananda." As of 2017, Tulsi's daughter, Hassi
   Mukherjee, lived there amid photos and mementos of spiritual luminaries
   who have visited, including Yogananda, of course, and his guru, Sri
   Yukteswar, and the famous female saint, Ananda Moyi Ma, about whom
   Yogananda wrote in the *AY*.

7 Swami Satyananda Giri, *A Collection of Biographies*, 153.

8 Swami Satyananda Giri, *A Collection of Biographies*, 193.

9 The criticism appears in print in a book by Swami Satyeswarananda Giri, a
   disciple of Swami Satyananda (*Biography of a Yogi—Yogananda*, Sanskrit
   Classics, 1985). It should be noted that Satyeswarananda was strongly
   critical of Yogananda in general and that SRF officials contend that some
   of his claims are inaccurate and rooted in personal feelings from his time
   as a Yogoda Satsanga monk in India. Swamis and scholars I interviewed
   said that teenagers taking it upon themselves to teach traditional practices
   would usually be frowned upon. The remarks were typically made
   lightheartedly and in the context of admiration for Yogananda's body of
   work.

10 Paramahansa Yogananda, *Autobiography*, 2013 edition, 32.

11 Paramahansa Yogananda, *Autobiography*, 2013 edition, 33.

12 Paramahansa Yogananda, *Autobiography*, 2013 edition, 36.

13 The Bose Institute, located in the vicinity of Garpar Road, was founded in 1917.

14 The Levitating Saint's story is told in Chapter 7 of *Autobiography of a Yogi*. This quote is on page 54 of the 2013 edition. It is interesting to note that in the 1970s Maharishi Mahesh Yogi introduced a set of practices based on Patanjali's treatise on siddhis. He claimed that sacred texts identify hopping like a frog as a preliminary stage of levitation. It appears that Yogananda would have agreed.

15 Paramahansa Yogananda, *Autobiography*, 2013 edition, 54.

16 The Levitating Saint's ashram, Nagendra Math, is in a different location from the one Yogananda spent time in. It is now at 2B Rammohan Roy Road, Kolkata.

17 The street is now called Raja Rammohan Sarani, but the building still houses a school.

18 Swami Nikhilananda, tr., *The Gospel of Sri Ramakrishna* (New York: Ramakrishna-Vivekananda Center, 1942). Swami Nikhilananda was assisted on the project by the young Joseph Campbell.

19 Paramahansa Yogananda, *Autobiography*, 2013 edition, 67.

20 Master Mahasaya is the focus of Chapter 9 of the *Autobiography*. This quote is on page 69 of the 2013 edition.

21 The entire incident is described in Chapter 9 of *Mejda*.

Chapter 5

1 Swami Satyananda Giri, *A Collection of Biographies*, 174.

2 Paramahansa Yogananda, *Autobiography*, 2013 edition, 73.

3 This story is told in Chapter 10 of the *Autobiography*. This quote is on page 74 of the 2013 edition.

4 On the site of Metropolitan Institution is now Vidyasagar College.

5 These details, about Mukunda enrolling in college and meeting Dayananda in Calcutta, are from Swami Satyananda's memoir. Neither *Autobiography of a Yogi* nor *Mejda* makes any mention of them.

6 Paramahansa Yogananda, *Autobiography*, 2013 edition, 75.

7 The house, at 31/58 Madanura Lane, is now maintained as a shrine.

8 Paramahansa Yogananda, *Autobiography*, 2013 edition, 77.

9 From the Sanskrit root *kas*, "to shine," hence the epithet "City of Light."

10 Paramahansa Yogananda, *Autobiography*, 2013 edition, 78.

11 Yogananda would have specified that these were the guru's first words to him in this particular lifetime. "This was not the first sun to find me at these holy feet!" he says in the *Autobiography*, and at other times cited previous incarnations when they had known one another.

12 Yogananda's first encounter with Sri Yukteswar is the subject of Chapter 10 in the *Autobiography*. The moment they meet takes place on page 79 of the 2013 edition.

13 The entire talk was recorded and is available from Self-Realization Fellowship as a CD titled *In the Glory of the Spirit*.

14 The initial encounter with Sri Yukteswar is recounted in Chapter 10 of the *Autobiography*; the second meeting is described in Chapter 12.

15 Specifically, Ananta was a supervising accountant in Agra's Public Works Department.

16 This is Yogananda's translation of Chapter 3, Verse 35, from Yogananda, *God Talks with Arjuna: The Bhagavad Gita, Royal Science of God-Realization* (Los Angeles: Self-Realization Fellowship, 1995), 402.

17 Here and elsewhere, I use Yogananda's spelling when there is a choice.

18 J.D. Salinger, "Seymour: An Introduction" in *Raise High the Roof Beam, Carpenters and Seymour: An Introduction* (Boston: Little, Brown, 1963), 61.

19 The day in Brindaban is described in Chapter 11 of the *Autobiography*. Ananta is quoted on page 89 of the 2013 edition.

Chapter 6

1 Serampore was originally Sri Ram Pur (City of Lord Rama) and many townsfolk still call it that.

2 Sri is a common honorific, a sign of respect, and in this case also part of a name. Giri, meaning "mountain," signifies one of the recognized orders of swamis. Yukteswar means union (from the same root as yoga) with Ishwara (God or Supreme Being).

3 The original ashram is now a private residence. In 1977, a memorial temple was built on part of the property. Maintained by the Yogoda Satsanga Society of India, it is called the Sri Sri Swami Sri Yukteswar Giri Smriti Mandir and is located at 3/A Buro Bibi Lane.

4 Yogananda translated that verse (4:34) this way: "Understand this! By surrendering thyself (to the guru), by questioning (the guru and thine inner perception), and by service (to the guru), the sages who have realized truth will impart that wisdom to thee."

5 Yogananda's account of his reunion with Sri Yukteswar in Serampore is at the beginning of Chapter 12 of the *Autobiography*.

6 Among them are Sri Ramakrishna, Sri Aurobindo, Ramana Maharshi, Swami Sivananda, Neem Karoli Baba, Brahmananda Saraswati, and Swami Nityananda.

7 Their presence on the cover was George Harrison's doing. He had been deeply affected by *Autobiography of a Yogi*, and kept stacks of the book around to give away.

8 Paramahansa Yogananda, *Autobiography*, 2013 edition, 93.

9 The school's long roster of distinguished former students includes Swami Vivekananda and A. C. Bhaktivedanta Swami, the founder of the Hare Krishna movement.

10 The income tax and the direct election of Senators, respectively.

11 Swami Satyananda Giri, *A Collection of Biographies*, 193.

12 Ghosh, *Mejda*, 165–6.

13 Paramahansa Yogananda, *God Talks with Arjuna*, 292.

14 Paramahansa Yogananda, *Autobiography*, 2013 edition, 113.

15 Quoted in the SRF Lessons, Lesson #29.

16 Paramahansa Yogananda, *Autobiography*, 2013 edition, 99. Sananda reports in *Mejda* that Yogananda "suffered from acute indigestion, aggravated by his irregular hours and eating habits, and by drinking too much tea, which he used to get on the way to his daily visit with Sri Yukteswarji." Once, he was incapacitated for two days. Then: "Father cured him by massaging his abdomen with a mixture of coconut oil and water, beaten into a froth."

17 Swami Sri Yukteswar, *The Holy Science* (Los Angeles, Self-Realization Fellowship, 1999).

18 Yogananda's *Bhagavad Gita* translation and commentary is titled *God Talks With Arjuna* (Los Angeles: Self-Realization Fellowship, 1995). His commentary on Jesus is *The Second Coming of Christ: The Resurrection of the Christ Within You* (Los Angeles: Self-Realization Fellowship, 2004).

19 Paramahansa Yogananda, *Autobiography*, 2013 edition, 102.

20 This exchange and Yogananda's subsequent adventure are described in Chapter 13 of the *Autobiography*, page 118.

21 Paramahansa Yogananda, *Autobiography*, 2013 edition, 121.

22 So significant was this event that Yogananda devoted an entire chapter to it in the *Autobiography*. It is Chapter 14, "An Experience in Cosmic Consciousness." This quote appears on page 126.

23 The boarding house is now a vacant hulk of loose bricks and faded paint, a point of interest and a photo op for touring devotees of Yogananda.

24 Paramahansa Yogananda, *Autobiography*, 2013 edition, 187.

25 Five days in the *Autobiography*, 188; two days in Yogananda's interview with Wendell Thomas, cited in *Hinduism Invades America* (New York: Beacon Press, 1930), 142.

26 Thomas, *Hinduism Invades America*. Thomas devotes Chapter VI to Yogananda. These quotes appear on page 143.

27 Details about the events surrounding those exams can be found in Chapter 23 of the *Autobiography*.

Chapter 7

1 Ghosh, *Mejda*, 184.

2 This quote is on the first page of Chapter 24 of the *Autobiography*, the same chapter in which Mukunda becomes Swami Yogananda. 2013 edition, 194.

3 Prabhas Chandra Bose would later serve as vice president of Yogoda Satsanga Society, the Indian branch of Yogananda's organization, for nearly 40 years.

4 Swami Satyananda Giri, *A Collection of Biographies*, 187.

5 Yogananda does not name all 10 subdivisions. This is the list as defined by the Himalayan Institute: Bharati (full of light), Giri (live in the mountains), Puri (live in the cities), Saraswati (scholars), Van (live in forests), Aranya (live in groves), Tirtha (live in pilgrimage places), Parvat (live in the high mountains), Sagar (live at the ocean), and Nath (defenders of the faith).

6 Paramahansa Yogananda, *Autobiography*, 2013 edition, 197.

7 The title *Nirvana Shatakam* is translated "Six Stanza Ode on Realization." It has also been called *Atma Shatakam* (Six Stanza Ode on Atman).

8 The structure of the poem mimics the classic "Neti Neti" discourse in Vedanta, as in "I am not this, not this," etc. In some translations, "He" is rendered "That," as in the familiar *mahavakya* (great utterance) from the Upanishads, "Thou art That" (*tat tvam asi*). "That" points to the formless aspect of Divinity, whereas "He" signifies a personal, and to our ears male, God.

9 Swami Satyananda Giri, *A Collection of Biographies*, 216.

10 The story is told in Chapter 25 of the *Autobiography*, 2013 edition, beginning on page 202.

11 Ghosh, *Mejda*, 186.

12 Paramahansa Yogananda, *Autobiography*, 2013 edition, 202.

13 Ghosh, *Mejda*, 150.

14 Thomas, *Hinduism Invades America*, 144. The word *risi* is more commonly spelled *rishi* in the West.

15 Tagore was knighted by the British Government in 1915. He later renounced the honor to protest British policies in India. Santiniketan became Visva Bharati University, whose motto translates to "Where the whole world meets in a single nest." It is still best known as Santiniketan.

16 Rabindranath Tagore, *Personality* (New York: Macmillan, 1917) 116–17.

17 According to Satyananda, these were actually affectionate nicknames Yogananda gave to each of his friends.

18 The occasion also marks the birth of the Yogoda Satsanga Society, as Yogananda's organization is known in India. In 2017, the government of India released a special stamp to commemorate the centenary.

19 Swami Satyananda was still the college student Manomohan Mazumdar when the school moved to Dihika. Hence, he stayed in Calcutta and ran the ashram at Pitambar Bhattacharya Lane (Sri Yukteswar evidently came every

Saturday to conduct satsang). He probably visited Dihikar and worked at the school during breaks in the college schedule.

20 Swami Satyananda Giri, *A Collection of Biographies*, 231.

21 Swami Satyananda Giri, *A Collection of Biographies*, 233.

Chapter 8

1 Paramahansa Yogananda, *Autobiography*, 2013 edition, 217.

2 The story of the fawn's death is told in Chapter 27 of the *Autobiography*, "Founding a Yoga School in Ranchi." The pond has long since become public property, and the original 25 acres have been reduced to 18. Still tranquil and beautifully landscaped, what is now called Yogoda Satsanga Sakha Math is used mainly as a retreat center and ashram. A handsome modern building serves as an administrative center for Yogananda's work in India. Yogananda's room has been preserved as a memorial. There is now a small girls' school on the site, and a campus on the outskirts of Ranchi houses a school and college.

3 Swami Satyananda Giri, *A Collection of Biographies of 4 Kriya Yoga Gurus* (Battle Creek, MI: Yoga Niketan, 2004), 257.

4 Maharaj(a) means, essentially, "great king." Hence, Guru Maharaj, a not uncommon title for a revered teacher, ascribes the qualities of a great royal leader to a guru.

5 Paramahansa Yogananda, *Autobiography*, 2013 edition, 217.

6 Vidal, *Sun, Moon, and Earth*, 126.

7 In *A Collection of Biographies*, Swami Satyananda Giri recalled that Yogananda was "enthused and excited" by a text written by "a German physical culturist named Miller." Perhaps he misstated Sandow's birth name, Müller, and was referring to his book *Strength and How to Obtain It*.

8 Paramahansa Yogananda, *Autobiography*, 2013 edition, 218.

9 The restaurant on Highway 101 in Encinitas opened in 1948; the one on Sunset Boulevard in Hollywood opened in 1951.

10 Ghosh, *Mejda*, 191.

11 The issue of Dhirananda's contribution came up in the 1935 lawsuit described in Chapter 15 of this book. Yogananda's statement on the subject is on page 209.

12 One of those early students was Bishnu Charan Ghosh, Yogananda's youngest sibling. Thanks in large part to the Yogoda exercises he learned at Ranchi, Bishnu went on to become a widely acclaimed teacher of yoga asanas and physical culture.

13 Where the storeroom stood is now a hexagonal temple called Smriti Mandir. Marble, with lace-like walls on all sides and a lotus-shaped dome, it is a shrine to the mission that was launched on that spot.

14 Paramahansa Yogananda, *Autobiography*, 2013 edition, 301.

15 Chapter 37 of the *Autobiography* describes the vision and everything that followed from it.

16 From "A Time for Remembering," a talk he gave at Mt. Washington, December 26, 1944, reproduced in *Pictorial History of Self-Realization Fellowship*, SRF, 1970.

17 There are minor discrepancies in Yogananda's statements about the events preceding his departure for America. The details here are pieced together from various accounts in a sequence that seems most logical.

18 Paramahansa Yogananda, *Autobiography*, 2013 edition, 302.

19 One can listen to Yogananda himself tell this story on the CD *In the Glory of the Spirit*, a recording of a talk he gave in Los Angeles on his birthday sometime in the late 1940s. It is available from Self-Realization Fellowship, along with other CDs of Yogananda speaking.

20 Paramahansa Yogananda, *Autobiography*, 2013 edition, 303.

21 Yogananda revealed this story for the first time in the *Autobiography*. He also included a drawing of Babaji's likeness, which was rendered by an artist based on Yogananda's description. Prints of that image can be seen on millions of altars in temples, meditation centers, yoga studios, and homes around the world.

22 Paramahansa Yogananda, *Autobiography*, 2013 edition, 57.

23 The entirety of Sri Yukteswar's parting advice, and the visitation from Babaji, are in Paramahansa Yogananda, *Autobiography*, 2013 edition, 303–304.

24 It is not clear if the handwritten notes were made by British officials in Calcutta or by American officials in Boston; either way, it speaks to a high level of postwar security.

25 Paramahansa Yogananda, *Autobiography*, 2013 edition, 294.

26 Paramahansa Yogananda, *Autobiography*, 2013 edition, 304.

Chapter 9

1 From the poem "On Coming to the New-Old Land–America," which is reprinted in *Songs of the Soul*. Paramahansa Yogananda, *Songs of the Soul* (Los Angeles: Self-Realization Fellowship, 1983), 62.

2 Yogananda's passport photo, a unique look at him at 27 with facial hair, can be found in recent editions of the *Autobiography*.

3 *The Boston Globe*, Monday, September 20, 1920, 7.

4 In the *Autobiography*, Yogananda wrote only this about his time in Boston: "Three happy years were spent in humble circumstances in Boston. I gave public lectures, taught classes and wrote a book of poems . . ." The material in this chapter, therefore, was culled entirely from other sources.

5 You can hear Yogananda himself tell that story on the CD *Beholding the One in All*, available from SRF Publications.

6 Sri Durga Mata, *A Paramhansa Yogananda Trilogy of Divine Love* (Pasadena, CA: Joan Wight Publications, 1992). Interesting descriptions of Yogananda's

physiognomy, modes of dress and grooming, and other characteristics are on pages 166 to 194. The book was lovingly assembled after Durga Mata's death by her close friend and fellow devotee Joan Wight.

7 Sri Durga Mata, *A Paramhansa Yogananda Trilogy*, 168.

8 That outing occurred on October 5, the day before his talk at the congress. There is photo of him sitting on Plymouth Rock.

9 As a point of historical interest, the article appears directly under a piece about the trial of Charles Ponzi, whose shenanigans gave us the term Ponzi Scheme.

10 Paramahansa Yogananda, *The Science of Religion* (Los Angeles: Self-Realization Fellowship, 1982), 4–5.

11 Paramahansa Yogananda, *The Science of Religion*.

12 Paramahansa Yogananda, *Autobiography*, 2013 edition, 306.

13 The church was located at 115 College Avenue in West Somerville, nowadays a half-hour ride by subway or car, but surely a more formidable trip then.

14 From "A Time for Remembering."

15 Alice Hasey and her husband, Ward B. Hasey, lived at 9 Lester Terrace in West Somerville, close to Davis Square.

16 The Lewises' account of their meeting and subsequent relationship with Yogananda is told in the book by their daughter, Brenda Lewis Rosser: *Treasures Against Time* (Borrego Springs, CA Borrego Publications, 2001).

17 Could it have been the weather? The average Boston temperature on Christmas Day is 32 degrees Fahrenheit; in Calcutta it's 77.

18 The scenario that follows is taken from Rosser, *Treasures Against Time*, 41–44.

19 Matthew 6:22.

20 Rosser, *Treasures Against Time*, 4.

21 Rosser, *Treasures Against Time*, 65.

22 If you're on a Yogananda tour of Boston, don't look for 30 Huntington Ave. The original building was torn down long ago, and in the 1980s a massive urban complex was built, replete with hotels and a huge shopping mall.

23 Yogananda translated "Sat-Sanga" as "Fellowship of Truth."

24 *Harvard Crimson*, February 24, 1923.

25 The structure is long gone, but the setting can be seen by entering the address on Google Maps: 70 Hiawatha Avenue, Waltham, MA.

26 "Yogi 'Will-Stunts' Go Coue One Better—Making Hub Muscular," *Boston Sunday Post*, February 23, 1923.

27 Coué's famous autosuggestion phrase was even sampled by John Lennon, with a minor tweak ("Every day in every way, it's getting better and better") in the song "Beautiful Boy."

28 Some sources say he spoke at Girls' Trade School, giving the impression he spoke to female students. The Applied Psychology Club simply used a lecture hall at the school.

29 Rosser, *Treasures Against Time*, 17.

30 *New-York Tribune*, November 23,1923. A movie camera was operating at the time, and silent, choppy footage of the quintet can be found online, with Yogananda flashing a winning smile for the camera. One half expects Charlie Chaplin's Little Tramp to waddle by at any moment and do a double take.

31 An inveterate seeker, Ms. Wilson later became a devotee of Sri Aurobindo and spent her final years at his ashram in India.

32 The 22-story Hotel Pennsylvania, at 7th Avenue and 33rd Street, now overlooks Madison Square Garden, which replaced the original Penn Station in 1963. Some of the hotel's original architectural touches remain intact.

33 The three gunas are sattwa, rajas, and tamas. Sattwa produces all that is good, harmonious, and supportive of spiritual virtues and physical well-being; rajas governs action, passion, dynamism, and drive; tamas represents inertia, dullness, and disorder.

34 Louis Sahagun, "Guru's Followers Mark Legacy of a Star's Teachings," *Los Angeles Times*, August 6, 2006.

Chapter 10

1 Paramahansa Yogananda, *Autobiography*, 2013 edition, 294.

2 In 1920, Americans spent $2 million on radio sets, parts, and accessories; in 1922 they spent $60 million, and in 1924 the figure exceeded $350 million.

3 Yogananda met some of the New Thought leaders and was likely to have visited the Vedanta Society at 34 W. 71st Street, where it is still located.

4 A Punjabi Sikh, Thind contested what was clearly a racially discriminatory immigration policy and lost in the Supreme Court; the case had the unintended consequence of tightening the restriction on Asian immigration.

5 For the whole story of Governor Henry Simpson Johnston's travails as a yoga enthusiast, see Philip Deslippe, "The American Yoga Scare of 1927: How Traveling Yogis Toppled the Oklahoma State Government," South Asian American Digital Archive, September 10, 2015.

6 According to Anya P. Foxen in *Biography of a Yogai: Paramahansa Yogananda and the Origins of Modern Yoga* (New York: Oxford, 2017), p. 127, citing Robert Love's book *The Great Oom*, Yogananda visited Pierre Bernard in Nyack in late 1920. It could not have happened; Yogananda did not visit New York for another three years. Either the meeting never occurred or the date was incorrect.

7 Foxen, *Biography of a Yogi*.

8 Mabel Potter Daggett, "The Heathen Invasion," *Hampton-Columbian Magazine*, 27(4)(October 1911): 399–411.

9 The law restricted the annual number of immigrants from any country to 2 percent of the number of their countrymen who had been counted in the 1890 census.

10 That would be about $350 today.

11 Steve Hannagan, "NEA Service," *Honolulu Star-Bulletin*, December 29, 1923, 14.

12 Readers should not interpret the descriptions of these techniques as instructions. For the best results, one should obtain instruction based on the Lessons that Yogananda developed.

13 The mantra's meaning is usually given as "I am He" or "I am That," although in the Vedic tradition a mantra's vibratory quality, not its literal meaning, is paramount.

14 Again, for the student's sake, yogic methods are best learned under reputable auspices from trained and authorized teachers.

15 Chapter 26 of the *Autobiography* is titled "The Science of Kriya Yoga." It contains a thorough description of its history and practice. This quote is in the 2013 edition, 210.

16 To repeat, this is a brief description of a technique, and is not meant to be instruction.

17 Lola Williamson, *Transcendent in America: Hindu-Inspired Meditation Movements as a New Religion* (New York: New York University Press, 2010), 60.

18 For example, Sri Sailendra Bejoy Dasgupta in *Paramhansa Swami Yogananda: Life-Portrait and Reminiscences* (Battle Creek, MI: Yoga Niketan, 2006), and Swami Satyeswarananda Giri in the aforementioned *Biography of a Yogi: Yogananda* (San Diego: Sanskrit Classics, 1985).

19 The revered Swami Sivananda of Rishikesh, for example, called Yogananda "an ideal representative of the ancient sages and seers, the glory of India."

20 The letter, dated January 7, 1924, is reproduced in Rosser, *Treasures Against Time*, 70.

21 Rosser, *Treasures Against Time*, 72. The letter is dated March 4, 1924.

22 Rosser, *Treasures Against Time*, 73. The letter is dated April 26, 1924.

23 As Vice President, Coolidge had succeeded the deceased Warren G. Harding in 1923.

24 *Pictorial History of Self-Realization Fellowship* (Yogoda Satsanga Society of India), 14.

25 We don't know what became of Ralph, but Yogananda noted Arthur's presence in the audience at a 1950 lecture in Los Angeles.

26 It is said that Yogananda learned how to drive on that trip. If he did, it was a skill he used rarely, if ever. He preferred to be driven.

27 *Pictorial History of Self-Realization Fellowship (Yogoda Satsanga Society of India)*, 15.

28 Ibid.

29 Since there were no tunnels or bridges connecting either New York City or Philadelphia with New Jersey at that time, the journey would have involved ferryboats.

30 *Pictorial History of Self-Realization Fellowship (Yogoda Satsanga Society of India)*, 15.

31 The entire poem is in Paramahansa Yogananda, *Songs of the Soul* (Los Angeles: Self-Realization Fellowship, 1983), 114.

32 From Paramahansa Yogananda, *Journey to Self-Realization* (Los Angeles: Self-Realization Fellowship, 1997), 84–85. The talk was given on June 15, 1947, in San Diego.

33 The dates were August 11, 13, and 14, and the respective titles were: "Mastering the Subconscious Mind," "Magnetic Healing," and "Concentration and Life Force." At City Auditorium, an organist ushered Yogananda to the stage with "Song of India," a tune based on an aria in a Rimsky-Korsakov opera called *Sadko*. The song would later become popular with jazz orchestras.

34 Paramahansa Yogananda, *Autobiography*, 2013 edition, 176. A photo of Yogananda leaning out of the window of the Maxwell to feed a bear in Yellowstone can be seen online and in some SRF publications.

35 "Miracles of Raja Yoga" in Paramahansa Yogananda, *Journey to Self-Realization*.

36 The boat left Vancouver on September 9. In the *Autobiography*, Yogananda calls the trip a 26-day vacation. That is plausible since his first lecture in Seattle was on October 7. A postcard to the Lewises, however, has him returning to Seattle on September 22.

37 The passage is part of an article in the inaugural (November 1925) issue of *East–West*, the original name of Yogoda Satsanga's in-house magazine.

38 The Masonic Auditorium, on the corner of Harvard and Pine, later became the Egyptian Theatre. Coincidentally, in 2014, the first public screening of the documentary *Awake: The Life of Yogananda* was held in that very theater during the Seattle International Film Festival.

39 The Golden Gate Bridge opened in 1937, six months after the San Francisco–Oakland Bay Bridge.

40 Located at 1290 Sutter Street, at Van Ness, it was then a Freemason center and temple. It is now the Regency Center.

41 The original "Standard Pose" was black and white; the image most often seen now is a colorized version.

42 Paramahansa Yogananda, *Autobiography*, 2013 edition, 312.

43 Most of Yogananda's other major works were completed after Tara Mata's passing by Mrinalini Mata, the disciple designated by Yogananda to succeed her as editor in chief. She was president of SRF from 2011 to 2017.

44 Paramahansa Yogananda, *Autobiography*, 2013 edition, 176.

Chapter 11

1 Yogananda also become close with popular New Thought author (e.g., *In Tune with the Infinite*) Ralph Waldo Trine. Their visits with one another were noted on a few occasions in *East–West* magazine.

2 The sponsors named by reporter Alma Whitaker in the *Los Angeles Times* were "Captain and Mrs. Richmond Pearson Hobson, Mrs. Rufus von Kleinsmid, Mrs. Isadore Dockweiler, Mrs. Willoughby Rodman, and Harry Haldeman."

3 *LA Times*, January 19, 1925.

4 "Coal to Newcastle," *Los Angeles Times*, January 28, 1925, B4.

5 The information and quotes are from the memoir *The Flawless Mirror* by Kamala. The quote "Always keep your dignity . . ." is from page 19. The book offers useful insight into Yogananda's personal side and the soul of a disciple. Copyrighted by Kamala in 1964, and distributed by Crystal Clarity Publishers, it can be found online.

6 Rosser, *Treasures Against Time*, 83.

7 That vision is described in the *Autobiography*, Chapter 21, page 174 in recent editions.

8 *Pictorial History of Self-Realization Fellowship*, 16. That's $628,000 in 2017 dollars, which makes the deal one terrific bargain, as the property is probably worth at least 10 times that amount.

9 An interesting historical note: F. Scott Fitzgerald's classic portrait of the 1920s, *The Great Gatsby*, was published on April 10. Initial sales were terrible.

10 *LA Times*, April 11, 1925.

11 *Inner Culture* magazine, April 1940, 52.

12 *Pictorial History of Self-Realization Fellowship*, 16.

13 Dated May 30, 1925, and sent from Portland, Oregon, the letter appears in Rosser, *Treasures Against Time*, 84.

14 According to my research, Yogananda was in Spokane on September 14. He may have composed and signed the letter earlier, and had a typist add the date it was to be mailed.

15 *East–West* magazine, November–December 1925, 29.

16 From the transcript of the speeches given at the Mt. Washington dedication ceremony.

17 SRF sources say that the 1956 edition contains essentially the same series of lessons as the earlier edition, with some reordering and material by authors other than Yogananda removed (e.g., food recipes). Further details regarding what was changed in different iterations of the Lessons can be

found online. Predictably, people still argue over which modifications were actually authorized by Yogananda and which constitute liberties taken and missteps made after his passing.

18 From the draft of a letter published in *Bulletin of Sri Aurobindo International Centre of Education* 28, no. 3 (August 1976): 48.

19 Paramahansa Yogananda, *Autobiography*, 2013 edition, 409.

20 Los Angeles Superior Court, case number 181261, October 13, 1925.

21 Los Angeles Superior Court, case number 181768, October 22, 1925.

22 One account was at the Security Trust and Savings Bank, the other at Pacific Southwest Trust and Savings Bank.

23 *East–West*, September–October 1926, 28. Subsequently, Rashid reportedly married a wealthy Englishwoman, lived in Europe for a while, and then resettled in India.

24 The entire poem can be found in Paramahansa Yogananda, *Songs of the Soul* (Los Angeles: Self-Realization Fellowship, 1983), 134. The book is a collection of Yogananda's verse.

25 *East–West* magazine, November–Dececember 1925, 13.

26 The magazine would later be published monthly and then quarterly; its size was reduced; its name became *Inner Culture* for a while and ultimately *Self-Realization*.

Chapter 12

1 At his first public lecture, Yogananda was introduced by Dr. Julian P. Arnold, whose father, Sir Edwin Arnold, was the author of a poetic translation of the *Bhagavad Gita* titled *The Song Celestial*. It was widely read in the late 19th and early 20th centuries, as was Arnold's life of the Buddha, titled *The Light of Asia*.

2 *East–West*, January–February 1926, 29.

3 *East–West*, January–February, 1926, 11. That issue also contained an article about Guru Nanak, the founder of Sikhism, and one about the Buddha. Yogananda was clearly displaying his multireligious perspective.

4 Thomas, *Hinduism Invades America*, 137.

5 Kamala, *The Flawless Mirror*, 13.

6 The crowd size at Yogananda's Carnegie Hall series is often said to have been 3,000, but the official seating capacity is 2,804.

7 In the *Autobiography*, Yogananda refers to the song as "an old Hindu chant." Sikhs might take offense at that. Perhaps Yogananda was thinking of "Hindu" in its original sense, pertaining to the geographical entity that was named for the Indus River and came to be called India. Or perhaps he meant that Guru Nanak, like Buddha, was a Hindu religious innovator whose work was later codified as a new religion.

8 Paramahansa Yogananda, *Cosmic Chants* (Los Angeles: Self-Realization Fellowship, 1974), xiii.

9 Paramahansa Yogananda, *Cosmic Chants* (Los Angeles: Self-Realization Fellowship, 1938), 11. The Carnegie Hall story is told in the Introduction. In addition, SRF has produced a CD of recorded chants led by Yogananda himself. Remastered with modern technology, the collection is titled *Songs of My Heart*. "O God Beautiful" is one of the songs.

10 The usual spelling is *brahmachari*, but publications and correspondence in Yogananda's domain used *brahmacharee* in reference to Sri Nerode.

11 509 5th Avenue became the legal address for *East–West* magazine; Yogananda was listed as owner and editor. The building is now occupied by the Lubavitch branch of Hasidic Judaism.

12 According to an in-house report, by the end of 1926, about 25,000 people had attended lectures, classes, and Sunday school meetings at the Mt. Washington Educational Center in the 15 months since its inception.

13 Rosser, *Treasures Against Time*, 9.

14 The letter, with additional instructions, is in Rosser, *Treasures Against Time*, 90.

15 Kamala, *The Flawless Mirror*, 25–26.

16 The translation was printed in the September–October 1926 issue of *East–West*, 32, and also in Chapter 31 of the *Autobiography*, 2013 edition, 306.

17 *East–West* magazine, July–August, 1926, 25.

18 *The Washington Post*, January 17, 1927. Yogananda surely would have used "art," not "are."

19 This should obviously be "Cosmic." The error was made by the *Washington Post* and repeated in *East–West* magazine, from which I derived the passage.

20 According to the *Washington Herald*, it was the first time a swami had been received officially by a U.S. President.

21 "Meatless Coolidge Meals Prescribed by Yogananda," *The Washington Post*, January 15, 1927, 8.

Chapter 13

1 As with other direct quotes in this book, this one is faithful to the grammar, spelling, and punctuation of the original source.

2 *The Los Angeles Examiner*, January 9, 1928.

3 Ten thousand dollars then would be about $140,000 in 2017. The telegram was dated April 26, 1926.

4 Paramahansa Yogananda, "Yellow Journalism versus Truth: Are Eastern Teachings 'Dangerous'?" *East–West*, January–February 1928, 3–8.

5 Anya P. Foxen, *Biography of a Yogi: Paramahansa Yogananda and the Origins of Modern Yoga* (New York: Oxford University Press, 2017), 54.

6 Essays about India by Lillian Gish and the scholar Dale Stuart appeared in the September–October 1927 issue of *East–West*. Yogananda's article,

"Yellow Journalism versus Truth," and another piece by Stuart appeared in the January–February 1928 issue. Yogananda's counterattack on yellow journalism continued in the March–April edition with a long piece titled "Spiritualizing the Newspapers." That issue also contained other critiques of the Mayo book.

7 *Time* magazine, February 20, 1928.

8 *Miami Daily News*, February 5, 1928.

9 The correspondence among British officials was obtained from the British Foreign Office by Anil Nerode, professor of mathematics at Cornell University and son of Nirad Ranjan Chowdhury, the Brahmacharee Nerode (later Sri Nerode) mentioned earlier.

10 A little more than a month after Yogananda left town, Chief Quigg was arrested for the murder of an African American prisoner who'd been killed while in his custody two years earlier. He was acquitted, then fired from his job when a grand jury investigation condemned his department for corruption, cruelty, torture, and even summary executions. He never served time, and in 1937, he got his job back.

11 Rosser, *Treasures Against Time*, 110.

12 Thomas, *Hinduism Invades America*, 139.

13 Thomas, *Hinduism Invades America*, 140.

14 The May–June issue of *East–West* lists centers in LA, Philadelphia and Merion Station (Pennsylvania), Boston, Cleveland, Cincinnati, Buffalo, Detroit, both Minneapolis and St. Paul (Minnesota), Pittsburgh, and two in Washington, D.C., one of which was the "Afro-American Yogoda Sat-Sanga," plus India and Scotland.

15 *East–West* magazine, May–June 1929, 43.

16 $8,000 in 1929 was equivalent to about $114,000 in 2017.

17 B. K. Bagchi, "Adventures of Indian Philosophy in America," *The Modern Review*, February 1936, 165–69.

18 *East–West* magazine, May–June 1929, 40.

19 Rosser, *Treasures Against Time*, 112.

Chapter 14

1 Yogananda, *God Talks with Arjuna*, 264.

2 *East–West* magazine, November–December 1929, 26.

3 For Kamala's description of the visit, see *The Flawless Mirror*, 54–57.

4 His New York hosts were Amelita Galli-Curci and her husband; during that visit the singer wrote the foreword to *Yogananda's Whispers from Eternity*, which would be published that December.

5 Said in conversation with Edwin Montagu, secretary of state for India, 1921. Richard Toye, *Churchill's Empire: The World That Made Him and the World He Made* (New York: Henry Holt and Company, LLC, 2010), 172.

6 *East–West*, April 1932, 5–8.

7 *East–West*, December 1933, 25.

8 *East–West*, February 1934, 3.

9 An e-mail exchange with Yogoda Satsanga in India suggests that Sananda Ghosh's dating may have been inexact and the father's contributions may have continued until 1932, when Yogananda's financial situation had changed.

10 Sri Durga Mata, *A Paramhansa Yogananda Trilogy*, 22.

11 A 1935 dollar was equivalent to about $18 in 2017.

12 Sri Gyanamata, *God Alone: The Life and Letters of a Saint* (Los Angeles: Self-Realization Fellowship, 1984), 248.

13 The date of his speech was September 10, 1933, one day shy of 40 years since Vivekananda's historic address at the World's Parliament of Religions in the same city. His topic was "Realizing World Unity Through the Art of Living."

14 Strictly speaking, interracial marriage was not against California law, but clerks were instructed not to give marriage licenses to mixed couples.

15 One such ad appeared in the *San Francisco Chronicle*, January 4, 1932.

16 Hamid Bey went on to create the Coptic Fellowship in Los Angeles. He died in 1976. The Fellowship is now located in Grand Rapids, Michigan.

17 Private e-mail correspondence.

18 Sri Durga Mata, *A Paramhansa Yogananda Trilogy*; Sri Gyanamata, *God Alone*; Kamala, *The Flawless Mirror*.

19 Private e-mail from an SRF official.

20 The Self-Realization Fellowship says that the use of "Praecepta" "was intended to emphasize that they were the teachings and instructions of SRF's spiritual preceptor or guru"—meaning Yogananda. The name would later change to the Self-Realization Fellowship Lessons.

21 According to SRF, the 1956 changes had been in the works prior to Yogananda's death in 1952, and were made in accordance with his wishes. As of this writing, the course is undergoing another long-awaited revision.

22 No official date marks the origin of the monastic order, but it is generally considered to be November 1931.

23 Vivekananda ordained some Western swamis, but his order has always trained monastics at the Ramakrishna Mission in India. Yogananda was really the first to establish Hindu-based monasteries in America and to institute training programs exclusively for Western monks and nuns.

24 The entire speech by James Lynn (later Rajarsi Janakananda) is reproduced in the book *Rajarsi Janakananda: A Great Western Yogi* (Los Angeles: Self-Realization Fellowship, 1996). It begins on page 135.

25 In his book *Conversations With Yogananda* (Nevada City, CA: Crystal Clarity, 2004), Swami Kriyananda, a direct disciple, quotes Yogananda as saying: "I've had many people say to me, 'If ever I get money, I'll give most of it

to you.' If ever they had a sudden 'windfall,' however—an inheritance, perhaps, or a soaring return on a stock market investment—it was only rarely that they fulfilled their promise."

26 Sri Durga Mata, *A Paramhansa Yogananda Trilogy*, 119.

27 The magazine went through name changes in the ensuing years. It became *Inner Culture* for some time, and eventually became *Self-Realization*, its current name.

28 Late in life, James Lynn took monastic vows. Yogananda named him Rajarsi Janakananda. He became president of Self-Realization Fellowship upon Yogananda's death in 1952, but lived only three more years.

29 The all-day meditations were originally on December 24. They were later changed to the 23rd.

30 Paramahansa Yogananda, *Autobiography*, 2013 edition, 313.

31 Superior Court of the State of California, in and for the County of Los Angeles, number 387 391. Dhirananda had originally sued late in 1929. According to the 1935 court documents, the papers for that earlier suit were either lost or destroyed. For unknown reasons, Dhirananda chose not to pursue the case in the intervening years.

32 While some Yogananda detractors conjecture that he left for India to avoid the lawsuit, the opposite is more likely the case. Since the India trip had been announced earlier, Dhirananda may have seen the need to act before Yogananda left.

Chapter 15

1 Richard Wright drove the car across the country.

2 *Inner Culture*, October 1935, 23.

3 Paramahansa Yogananda, *Autobiography of a Yogi*, Chapter 39.

4 This and other observations from his journey to India are in "Letter to Students and Friends of Self-Realization" in *Inner Culture* magazine, October 1935, 23, and in other issues of the magazine.

5 Durga Mata, *A Paramhansa Trilogy*, 50.

6 Swami Kriyananda, *Paramhansa Yogananda: A Biography, with Personal Reflections and Reminiscenses* (Nevada City: Crystal Clarity Publishers, 2011), Chapter 15. According to Swami Kriyananda, Yogananda assigned the following incarnations to famous historical figures: Joseph Stalin, Genghis Khan; Winston Churchill, Napoleon; Mussolini, Mark Antony; Charles Lindbergh, Abraham Lincoln; Therese Neumann, Mary Magdalene; the Three Wise Men, Babaji, Lahiri Mahasaya, Sri Yukteswar.

7 Yogananda describes some of the Alexander tales in Chapter 41 of the *Autobiography*.

8 Kriyananda, *Paramhansa Yogananda*, 131.

9 *Inner Culture* magazine, October 1935, 23.

10 *Rajarsi Janakananda: A Great Western Yogi* (Los Angeles: Self-Realization Fellowship, 1996), 67.

11 *Rajarsi Janakananda: A Great Western Yogi* (Los Angeles: Self-Realization Fellowship, 1996), 68. Schools under British rule taught European history better than they did India's.

12 The complete letter is in *Rajarsi Janakananda: A Great Western Yogi*, 82.

13 Paramahansa Yogananda, *Autobiography*, 2013 edition, 320.

14 *Inner Culture*, October 1935, 23.

15 Self-Realization Fellowship, *Rajarsi Janakananda*, 71–72.

16 The October 1935 issue of *Inner Culture* contained a stunning photo of Yogananda, Richard Wright, and Ettie Bletsch on camels, with the Great Pyramid of Giza behind them.

17 Also known as the Taj Mahal Palace, and colloquially as "the Taj," the hotel was one of the targets of the 2008 Mumbai terrorist attack.

18 Paramahansa Yogananda, *Autobiography*, 2013 edition, 321.

19 They could not drive across India because the roads had been flooded by monsoons. Wright also said the trains were "better as massage machines than conveyances" ("News from India," *Inner Culture*, December 1935).

20 The Gandhi visit is recalled in Chapter 44 of the *Autobiography*, 2013 edition, 383.

21 *The Collected Works of Mahatma Gandhi*, Vol. 61 (Publications Division, Ministry of Information and Broadcasting, Government of India, 1958).

22 Paramahansa Yogananda, *Autobiography*, 2013 edition, 321.

23 Ghosh, *Mejda*, 199.

24 From a short memoir, Hare Krishna Ghosh, *Experiences with My Guru, Paramhansa Yogananda*, published online at www.ananda.org. https://www.ananda.org/free-inspiration/books/experiences-with-my-guru-paramhansa-yogananda/experiences-the-book/.

25 Wright's diary entry for that day is reproduced in Chapter 40 of the *Autobiography*, 2013 edition, 322–24; his description of Sri Yukteswar and his hermitage is insightful and vivid.

26 The journey and arrival are affectionately described in both the *Autobiography*, Chapter 40, and in Ghosh, *Mejda*, 199–201.

27 Paramahansa Yogananda, *Autobiography*, 2013 edition, 325.

28 From Self-Realization Fellowship, *Rajarsi Janakananda*, 75–76.

29 Hare Krishna Ghosh, *Experiences with My Guru*.

30 *The Indian Express*, November 23, 1935.

31 *The Indian Express*, November 23, 1935.

32 B. K. Bagchi, "Adventures of Indian Philosophy in America," February 1936.

33 I gained access to some unpublished letters, and cannot legally quote them directly.

34 That suit, for $10,000, claimed that Bagchi had "wrongfully and maliciously acquired an improper influence over [Tandon's] wife."

35 This was Swami Kriyananda's contention in *Paramhansa Yogananda: A Biography*, 132.

36 Chapter 41 is titled "An Idyl in South India" (*idyl* may be an antiquated spelling).

37 Paramahansa Yogananda, *Autobiography*, 2013 edition, 330.

38 Sri Munagala Venkataramiah, *Talks with Sri Ramana Maharshi* (Tiruvannamalai, India: Sri Ramanasramam, 2013), 103–5.

39 Her name is more commonly rendered "Anandamayi Ma." Yogananda describes his visit with her in Chapter 45 of *Autobiography*.

40 For some reason, Yogananda did not visit Sri Aurobindo, although he spent time in Madras (now Chennai), only 150 kilometers from the Aurobindo ashram in Pondicherry.

41 Hare Krishna Ghosh, *Experiences with My Guru*.

42 The recording of the talk, titled "Removing All Sorrow and Suffering," can be purchased from Self-Realization Fellowship. The anecdote about his father is on Track 10 of the CD.

43 See the *Autobiography*, Chapter 42, "Last Days with my Guru." The poignant moment described here is on page 340 of the 2013 edition.

44 He originally spelled it Paramhansa. The additional "a" was inserted some years after his death by SRF. Curious readers can find the explanation online or in the Publisher's Note in SRF's 1981 reprinting of Yogananda's *Whispers From Eternity*. I chose to use the spelling most familiar to the public, to avoid confusion.

45 Sailendra Bejoy Dasgupta (a disciple of Sri Yukteswar) and Swami Satyeswarananda (a disciple of Swami Satyananda) disputed this story in their books, and Yogananda detractors on the Internet have essentially accused him of being a self-proclaimed Paramahansa. SRF points out that the November–December 1951 issue of its magazine contains a quote from an eyewitness, Ananda Mohan Lahiri (Lahiri Mahasaya's grandson) that confirms Yogananda's account. It should also be said that Yogananda clearly did not make up the story sometime later on; he mentioned the incident in a private letter from India (*Rajarsi Janakananda: A Great Western Yogi*, 100).

46 Sananda Ghose's account in *Mejda* suggests that Bishnu's wife and children may also have been stuffed into the Ford.

47 Excerpts are from Self-Realization Fellowship, *Rajarsi Janakananda: A Great Western Yogi*.

48 This was part of Yogananda's research for the Lahiri Mahasaya biography that Sri Yukteswar asked him to write. The material he accumulated was used in *Autobiography of a Yogi*.

49 The experience is described in Chapter 22 of the *Autobiography*.

50 Paramahansa Yogananda, *Autobiography*, 2013 edition, 343.

51 Photos and movie footage of the period before the burial, with mourners paying last respects and Yogananda seated beside his guru's lifeless body, occasionally propping up his chin to keep his face visible, can be seen in the excellent documentary *Awake: The Life of Yogananda* and in the coffee-table book of the same name.

52 The *Autobiography*, Chapter 43, "The Resurrection of Sri Yukteswar."

53 One thing is clear: he did not invent the story to spice up his autobiography; he mentioned the event in letters to Lynn and the Lewises while still in India.

54 Paramahansa Yogananda, *Autobiography*, 2013 edition, 368.

55 *Inner Culture*, December, 1936, 25.

56 Paramahansa Yogananda, *Autobiography*, 2013 edition, 347.

57 Paramahansa Yogananda, *Autobiography*, 2013 edition, 400.

Chapter 16

1 Paramahansa Yogananda, *Autobiography*, 2013 edition, 400.

2 In *Inner Culture*, January 1937, pages 3–4, Yogananda made a surprisingly strong statement supporting King Edward VIII and criticizing the Church of England for "religious bigotry." He said, in part: "King Edward, by renouncing the throne and clinging to love, is not indulging in selfish private pleasure, but he is showing the young people of the world how, for ideal love and true happiness, one should renounce material pomp, money, and power."

3 Sri Durga Mata, *Trilogy of Divine Love*, 99.

4 Paramahansa Yogananda, *Autobiography*, 2013 edition, 101.

5 Sri Durga Mata, *Trilogy of Divine Love*, 30.

6 The building may once have been home to a synagogue. On the site now is one of the busiest freeway intersections in the country (the 10 and the 110).

7 Seva Devi died in November 1938.

8 In January 1937, the following books were available: *Whispers from Eternity*; *Metaphysical Meditations*; *Scientific Healing Affirmations*; *The Science of Religion*; *Songs of the Soul*; *Psychological Chart*.

9 Though its form has changed somewhat, the Horn of Plenty Bank remains one of SRF's many offerings to this day.

10 The organization's magazine not only changed its name at various times, but also its format and frequency. In May 1937, it shrank from letter-size pages to booklet-size. In July 1940, it became a quarterly publication.

11 Most useful in this regard are: Sri Gyanamata, *God Alone*; Sri Daya Mata, *Finding the Joy Within You* (Los Angeles: Self-Realization Fellowship, 1990); Self-Realization Fellowship, *Rajarsi Janakananda*; Sri Durga Mata, *A Paramhansa Trilogy*; Roy Eugene Davis, *Paramahansa Yogananda As I Knew Him* (Lakemont, GA: CSA Press, 2005); Swami Kriyananda, *Conversations with Yogananda*; Swami Kriyananda, *Paramhansa Yogananda*.

12 These and other glimpses of Yogananda's personality and human traits
    are in the third section of Sri Durga Mata, *Trilogy of Divine Love*, titled
    "Reflections of My Guru, Paramhansa Yogananda."

13 I was told that he did much the same with "Indian Love Call," and converted
    "I Love You, California" to "I Love You, India" and "Roamin' in the
    Gloamin'" to "Sitting in the Silence."

14 Roy Eugene Davis, *Paramahansa Yogananda As I Knew Him*, 37–38.

15 It is said that he ate chicken or fish on occasion, out of deference to a host, but
    there are also tales, perhaps apocryphal, of him imbibing surreptitiously.

16 Sri Daya Mata, *Finding the Joy Within You*, 246.

17 She was elected after the passing of Daya Mata in 2010.

18 "If You Would Know the Guru: An Informal Talk by Sri Mrinalini Mata,"
    audio CD available from SRF.

19 Sri Gyanamata, *God Alone*, 120.

20 Sri Gyanamata, *God Alone*, 111.

21 Sri Gyanamata, *God Alone*, 260.

22 *Inner Culture*, March 1938, 11.

23 The dismissal letter was sent by Wilson and Thomas, Attorneys at Law, on
    September 26, 1939.

24 The Nerode family eventually settled in Chicago. Sri Nerode taught Yoga and
    wrote numerous philosophical and practical treatises. He died in 1983.

25 Anil Nerode contends that his father did not want the sexual allegations to be
    made public, but they became so due to a lawyer's incompetence.

26 In my review of available documents, I saw no suggestion that Yogananda
    ever considered paying off the Nerodes or settling the lawsuit out of court.
    He did contend that he offered them what would now be called severance
    pay when they were dismissed.

27 Daya Mata was deposed in a lawsuit between Self-Realization Fellowship and
    what was then called Ananda Church of Self-Realization that lasted from
    1990 to 2002.

28 The woman who wrote the letter is now deceased. For the sake of any
    surviving family members, I elected not to reveal her name or personal
    details.

29 A few Internet voices allege that Yogananda fathered children with two other
    disciples as well. Historical evidence indicates that one of the children was
    fathered by another man, and the actual existence of the second child is
    more a matter of hearsay and speculation than established fact. Neither of
    the two women mentioned in these allegations ever even hinted at a sexual
    relationship with Yogananda, nor is there any evidence of one.

30 Ben Erskine himself did not choose to go public with his conviction that
    he was Yogananda's son; the story got out because his daughter sought to
    pressure SRF to give her money in 1995.

31 Genetic Technologies of Glencoe, Missouri, and ReliaGene Technologies of New Orleans.

32 Anil Nerode asserts that the legal procedures for "chain of custody" of the tested samples were not precisely followed. When the results were announced, G. Michael Still told the *Los Angeles Times*, "In my opinion, this is airtight." (See Teresa Watanabe, "DNA Clears Yoga Guru in Seven-Year Paternity Dispute," *Los Angeles Times*, July 11, 2002.) It seems likely that some people would mistrust any test arranged and paid for by SRF, but no other entity has ever undertaken the task. Ben Erskine, who is still alive as of this writing, said he has no interest in pursuing the matter.

33 It has been argued that spicy matters nearly eight decades old do not warrant mention in this book. But Yogananda had to deal with some of the accusations during his lifetime, and the heirs to his legacy had to deal with the Erskine charges not very long ago. And, as noted, the issues are amplified today on social media platforms, even if they are discussed by only a small group of Yogananda devotees and former devotees.

34 *Paramahansa Yogananda: In Memorium: Personal Accounts of the Master's Final Days* (Los Angeles: Self-Realization Fellowship, 1958), 10.

35 Rosser, *Treasures Against Time*, 86.

36 He took to that designation slowly; it was not until the June 1938 issue that the SRF magazine referred to him as Paramhansa. Disciples who found "Paramahansaji" a mouthful continued to address him as "Swamiji" or "Master," or "Guruji" or "Gurudeva," and sometimes, when addressing him directly, as simply "Sir."

37 Bishnu also lectured at Columbia University in New York.

38 Paramahansa Yogananda, *The Second Coming of Christ: The Resurrection of the Christ Within You* (Los Angeles: Self-Realization Fellowship, 2004).

39 Called Yogoda Satsanga Math, it remains in operation as a YSS retreat and administrative center.

40 The room has been preserved as it was in Yogananda's time, for viewing by appointment and on special occasions.

41 This was the first time an image of Krishna was placed in any of Yogananda's facilities. It was also the *only* place during Yogananda's lifetime. It was no doubt deemed too controversial in Christian America, at a time when critics were eager to depict Hindus as idol-worshipping pagans. Krishna was restored to the SRF altars, and Yogananda's "Standard Pose" was added, sometime after his passing. The altars of the Ananda community, founded by Swami Kriyananda, remain sans Krishna.

Chapter 17

1 From "A World Without Boundaries," a talk he gave on February 26, 1939, in *The Divine Romance* (Los Angeles: Self-Realization Fellowship, 1986), 345.

2 According to documents I've seen, his Petition for Naturalization was approved on August 26, 1949. It is interesting to note that, in a 1939 speech, he said he

had not attempted to become a U.S. citizen because he considered himself a citizen of the world, not of any one country.

3 John Barnes and David Nicholson, eds., *The Empire at Bay: the Leo Amery Diaries, 1929–45* (London: Hutchinson, 1988), 832.

4 The communal violence came to be known as the "Great Calcutta Killings."

5 *East–West* magazine, November–December, 1947, 4.

6 The partition resulted in East Pakistan, which became independent Bangladesh in 1971.

7 Another great hero of his, Rabindranath Tagore, passed away due to illness in 1941, at age 80.

8 *Los Angeles Times*, February 2, 1948, 2.

9 As an interesting historical note, Yogananda did not give many of his monastics Sanskrit names. Most of them went by their given names. After his passing, a name change became customary. Similarly, during Yogananda's lifetime the monastics wore modest Western clothing. "Our boys and girls dress as Americans," he said in 1950, "but their hearts are different." Uniform orange attire became standard six or seven years after the guru passed.

10 Quotes in this paragraph are from private correspondence with Brother Chidananda.

11 The space once occupied by the lost temple contains an exquisite meditation garden, with a koi pond, a variety of flowers and plants, shade trees, benches, and ocean views. Services are held off campus in a spacious temple nearby.

12 As was mentioned earlier, the "ananda" suffix means bliss. Janaka was a legendary ruler and self-realized yogi. Rajarsi is a compound of *raja*, meaning king or royal, and *rishi* (or *rsi*), meaning illumined sage. Yogananda preferred "king of saints." For the remaining months of Yogananda's life, Rajarsi was still referred to as St. Lynn. Later, when his renunciate name entered usage, it was misspelled as Rajasi (without the "r," making the meaning more mundane). After a handwritten note of Yogananda's was found in which he spelled it Rajarsi, that became the spelling.

13 Over the years, Yogananda supported several ideas for generating income, including something called the Temple of Silence, a helmet-like appliance to block out sound during meditation.

14 James Lynn bequeathed a plentiful sum to SRF (reportedly $1 million, plus more when his wife passed away). The Lynns had no children, but a nephew, Eugene Lynn, was also a beneficiary. He used his inheritance to create Lynn University in Boca Raton, Florida.

15 *Inner Culture*, October 1942, 40.

16 Ibid.

17 At the time, SRF also ran a restaurant in Encinitas, on a main road a short walk from the ashram.

18 San Diego SRF temple website: http://sandiegotemple.org/about-2/.

19 Her mother, Vera Brown, also became a monastic; she took the name Meera Mata.

20 About 700 attended the first convocation. Now they are held every August at the Westin Bonaventure Hotel in downtown LA. In 2017 about 4,000 people came, from 43 countries.

21 The Lake Shrine heritage includes some celebrity lore. A memorial service for George Harrison was held in the Windmill Chapel at his family's request; the actor Dennis Weaver (Chester on *Gunsmoke*) spoke in the chapel once a month for 17 years; Elvis Presley reportedly loved to walk around the lake (brochures he obtained there led to 12 years of meetings with Daya Mata, who served the King as a spiritual adviser); and in 2017, rock star Tom Petty's funeral service was held there.

22 Paramahansa Yogananda, *Man's Eternal Quest* (Los Angeles: Self-Realization Fellowship, 1975), xi–xii.

23 The "Collector's Series of Informal Talks," a series of 10 CDs, is available online through SRF Publications.

24 He also had young monks demonstrate yoga postures at events. While he touted the physical benefits of asana practice, he always emphasized that their main purpose was to foster the higher mental and spiritual goals of classical Yoga.

25 *Inner Culture*, April 1932, 14.

26 The vision, with additional detail, is described in the *Autobiography*, 2013 edition, 413.

27 As Yogananda tells it, Lahiri Mahasaya once said, "About fifty years after my passing my life will be written because of a deep interest in yoga which the West will manifest." Lahiri died in 1895. Fifty years later, in 1945, Yogananda completed his autobiography.

28 Modern readers, accustomed to the orange cover, may be surprised to learn that the initial cover was blue.

29 As a point of interest, in his correspondence Yogananda frequently used "ceaseless blessings" as a salutation.

30 *Louisville Times*, March 7, 1947.

31 *New York Times*, March 15, 1947.

32 *The San Jose Mercury-News*, March 9, 1947.

33 *The News and Courier*, March 16, 1947.

34 *The Review of Religion*, May 1948.

35 The *Newsweek* and *Time* reviews were in the March 10 and March 17, 1947, editions respectively.

36 It is well documented that some Indian ascetics use stagecraft and sleight-of-hand tricks to get the attention of seekers, sometimes as a teaching tool and

sometimes to take advantage of their credulity. Which does not, of course, rule out that others are genuine masters with extraordinary mind power.

37 According to SRF records, the first print run was 7,000 copies. The second printing, in 1948, was for half that amount. A third printing of 5,000 copies, with minor revisions, was published in 1949.

38 In addition to the three mentioned here, Swami Premananda (formerly Brahmachari Jotin) also split with SRF after Yogananda's passing, in this case over a policy dispute. His Self-Revelation Church of Absolute Monism is still in operation in Bethesda, Maryland, run by an American disciple named Srimati Kamala since Premananda's death in 1995. As mentioned earlier in the book, Mildred Hamilton and Oliver Black also struck out on their own. Swami Premananda died in 1995.

39 Davis's principal disciple has been Yogacharya Ellen Grace O'Brian, the spiritual director of the Center for Spiritual Enlightenment in San Jose, California.

40 Unlike Roy Eugene Davis and Norman Paulsen, Kriyananda's separation from SRF was not amicable; the two organizations fought a bitter lawsuit over copyright issues for 12 years (interested parties can find details online). Kriyananda's successors, Nayaswamis Jyotish and Devi Novak, are a long-time married couple, reflecting the community's householder orientation.

41 *Awake: The Life of Yogananda* (2014), written and directed by Paola di Florio and Lisa Leeman. Produced and distributed by Counterpoint Films, Peter Rader, Paola di Florio, and Lisa Leeman, Producers. The companion book by the same title was published in 2015 by Self-Realization Fellowship.

42 The arguments on both sides, along with details about every change made to the seminal book after its initial publication, can be readily found online. Crystal Clarity Productions, the publishing arm of Swami Kriyananda's Ananda Sangha Worldwide, publishes the original 1946 version. It's the one with the blue cover and the spelling "Paramhansa."

43 George Harrison's song "Dear One" on his 1976 album *Thirty Three & 1/3* was dedicated to Yogananda. It's not the only rock music inspired by Yogananda. The album *Tales from Topographic Oceans* by Yes was inspired by a footnote in *Autobiography of a Yogi* (2013 edition, 77) about the Hindu *shastras*, or sacred texts.

Chapter 18

1 Paramahansa Yogananda, *God Talks With Arjuna*, xii.

2 These are Yogananda's succinct definitions in *Autobiography of a Yogi* (in a Chapter 43 footnote, page 353): "In *sabikalpa samadhi* the devotee has attained realization of his oneness with Spirit but cannot maintain his cosmic consciousness except in the immobile trance state. By continuous meditation he reaches the superior state of *nirbikalpa samadhi*, in which he may move freely in the world without any loss of God-perception."

3 *Self-Realization*, September 1948, 7.

4 *Time* magazine, August 4, 1952, 57.

5 It has been hypothesized that Indians could have a predisposition to the disorder, which ended Vivekananda's life at age 39.

6 *Bhagavad Gita*, Chapter 2, Verse 38.

7 Sri Daya Mata, *Finding the Joy Within You*, 254. For more details and eyewitness accounts of Yogananda's final days, see *Paramahansa Yogananda: In Memorium*, an SRF publication.

8 As per *Paramahansa Yogananda: In Memoriam*, 69. The complete poem can be found in *Songs of the Soul*, 168.

9 Korla Pandit was actually John Roland Redd, an African American from St. Louis. As a career move, he adopted a fabricated identity as the Delhi-born child of a Brahmin priest and a French opera singer.

10 In line with the tradition of preserving the bodies of realized masters intact, as we saw with Sri Yukteswar, Yogananda was not cremated.

11 SRF's hopes for moving the body to Mt. Washington have so far been dashed by legal constraints and neighborhood opposition to what would likely become a pilgrimage site. They have not given up on the Mother Center becoming his final resting place.

12 Paramahansa Yogananda, *Autobiography*, 2013 edition, 422.

13 *Integral Yoga Magazine*, Winter 2014, 20-22.

14 SRF says that "it was the Guru's express wish that the Board reinstate Krishna's picture when the time was right." When public appreciation of India's ancient teachings grew sufficiently, the board determined that the time had come. On their altars (but not those of every Kriya Yoga lineage) the placement of the images, from left to right, is: Lahiri Mahasaya, Babaji, Jesus, Krishna, Yogananda, Sri Yukteswar.

15 This talk, "Beholding the One in All," was recorded on January 5, 1949. A recording of the talk is available from Self-Realization Fellowship.

BIBLIOGRAPHY

Works by Paramahansa Yogananda

The following are all published by Self-Realization Fellowship, Los Angeles.

Autobiography of a Yogi, 1946.

Autobiography of a Yogi, Audio Edition, read by Sir Ben Kingsley, 1996.

The Divine Romance: Collected Talks and Essays on Realizing God in Daily Life, 1986.

God Talks with Arjuna: The Bhagavad Gita: Royal Science of God-Realization: The Immortal Dialogue Between Soul and Spirit, 1999.

Journey to Self-Realization: Collected Talks and Essays, Vol. 3, 1997.

Man's Eternal Quest, 1975.

The Science of Religion, 1982.

The Second Coming of Christ: The Resurrection of the Christ Within You, 2004.

Songs of the Soul, 1983.

The Yoga of Jesus: Understanding the Hidden Teachings of the Gospels, 2007.

Works about Paramahansa Yogananda

Awake: The Life of Yogananda. Based on the film by Paola di Florio and Lisa Leeman. Los Angeles: Self-Realization Fellowship, 2015.

Davis, Roy Eugene. *Paramahansa Yogananda as I Knew Him: Experiences, Observations, and Reflections of a Disciple*. Lakemont, GA: CSA Press, 2005.

Foxen, Anya P. *Biography of a Yogi: Paramahansa Yogananda and the Origins of Modern Yoga*. New York: Oxford University Press, 2017.

Ghosh, Hare Krishna. *Experiences with My Guru, Paramhansa Yogananda*. Ananda Sangha Worldwide, 1995. https://www.ananda.org/free-inspiration/books/experiences-with-my-guru-paramhansa-yogananda/.

Ghosh, Sananda Lal. *Mejda: The Family and the Early Life of Paramahansa Yogananda*. Los Angeles: Self-Realization Fellowship, 1980.

Kamala. *The Flawless Mirror*. Nevada City, CA: Crystal Clarity, 1964.

"Meatless Coolidge Meals Prescribed by Yogananda." *Washington Post*, January 15, 1927, 8.

Paramahansa Yogananda: In Memoriam: Personal Accounts of the Master's Final Days. Los Angeles: Self-Realization Fellowship, 1958.

Rosser, Brenda Lewis. *Treasures Against Time: Paramahansa Yogananda with Doctor and Mrs. Lewis*. Borrego Springs, CA: Borrego Publications, 1991.

Sri Durga Mata. *A Paramhansa Yogananda Trilogy of Divine Love*. Pasadena, CA: Joan Wight Publications, 1992.

Sri Sailendra Bejoy Dasgupta. *Paramhansa Swami Yogananda: Life-Portrait and Reminiscences*. Battle Creek, MI: Yoga Niketan, 1983.

Swami Kriyananda. *Conversations with Yogananda*. Nevada City, CA: Crystal Clarity, 2004.

———. *Paramhansa Yogananda: A Biography, with Personal Reflections and Reminiscences*. Nevada City, CA: Crystal Clarity, 2010.

Swami Satyananda Giri. *A Collection of Biographies of 4 Kriya Yoga Gurus*. Battle Creek, MI: Yoga Niketan, 2004.

Swami Satyeswarananda Giri. *Biography of a Yogi—Yogananda*. San Diego: Sanskrit Classics, 1985.

Related Sources

Albanese, Catherine L. *A Republic of Mind and Spirit: A Cultural History of American Metaphysical Religion*. New Haven: Yale University Press, 2007.

The Collected Works of Mahatma Gandhi, vol. 61. New Delhi: Publications Division, Ministry of Information and Broadcasting, Government of India, 1958.

Forsthoefel, Thomas A., and Cynthia Ann Humes, eds. *Gurus in America*. Albany: State University of New York Press, 2005.

Frawley, David (Vamadeva Shastri). *Astrology of the Seers*. Twin Lakes, WI: Lotus Press, 2000.

Goldberg, Philip. *American Veda: From Emerson and the Beatles to Yoga and Meditation, How Indian Spirituality Changed the West*. New York: Harmony, 2010.

McConnell, Marion (Mugs). *Letters from the Yoga Masters: Teachings Revealed Through Correspondence from Paramhansa Yogananda, Ramana Maharshi, Swami Sivananda, and Others*. Berkeley, CA: North Atlantic Books, 2016.

Parsons, Jon. *A Fight for Religious Freedom: A Lawyer's Personal Account of Copyrights, Karma and Dharmic Litigation*. Nevada City, CA: Crystal Clarity, 2012.

Rajarsi Janakananda: A Great Western Yogi: The Life of Paramahansa Yogananda's First Spiritual Successor. Los Angeles: Self-Realization Fellowship, 1996.

Salinger, J. D. "Seymour: An Introduction," in *Raise High the Roof Beam, Carpenters and Seymour: An Introduction*. Boston: Little, Brown, 1963.

Sri Daya Mata. *Finding the Joy Within You: Personal Counsel for God-Centered Living*. Los Angeles: Self-Realization Fellowship, 1990.

Sri Gyanamata. *God Alone: The Life and Letters of a Saint.* Los Angeles: Self-Realization Fellowship, 1984.

Sri Munagala Venkataramiah. *Talks with Sri Ramana Maharshi.* Tiruvannamalai, India: Sri Ramanasramam, 2013.

Swami Kriyananda. *The Path: One Man's Quest on the Only Path There Is.* Nevada City, CA: Crystal Clarity, 1977.

Swami Nikhilananda, tr. *The Gospel of Sri Ramakrishna.* New York: Ramakrishna-Vivekananda Center, 1942.

Swami Sri Yukteswar. *The Holy Science.* Los Angeles: Self-Realization Fellowship, 1990.

Syman, Stefanie. *The Subtle Body: The Story of Yoga in America.* New York: Farrar, Straus and Giroux, 2010.

Thomas, Wendell. *Hinduism Invades America.* New York: Beacon Press, 1930.

Tweed, Thomas A., and Stephen R. Prothero. *Asian Religions in America: A Documentary History.* New York: Oxford University Press, 1999.

Vidal, Mas. *Sun, Moon, and Earth: The Sacred Relationship of Yoga and Ayurveda.* Twin Lakes, WI: Lotus Press, 2017.

Williamson, Lola. *Transcendent in America: Hindu-Inspired Meditation Movements as New Religion.* New York: New York University Press, 2010.

INDEX

Note: Page references starting with "P-" (e.g., P-2) indicate pages in the photo insert.

A

Index

Chatterji, Ashutosh, 44
Chatterji, Pratap, 58, 59
Chidananda, 63, 90, 128, 195, 280
Childhood. *See also* birth
   ahimsa during, 16–17
   in Gorakhpur, 7–8
   letter to God, 9–10
   miraculous healing, 7
   mourning for mother, 15
   photo, P-2
   pilgrimages during, 16–18
   preoccupation with miracles, 12
   reverie during, 10
   seclusion and meditation during, 11
   spiritual training, 4
   traits displayed during, 8–9
   vegetarianism adopted during, 16
Cholera, 7, 13, 68
Chowdhury, Nirad Ranjan (Brahmacharee Sri Nerode), 166, 188, 199, 206, 235, 242–246, 248
Christ Consciousness, 110, 262

Christian Scientists, 107
Christianity, revival of, 149
"Christmas Message to the Nations of the World" (Yogananda), 195
Churchill, Winston, 194, 253
City of Sparta, 97, 99–100
Clairvoyance, 68, 110
Clark, J. Ross, 150
Clark, Miriam A., 150
Commemorative stamp, 283, P-16
Commercialism, 236
Concentration camps, 212
Congress of Religious Liberals, 105
Coolidge, Calvin, 101, 131, 140, 170–171
Cosmic Chants (Yogananda), 165, 237
Cosmic energy, 89, 90, 144
Cosmic Good, 198
Cosmic Spirit, 266
Coué, Émile, 116
Cox, James M., 101
Cuba trip, 163
Curthose, Robert, 223

D

Daggett, Mabel Potter, 125
Darling, Florina (Durga Mata)
   on Arjuna, 213
   on blessing, 234
   housecar and, 207
   on meals, 238
   memoir, 202
   on movies, 238
   operations and, 209, 254
   on overcoat, 103
   on photos, 104
   on salaries, 197
   travel with, 232
Darshan, 63, 215, 277
Das, Prokas Chandra, 41–42
Das, Ranendra Kumar, 184, 254
Datta, Narendranath, 41
Davis, Roy Eugene, 239, 268–269, 275
Dayananda, 50–52, 56
Defense Bonds, 252
Devotional practices, 30
Dharma, 56, 161, 227
Dharmavijnana, 91
Dhirananda
   advantages from, 118

classes and sermons by, 166 167
as collaborator and lieutenant, 66
compensation demand by, 186, 188
duties of, 153–154
as ghostwriter, 92
initiation of, 87
lawsuit of, 208–210, 221–223
praise for, 153
renouncing swamihood, 187
sexual misconduct allegations against, 174–178
summoning of, 130
Sunday school classes taught by, 157–158
travel to America, 114–115
Diksha, 58, 63, 127
Disciples, 5–6, 40, 108, 275, 277, 278, 279
Divine Father, 185
Divine Grace, 188
Divine Light, 42, 198
Divine Mother
   appearance of, 47
   belief in, 12
   beseeching, 189, 205
   conversing with, 273

321

L

M

N

O

P

ACKNOWLEDGMENTS

My research for this book involved dozens of interviews, site visits in the U.S. and India, and countless hours of reading in books, newspapers, and documents stored in organizational, governmental, and personal archives. I am grateful to all those who gave me access to that material. Special thanks go to Brother Chidananda of Self-Realization Fellowship (he became president as this book was being completed), who responded patiently to my queries and showed me key archival documents. I am grateful for his cooperation, and to that of Lauren Landress, SRF's director of public affairs, for her input and for graciously facilitating my points of access to the organization that Yogananda founded. The leadership and staff members at Ananda Worldwide were similarly cooperative. For access to material from personal archives, I am indebted to Robert Ardito and Martine Vanderpoorten, and especially to Anil Nerode and Jon Parsons, all of whom were exceptionally gracious in responding to my requests.

A bow of gratitude to two indispensable collaborators: my astute and patient editor, Patty Gift; and my cherished friend and agent, Lynn Franklin.

My thanks to those who provided research assistance along the way: Shelley Miller (who also offered useful feedback on early drafts), Tracey Schuster, Joe Cadiff, Matthew Cochrane, and Laura Brickman.

Many others kindly shared information or provided other forms of help. I hope they forgive me for listing them alphabetically: Swami Amarananda, Arun Banerjee, Debashish Banerji, Todd Bettinger, Phil Bolsta, Helene Castera, Roy Eugene Davis, Nicole DeAvilla, Paola DiFlorio, Ben and Lorna Erskine, Michael

Flynn, Anya P. Foxen, David Frawley, Somnath Ghosh, Karen Mindt Howell, Nikki Johnson, Ulla-Maija Kivimäki, Lisa Leeman, Ron Lindahn, Debashis Maity, Craig Marshall, Hriman McGilloway, Patralekha Nath, Swami Nigamananda, Nayaswamis Jyotish and Devi Novack, David Nowe, Ellen Grace O'Brian, Rao Pantulu, Latika Parojinog, Marydale Pecora, Swami Prajnanananda, Peter Rader, Anita Rehker, Richard Salva, Dana Sawyer, Brother Shekhar, Fred Stella, Tim Tarbell, Mas Vidal, Swami Vidyadishananda, Brother Vishwananda, Priscilla Walker. Pranams to them all.

On a personal level, I extend my profound appreciation and big hugs to friends and family members who allowed me to use them as sounding boards, advisers, and sources of comic relief during the voyage from inception to completion of this book. Chief among them: my brother Bob Goldberg, Elliot Friedland, Jack Forem, and Dean Sluyter. Finally, to the person to whom I owe the most gratitude, my wife, Lori Deutsch: thank you for helping me stay healthy and sane throughout this process, for listening, for loving, for easing my concerns, and for understanding an author's need to be occasionally absent from "real life."

ABOUT THE AUTHOR

Philip Goldberg has been studying India's spiritual traditions for more than 45 years, as a practitioner, teacher, and writer. He is the author or co-author of more than 20 books, published in more than a dozen languages, including *The Intuitive Edge*; *Get Out of Your Own Way*; *Roadsigns on the Spiritual Path: Living at the Heart of Paradox*; and *American Veda: From Emerson and the Beatles to Yoga and Meditation, How Indian Spirituality Changed the West*. The last book chronicles the remarkable influence of India's traditional spiritual teachings on the West. It was named one of the top 10 religion books of 2010 by both *Huffington Post* and the American Library Association's *Booklist* and received the Award for Special Distinction by the Uberoi Foundation for Religious Studies. As a screenwriter and published novelist (*This Is Next Year*), Phil is a member of the Writers Guild of America and the Authors Guild.

An ordained interfaith minister, spiritual counselor, and meditation teacher trained in 1970 by Maharishi Mahesh Yogi, Phil is an illuminating and entertaining public speaker who has presented at yoga centers and festivals, universities, retreat centers, religious and spiritual institutions, and other venues throughout the United States and India. He leads workshops on Indian sacred texts, meditation, and related topics, both in person and online. He blogs, mainly about religion and spirituality, in *Elephant Journal*; contributes regularly to *Spirituality & Health* online about the intersection of spirituality and social issues; and sits on the board of *The Interfaith Observer*. Phil has been interviewed by a variety of newspapers, magazines, and radio and television outlets, and appears onscreen in the award-winning documentary *Awake: The Life of Yogananda*.

He also conducts journeys to sacred India through his company, American Veda Tours, and co-hosts the popular *Spirit Matters* podcast, which features interviews with a diverse array of spiritual teachers and leaders. Born and raised in Brooklyn, he now lives in Los Angeles with his wife, acupuncturist Lori Deutsch. His website is www.PhilipGoldberg.com.

Hay House Titles of Related Interest

YOU CAN HEAL YOUR LIFE, the movie,
starring Louise Hay & Friends
(available as a 1-DVD program, an expanded 2-DVD set,
and an online streaming video)
Learn more at www.hayhouse.com/louise-movie

THE SHIFT, the movie,
starring Dr. Wayne W. Dyer
(available as a 1-DVD program, an expanded 2-DVD set,
and an online streaming video)
Learn more at www.hayhouse.com/the-shift-movie

CHANTS OF A LIFETIME: Searching for a Heart of Gold,
by Krishna Das

MORE BEAUTIFUL THAN BEFORE: How Suffering Transforms Us,
by Steve Leder

PERFECTLY IMPERFECT: The Art and Soul of Yoga,
by Baron Baptiste

TRANSCENDENTAL MEDITATION: The Essential Teachings of
Maharishi Mahesh Yogi—The Classic Text Revised and Updated,
by Jack Forem

All of the above are available at your local bookstore,
or may be ordered by contacting Hay House (see next page).

We hope you enjoyed this Hay House book. If you'd like to receive our online catalog featuring additional information on Hay House books and products, or if you'd like to find out more about the Hay Foundation, please contact:

Hay House, Inc., P.O. Box 5100, Carlsbad, CA 92018-5100
(760) 431-7695 or (800) 654-5126
(760) 431-6948 (fax) or (800) 650-5115 (fax)
www.hayhouse.com® • www.hayfoundation.org

———

Published and distributed in Australia by:
Hay House Australia Pty. Ltd., 18/36 Ralph St., Alexandria NSW 2015
Phone: 612-9669-4299 • *Fax:* 612-9669-4144 • www.hayhouse.com.au

Published and distributed in the United Kingdom by:
Hay House UK, Ltd., Astley House, 33 Notting Hill Gate, London W11 3JQ
Phone: 44-20-3675-2450 • *Fax:* 44-20-3675-2451 • www.hayhouse.co.uk

Published in India by: Hay House Publishers India,
Muskaan Complex, Plot No. 3, B-2, Vasant Kunj, New Delhi 110 070
Phone: 91-11-4176-1620 • *Fax:* 91-11-4176-1630 • www.hayhouse.co.in

Distributed in Canada by:
Raincoast Books, 2440 Viking Way, Richmond, B.C. V6V 1N2
Phone: 1-800-663-5714 • *Fax:* 1-800-565-3770 • www.raincoast.com

———

Access New Knowledge.
Anytime. Anywhere.

Learn and evolve at your own pace
with the world's leading experts.

www.hayhouseU.com

Free e-newsletters
from Hay House, the Ultimate
Resource for Inspiration

Be the first to know about Hay House's free downloads, special offers, giveaways, contests, and more!

 Get exclusive excerpts from our latest releases and videos from *Hay House Present Moments*.

 Our *Digital Products Newsletter* is the perfect way to stay up-to-date on our latest discounted eBooks, featured mobile apps, and Live Online and On Demand events.

 Learn with real benefits! *HayHouseU.com* is your source for the most innovative online courses from the world's leading personal growth experts. Be the first to know about new online courses and to receive exclusive discounts.

 Enjoy uplifting personal stories, how-to articles, and healing advice, along with videos and empowering quotes, within *Heal Your Life*.

 Have an inspirational story to tell and a passion for writing? Sharpen your writing skills with insider tips from *Your Writing Life*.

Sign Up Now!

Get inspired, educate yourself, get a complimentary gift, and share the wisdom!

Visit www.hayhouse.com/newsletters to sign up today!

Hay House Podcasts
Bring Fresh, Free Inspiration Each Week!

Hay House proudly offers a selection of life-changing audio content via our most popular podcasts!

Hay House Meditations Podcast

Features your favorite Hay House authors guiding you through meditations designed to help you relax and rejuvenate. Take their words into your soul and cruise through the week!

Dr. Wayne W. Dyer Podcast

Discover the timeless wisdom of Dr. Wayne W. Dyer, world-renowned spiritual teacher and affectionately known as "the father of motivation." Each week brings some of the best selections from the 10-year span of Dr. Dyer's talk show on HayHouseRadio.com.

Hay House World Summit Podcast

Over 1 million people from 217 countries and territories participate in the massive online event known as the Hay House World Summit. This podcast offers weekly mini-lessons from World Summits past as a taste of what you can hear during the annual event, which occurs each May.

Hay House Radio Podcast

Listen to some of the best moments from HayHouseRadio.com, featuring expert authors such as Dr. Christiane Northrup, Anthony William, Caroline Myss, James Van Praagh, and Doreen Virtue discussing topics such as health, self-healing, motivation, spirituality, positive psychology, and personal development.

Hay House Live Podcast

Enjoy a selection of insightful and inspiring lectures from Hay House Live, an exciting event series that features Hay House authors and leading experts in the fields of alternative health, nutrition, intuitive medicine, success, and more! Feel the electricity of our authors engaging with a live audience, and get motivated to live your best life possible!

Find Hay House podcasts on iTunes, or visit www.HayHouse.com/podcasts for more info.